EDUCATION: A TIME FOR DECISIONS

Selections from the
Second Annual Conference of the Education Section
World Future Society

Edited by

Kathleen M. Redd
St. Cloud State University

and

Arthur M. Harkins
University of Minnesota

WORLD FUTURE SOCIETY
4916 St. Elmo Avenue (Bethesda)
Washington, D.C. 20014 • U.S.A.

The Sourcebook Series
of the
World Future Society's Education Section

Education: A Time For Decisions is the second in an
ongoing series of Sourcebook volumes featuring
papers first presented at the annual conference of
the World Future Society's Education Section.
Sourcebook I, Educational Futures, edited by Fred
Kierstead, Jim Bowman and Christopher Dede, contains 16 essays on educational futures theory,
models and methodologies, and selected special
topics of concern to futurist educators, from the
1978 Conference in Houston, Texas, and is available
from the World Future Society Book Service for
$5.95.

Published by
World Future Society
4916 St. Elmo Avenue
Washington, D.C. 20014 * USA

ISBN 0-93242-12-2

Price $6.95
        $6.25 to members of the World Future Society.
Please inquire for reduced multiple copy price for classroom use.

CONTENTS

Section III

Section IV

FOREWORD
Converting Our Dreams Into Realities

Edward Cornish
President, World Future Society

What can we do to create a better future world?

The best answer that I can offer is this: We need a great dream--a vision of a future that will be so compellingly desirable that we will all feel responsible for its realization.

Thousands of years ago, King Solomon said, "Where there is no vision, the people perish." His words are not just a warning to us; they are a prescription for saving our ailing civilization. Modern civilization has lost its vision of the future--the hope of a heaven in the afterlife or a utopia in the secular world-- and having lost that vision has become mired in confusion and conflict. But if that vision can be recreated in a new form, then civilization can again go forward confidently.

I believe that we are now in the process of creating that new vision, and that today's futurists are playing a crucial role in that task. What is needed is a strong positive image of a possible future world--a vision that will inspire people all over the world to do their best to achieve it. Can we create such a vision? I feel positive that we can and that is why I remain optimistic about the future. The future is dark only because we have not yet created light, but we can create light and I believe that we will.

Creating a credible vision of a desirable human future will not be easy. The Italian poet Dante tried to describe both hell and heaven in his epic poem La Divina Commedia, but despite his magnificent poetic gifts, he succeeded really in giving us only a view of hell. We can all visualize a place where the evil-doers of history are roasted eternally, but most people think that it would be rather boring to have to sit around heaven day after day strumming on a harp and waiting to catch a glimpse of the Almighty when He comes strolling by. No matter how you describe it, heaven always winds up sounding like a bore. And the same is true for any utopia. Even if you assure people that everyone in your utopia will be deliriously happy, it still sounds rather boring and even a bit sinister. It's a little like the old story of the Communist speaker who tells a crowd that "When the revolution comes, we'll all be eating strawberries and cream." A voice pipes up, "But I don't _like_ strawberries and cream." "When the revolution comes," says the speaker, "you will eat strawberries and cream and like it."

Creating a vision of utopia is virtually impossible, I think, so long as we insist that all the utopians should be the same--that we've all got to play on our harps or eat strawberries and cream, regardless of whether we wish to do so or not. Instead, I think that we should create a world in which a hundred utopias can bloom--even a million or a billion utopias. I challenge everyone to devise a concept of the ideal life and imagine living in it. In your own private utopia, you can make whatever rules you like, so long as your rules do not conflict with anyone else's utopia. It is the nature of human beings to be free and therefore to be different, peculiar, contradictory, and ornery--in short to be _individuals_--and if we are to have a true utopia, we must recognize that it may be suited for only a single person--and then only for a short period of time. So we must envision, I believe, not a utopian world but a world of utopias; that is the desirable future which is big enough for all our dreams.

But it is not enough to create a vision; we must also struggle to realize that vision. Dreams do not become realities simply by the dreaming of them; something else is needed--human effort. Dreams become realities not by waving a magic wand over them, but by means of a great deal of boring, frustrating, painful work. We transmute dreams into achievements by means of a philosopher's stone available to all of us--blood, sweat, and tears. To make dreams real, we must struggle in the frustrating swamp of present conditions. Inevitably, the struggle entails a seemingly endless experience of petty details, angry misunderstandings, frustrations, and failures.

The best dreams of all are those that we can never fully realize but in attempting to achieve them, we surpass ourselves; we become something more than intelligent beasts; we may even feel stirring within us a sense of the divine, because our striving to achieve a great and noble dream lifts our spiritual life toward the sublime.

We today are shaping the future world by our actions, but our actions are guided by our visions, our dreams. Thus it is essential that we pay more attention to our dreams for the future. Educators have a special responsibility here, for they are the ones who transmit dreams to the citizens of tomorrow. If these dreams are good dreams, they can form the great vision that we need to have a desirable future world.

ACKNOWLEDGEMENTS

Christopher J. Dede is the force behind the organization of annual conferences for the Education Section of the World Future Society and for the preparation of post-conference publications. We are indebted to him for his leadership in the Section and his support in the preparation of Sourcebook II. In addition, we would like to thank the authors for their contributions to this volume, for their cooperation in the selection and editing process, and for their commitment to the research and reflection that resulted in these articles. T. Lance Holthusen deserves special recognition for his role as General Chairperson of the 2nd Annual Conference, as do all of the individuals who worked so diligently to make the 2nd Annual Conference a success.

Ann Shaw and Brenda Tritz contributed greatly to the preparation of this volume; they handled the typing of the manuscript and its many revisions with skill, good humor and much patience. Finally we wish to thank our families for their patience and understanding while this volume was being prepared.

GENERAL INFORMATION

Education and society are inextricably linked. Society
provides the larger context within which education occurs;
education is the means through which individuals learn to
participate in the larger society. Education in modern societies
occurs in many settings: schools, families, corporations, mass
media, and community. Yet formal schooling continues to be the
primary focus when education is discussed, even among futurists.
Moreover, there are implicit suggestions that schooling continues
to be viewed very narrowly as a prescriptive, authoritarian, one-
way process, something done by teachers to students. The old
thought patterns from a simpler era are still deeply engrained.
However, among some educators and futurists this seems to be
diminishing.

Many of the presentations at the 2nd Annual Conference of
the World Future Society's Education Section held in Minneapolis,
October 18-21, 1979, were marked by growing feelings of concern,
and even impotence, as the pressures of societal and educational
changes, which permeated the Sixties and Seventies, have become
more demanding. The euphoria and delight in finding, at the 1st
Annual Conference, kindred spirits to whom one did not have to
explain futures studies were tempered a bit. The tone of the 2nd
Annual Conference was serious but not pessimistic. This is
reflected throughout the twenty papers selected for inclusion in
Sourcebook II. The presentations on which these papers were
based included invitational general sessions, presenter proposed
clinics and sectionals, and working groups which focused on
emergent issues in futures studies. Of necessity Sourcebook II
contains only a sampling of the more than 150 sessions presented
at the conference. The call for proposals for the conference
stressed dialogue, activity oriented sessions, and demonstra-
tions. One had to participate to capture the full flavor of many
of the sessions and of the conference as a whole. However, as
editors, we feel that the papers included in Sourcebook II
reflect the major thrusts planned into the conference as well as
those generated synergistically during the conference.

Throughout the conference, participants were reminded repeatedly that educational futurists must be concerned with policies, planning, problematic areas, and philosophic issues as well as currently practiced and proposed programs. In addition, there must be awareness of present circumstances as well as preparation for the range of alternative futures. These concerns are reflected in the organization of Sourcebook II. In Section I, there are discussions of planning and policies for the present and for the future. While the focus is generally on the short- to medium-range future, there are repeated analyses of the interface between education and society. Section II includes papers in which questions are raised about what ought to be some of the focal points of education and about some of the settings in which non-school education occurs. The papers in Section III all have a broad visionary, theoretical tenor which, it is hoped, will encourage all of us to think about new possibilities and paradigms. Application of a futures focus to school based education is the theme of Section IV. Programs discussed here, whether proposed or already in practice, involve teachers and learners from kindergarten through college.

Futures studies is often characterized by the diversity of specializations of its adherents and practitioners and is often faulted for being a field dominated by white Western males. The authors of the papers included in this volume are from varied backgrounds and geographical locations. The areas of specialization and early training range from the humanities, the law, and journalism through the natural and social sciences. Ten of the twenty-two authors are women. And yet there is a dearth, in this volume as there was in the conference as a whole, of non-Western, non-white perspectives. Several of the authors, including Thomas Sork and William Smith, make reference to this. It is important to note, however, that the focus of the 3rd Annual Conference of the Education Section is on diversity. Thus it is expected that these issues will be explored in depth in upcoming Sourcebooks and conferences.

Kathleen M. Redd
Arthur M. Harkins
Editors

Section I
Policies and Plans for the Present and the Future

Section I
Policies and Plans for the Present
and the Future

INTRODUCTION

Regardless of whether education is viewed as pushing society into the future or as being pulled by societal changes into confrontation with the present, education occurs in a societal context. Societal supports and demands shape both the content and the process of education. This creates a multi-layered phenomenon as well as a multi-faceted challenge. Schools, the educational agency most often focused on, do not exist in isolation; they are an integral part of a changing social milieu.

Christopher Dede, Florence Hood, Harold Shane, William Smith, and Edith Weiner all discuss education and schooling in a societal context. Common to all is an emphasis on the importance of understanding the process of change, complex though it may be. In addition, there is a need to recognize that not all individuals and institutions change in exactly the same way nor at the same rate. But lag-time and unevenness in change cannot and should not be used as excuses to avoid preparing for, and managing, change. Preparation for change necessitates envisioning what alternatives are available, determining what is preferable, and working toward the achievement of these images of the future. Change, whether short- or long-term, takes time to implement, and change, by its very nature, is a destabilizing force on individuals and on society as a whole.

The contributors in this section discuss policies and plans for education from varied perspectives--those of the corporate sphere, governmental service, professional education, and academic disciplines. And yet their admonitions and conclusions about education and the future are often overlapping and complementary.

Dede describes variables which may shape "The Next Ten Years in Education." In so doing, he is reminding all of us that the future is not fixed or predetermined, that it is open to human intervention. Dede exhorts educators to shift from a reactive to a proactive reconstructionist view. In addition, he encourages educators to prepare for "legitimate indeterminacy" in areas where the options are diverse. The process of education, as well as the agencies through which it occurs, need to become more integrative with the process of societal change.

Weiner discusses change in terms of technology, the family as an institution, the acceptance of authority and expertise, and credentialism. Throughout her paper, Weiner encourages a holistic world view, one that would help to counter what she sees as "educated incapacity." In addressing the education/corporation interface, Weiner points out the deficiencies of current schooling in preparing individuals to function in the corporate world and encourages cooperative, mutually beneficial inter- actions between the educational and corporate sectors. She strongly suggests that educators at all levels, need to better develop their scanning capacity to detect potential changes, to learn to look for patterns of changes in disparate fields and to prepare for new arenas, new markets for education.

Social change from the perspective of the social science disciplines is the primary focus of Shane's paper. He characterizes the upcoming decade as the "Uneasy 80's," replete with continued, destabilizing, transnational social change. In addition, he discusses, from the perspectives of the social sciences, the phenomena of "present shock" and experience com- pression which rapid change often produces. Along with this may go a confused sense of spatial and temporal congruity. Shane supports the contention that the social sciences are being woven into a seamless web with the boundaries of the disciplines becoming more permeable. In addition he seems to be suggesting implicitly that the experts cannot provide all the answers nor solve all the problems. Based on his analysis of social change, Shane makes suggestions for the improvement of instruction, encouraging involvement with real world situations, stress on alternative choices and the development of skills to make reasoned choices.

Hood, like Shane, explores the process of change as a major focal point in her paper. She places great emphasis on the need to understand the process of change at the macro and micro levels and to use this knowledge proactively. In this, Hood is provi- ding an expansion of the concerns discussed in Dede's paper. Hood argues quite forcefully for the need to rethink the meaning of public education. Hood's concerns about the Electronic Revo- lution are amplified in the papers by John Deethardt, Arthur Harkins and Earl Joseph. In addition, Hood reminds us of the continuity of past, present and future education by citing the Seven Cardinal Principles of Education prepared in 1918.

In "Bridging the Future," William Smith stresses the continuity and interconnectedness of events and times. He discusses the pace of change and the change of scale with which we all must deal. Not only must educators learn to read the signposts that mark continuities and portend changes, but they must also learn to apply systems theory to schools as formal organizations. Smith, who was appointed U.S. Commissioner of Education in January of 1980 after serving as Director of the Teacher Corps for several years, is well acquainted with the slowness of institutional change despite strident demands from many groups for easy solutions. From his vantage point in government, he is able to comment knowingly on the pervasiveness of social pessimism and the dearth of ready answers to social problems. However Smith is also able, in his paper, to convey a sense of his personal optimism and his commitment to education.

The Next Ten Years in
in Education

Christopher J. Dede

Last year, at the First Conference of the Education Section, World Future Society, I discussed how we might best conceptualize our role as educators concerned with the future. In particular, I spent some time developing a perspective on where we are in history and what long-term challenges and opportunities we face.[1] This year, I will take a very different approach, building on that overview, and will set forward some forecasts on the nature of the immediate future, the next decade.

Making these predictions is a very risky thing for me to attempt professionally, because you will still be around at the end of the next 10 years to check the validity of my forecasts. By 1989, I will either be a futuristic hero or be selling hotdogs in Yankee Stadium to make a living! Nonetheless, I will take my chances on what the future brings, because I see so many incredibly short-sighted decisions being made today that I feel all of us must speak out on what we see coming.

Ultimately, a person's beliefs about the future are very powerful in shaping his actions. In a sense, what we strive to do as educators is to change students' lives by giving them visions of what their personal future might be and the knowledge they need to actualize these possibilities. One of the aspects of futures research that has always fascinated me is the extent to which one can change someone's behavior by altering the image of the future that he holds. If we are to be effective in building a positive future for education, we need to examine our own professional beliefs about the future and ensure that our images are appropriate. Here are four metaphors from Draper Kauffman's Teaching the Future to use in reflecting on your conceptualizations of change. Which do you find best describes your day-to-day vision of the future of education?

The future can be seen as similar to a rollercoaster on a dark night. All of us are in a car on the rollercoaster, speeding along the rails. We know that we're on a fixed track which the car must follow, that our future is already determined, but we don't know where the track is going because everything is black as pitch. Now and then a flash of lightning comes and a bit of the track is exposed--we can see for just an instant what will happen next--but then it is dark again. This rollercoaster metaphor has been the dominant image of the future throughout history. In fact, one of the reasons the future did not begin to be researched until recently has simply been that, for much of the past, what would come was seen as predetermined, God's will, unknowable. Many of the early futurists may have died at the stake, because to speculate about the predetermined future was considered to be heresy.

A second metaphor is that the future is similar to a mighty river winding through the countryside. We are in a boat on that river. There is a generally predetermined course--the river has definite banks and a strong current--but we have more freedom to steer than on the rollercoaster. We have to follow the river, but we can avoid sandbars and, if the river forks, we can choose which direction we are to take. Many of us think about the future of the public schools in this manner; the tide of events in formal education sweeps us along, but we can choose where to steer along the surface.

A third metaphor is that the future is similar to an ocean. We are in a ship, acting as the masters of our fate, the captains of our soul. We can choose whatever future we will if we only work for it; though there may be storms and reefs, with care we can sail the ship to where we want to be. In the 1960s, many of us, for at least a brief time, felt this way about what we could accomplish in changing education.

Finally, one can conceptualize the future as being similar to a dice game. At any instant, the dice are shaken, a number comes up, and this number represents a decision. Then the dice are tossed again, another number appears, and through such a random series of actions the future chaotically emerges. I am working in Washington this year in the Planning Office of the National Institute of Education; as I watch how the political system works, I see many people who can empathize with the metaphor of the future as a dice game.

None of these metaphors is intrinsically right or wrong; each describes a different aspect of the ways in which the future is determined. As educators concerned with change, we need to be aware of our assumptions about these different aspects of the future, so that we can respond appropriately by clinging to the boat, steering, or mapping courses to new lands. What I want to discuss in the next portion of this article is the part of the future similar to a river.

Likely Developments in Education's Context
In the Next Decade

In the next 10 years, what are the likely constraints we face? The forecasts following are speculative; I cannot prove what I'm going to set forth. But since some assumptions about the future must be made, these are a reasonable set of predictions with which to begin.

Economy. The 1980s will be a time of major economic instability and uncertainty, as chaotic a period as has existed since the 1930s. The first half of the decade will likely cycle among periods of low growth with very high inflation, stagnation with high inflation, and recession with moderate inflation.

The second half of the decade will probably see: either massive capital investment, with emerging successes in technology and technocracy beginning to lay the foundations of new prosperity, or the relative impotence of technology and technocracy to solve current crises, followed by fiscal collapse to a new type of economic catastrophe (about 14% unemployment coupled with about 20% inflation).

Technology. The availability of inexpensive, powerful miniature computers will cause a massive shift in occupational roles over the next 10 years. Since capital-intensive industries outperform labor-intensive industries during inflationary periods, rote tasks will gradually become automated (especially in areas, such as information processing, in which no manipulative functions are required). Occupational demand will center on skills of decision-making given incomplete information, flexibility, and creativity (all of which machines are not well adapted to do).

New developments in instructional technology will offer, for certain subjects, cost-effective alternatives to traditional teaching methods. Micro-computer and videodisc hardware will be readily affordable. Limited availability of quality software will become the major restriction on use. Corporations will increasingly utilize these instructional systems to reduce industrial training costs; middle and upper income families will use these technologies for enrichment of personal time and to enhance their learning.

Demographics. The "baby bust" generation will pose sequential problems of enrollment decline for elementary, secondary, secondary, and college level education through the 1980s. However, an upturn in student population will begin in the lower elementary grades in the middle of the decade.

The increasing presence of women in the work force, as well as greater demands for occupational education, will create needs for extra-family supervision and socialization of children.

Many immigrants will settle in metropolitan areas, including significant numbers of non-English-speaking students.

High rates of mobility will cause regional flux in student populations. The Southern, Southwestern, and Rocky Mountain portions of the country will experience net population in-migration from the remainder of the United States. Out-migration of middle and upper class families to suburbs and rural areas will continue (despite gentrification). Minority and lower income students will increasingly become concentrated in urban school districts.

The proportion of elderly persons in the population will continue to rise, placing stress on income redistribution programs (such as Social Security and Medicare).

Cultural Values and Beliefs. Social instability and change and a growing sense of lack of control will create difficulties in "coping" for many people. Planning, leadership, and self-renewal will become increasingly problematic for institutions, as responding to crises in the "here and now" consumes ever greater amounts of time and energy. (This process is described in depth in O. W. Markley's Stanford Research Institute report, Changing Images of Man.)[2]

The technological and bureaucratic complexity of society will pose many problems for citizens. Reliance on the advice of "experts" for most choices will become increasingly necessary (yet simultaneously resented). Uniform socialization of the population to the multiple, higher order cognitive and affective skills required for participation in society will require major expenditures of resources, yet will be essential to the proper functioning of a high technology society.

Heightened values conflict will occur, as multiple special interest groups do battle on individual ethical issues such as abortion, individual rights and responsibilities, and biomedical manipulation. Perceived incapacities of technology and techno-cracy to deal with current crises will cause a major struggle between those who continue to espouse a narrowly rational, high technology-based, materialistic "American Dream" and those who proselytize for a shift to a more adaptive, ecological, spiritual lifestyle. One risk of this cultural "civil war" at a time of economic distress is the emergence of a charismatic dictator.

Governance. Financial pressures on citizens will intensify the existing "anti-taxes" movement, and business groups will attempt to link anti-regulatory arguments to this cause. The result will be a pervasive "reduce governance" stance. Conflicting pressures will come from those who see a single strong hand as needed to lead America out of current crises (a "charismatic leader" approach). Representative democracy will thus be eroded by pressures both for localism and for unitary authority.

Public response to emerging resources crises (e.g., water) will continue to be directed toward programs for crash priority replenishment. These will tend to be oriented toward high technological sophistication rather than conservation measures involving lifestyle changes. Competition among Federal priorities will become extremely intense, to the relative detriment of long-range needs and issues.

Demands for accountability and evidence of competence will force conservative decision-making and the production of large amounts of documentation of performance. These tendencies will create further problems in institutional ability to respond to change.

Many other likely developments in the 1980s can be cited. This representative list has been selected because these forecasts have major implications for educational equity and practice. Ultimately, a rigorous approach to anticipating educational challenges of the next decade would involve extending these forecasts to create detailed alternative scenarios of society in the mid-1990s. From such an overall environmental context, the role education must play to create a positive future can be inferred. (One such project is already in progress under the joint sponsorship of the Education Section, World Future Society and Old Dominion University, directed by Dwight Allen and myself.)

Illustrative Implications for Educational
  Equity and Practice

The developments cited above are based on fairly cautious and conservative assessments of probable societal changes in the next 10 years. Nonetheless, their impact on educational equity and practice is likely to be quite large, in part because many of these trends will interact in a mutually reinforcing manner. The negative feedback loops in social systems resist change so strongly that even a very powerful isolated trend frequently is suppressed. As a result, futures forecasts which rely on naive extrapolation of isolated trends tend to have low validity. However, a great many reinforcing events which combine to affect basic parameters of the society can overwhelm this inertia and lead to a basic redefinition of the social system itself. The 1980s seem to be such a period in history. A large number of major quantitative changes may well perpetrate an overall qualitative change.

An extended example of reinforcing developments may help to illustrate this point: formal education will experience very severe financial strains in the next decade because of the simultaneous impact of a number of trends. First, we seem to be approaching the maximum percentage of their income that people are willing to spend for education (currently about 8-1/2 to 9% of GNP). Over time, the "piece of the pie" that we've been able to claim from people's incomes has crept up and up and up--but now clients are saying, "no more."

The reason that our share of the fiscal "pie" has continually increased has not been because we've been particularly wasteful with money, but because education is labor-intensive rather than capital-intensive (that is, we use people to produce educational outcomes instead of using machines). Auto assembly plants and steel mills are examples of capital-intensive industries; medicine and government are labor-intensive industries. Over time, capital-intensive industries cost consumers progressively less, relative to labor-intensive industries, because salaries rise faster than capital costs. (For example, from 1965 to 1975 the Consumer Price Index rose 69%; educational costs rose 155%.) The initial expenditure on a huge machine and the interest that is paid on the debt from buying the machine on credit and the repairs and the maintenance costs all are less expensive over time than people's salaries (in part, because machines continuously improve in efficiency).

Second, even small yearly reductions in budget cumulate to an enormous drain on fiscal resources fairly quickly. Right now, inflationary losses for many educational agents are running at well over 14% per year, but revenues are growing at only around 7% per year. The result is an average yearly 7% net loss. In 10 years, 7% loss per year will leave formal education with one-half the revenues (in real terms) it now has. Further, given the general economic woes society will probably be experiencing, we can be sure that education will not have first claim on social priorities in terms of funding--nor second, nor fifth.

Third, on top of this general economic drain, education will face spiraling resource costs--not just in energy, but in such items as water, paper, and transportation. Politics being

what it is, in response to these increased costs we will see
wildly changing and inconsistent policies from government. So
far, the Federal response to the energy situation has been less
than ideal, and in general that will continue to be true for all
resource crises.

Finally, at the same time educators are facing economic woes
because of the factors above--and because of dwindling enrollments due to demographic changes--we are also confronted by
demands for "higher quality" education. We're supposed to train
for jobs, screen for jobs, train for further schooling, screen
for further schooling, socialize, entertain and babysit, keep
students off the job market, prepare for citizenship, prepare for
family life, and (in the remaining time available) create happy
healthy human beings . . . on 7% per year less! The simultaneous
intersection of all these trends will create very difficult times
for formal education (especially public schools) and will make
solving any one of these problems that much harder.

With this background, a few examples of the implications for
education of interactions among the future societal developments
listed earlier are given below.

Emergence of a Capital-Intensive Sector in Education. The
financial squeeze higher education will experience, when coupled
with two other factors, may provide the impetus for formation of
a nonformal, geographically dispersed, capital-intensive system
of instruction. One of these factors is the coming massive
redefinition of job roles as micro-computers are used to make
industries less labor-intensive as a way of coping with economic
woes. The existing formal educational system is neither equipped
nor cost-effective for the magnitude of adult retraining
involved.

The second factor is the emergence of high quality instructional technology at a reasonable cost. Industries are already
on the forefront of using these devices for teaching purposes
because their efficiency and reduced staffing expenses create
very high economic incentives. While the difficulties in
evolving a whole new model of instruction, evaluation, and
certification are substantial, the motivation for such innovation
is now present. (Books did not suddenly become central when the
printing press was developed; they were first widely used when an
economic incentive appeared.)

Such a non-formal instructional technology system, once
established for adult retraining, might quickly expand its
influence because of easy add-on capabilities. For example,
parents who could afford to do so would supplement their

children's schooling using system software packages, and eventually might lobby to substitute these cheaper methods for the
training portion of K-12 education. Within 15 years, through
such expansions, a capital-intensive system might rival the
labor-intensive system in importance. The unanswered equity and
practice questions of such a new educational model are numerous
and troubling.

"Disparate, But Equal" Education. The roles which formal
education plays in different types of communities may become
quite disparate by the 1990s. Communities with a large
percentage of two-wage families will expect schools to provide
much higher levels of supervision and socialization than areas
with a predominance of one-income households. In metropolitan
areas, demographic concentration of minority groups and
immigrants (many non-English-speaking) will create a set of
educational needs quite different from those of suburban, upper-
income areas. Schools (mostly private) that convert quickly to
capital-intensive instructional approaches will have a very
different classroom environment than the traditional one, as will
schools which respond to pressures for a meritocratic, high-
powered system of gifted/talented education to train an elite
capable of reversing America's problems.

High population mobility will ensure the need to smooth
transitions among these diverse environments. Moreover, the
uniformly high degree of socialization requisite for functioning
in a high technology society will require some degree of national
standardization and coordination. Substantial challenges for
educators will result from these emerging, diverging educational
roles.

Retrenching Traditional Approaches. The financial
constraints which trouble formal schooling in the 1980s may be
augmented by several other major problems. "Here and now"
concerns will become so dominant in society that planning and
leadership will become very demanding roles in education, as
multiple, continual crises drain time and resources. The strains
which students experience in their lives will make maintenance of
traditional academic standards very difficult. A pervasive sense
of lack of control will cause disillusionment, apathy, and
cynicism about the possibilities of preserving the current
schooling system. Voucher systems and the franchises which
develop in response will further complicate this situation.

National priorities and local mandates will continually be
in conflict, posing grave problems for educational decision-
makers. Demands for documented accountability and competence

will badly reduce the ability of educators to accomplish their basic duties. The current lack of consensus on what the basic content of education should be will widen.

In short, the existing model for formal education will become almost unworkable. Education will be cited as an example of a crisis area in the struggle between those who feel the "materialistic American Dream" is still possible to reach and those who argue for a less technological, more human-centered society. The challenge for educators will be to shift from a reactive to a proactive reconstructionist position which chooses among the options in this struggle by taking a united, professional stand on the future of schooling. (My ideas on the stance educators should choose are set forward in The Far Side of The Future.)[3] Whether or not this challenge is met, the consequences for American society will be very large.

My colleague, Jim Bowman, tells a story about a frog. He claims that one can take a pot of water, put it on the stove without a lid, place a live frog in it, and boil the frog without ever covering the pot! The trick which keeps the frog cooking is that the heat underneath the pot is turned on just a little bit, so the temperature in the water goes up very, very slowly (perhaps a degree an hour). It gets hotter and hotter and hotter in the pot, but the frog never knows when to scream and jump out because the change is so gradual--so it boils! Educators can learn from this story because every year the water in our pot is that much closer to boiling: our budgets are smaller, we've cut things we needed to keep, we assume once more that the erosion of funds is going to stop, and we're about to get cooked!

We behave like the woman who had some cocker spaniel puppies with very long tails. She wanted to be stylish and have their tails short, but she wanted to spare them the pain of cutting off their tails all at once, so she cut off an inch every day! I feel that we're beginning to do that in education, primarily because we've been unwilling to accept that the whole fiscal tail really must come off. Paring the first 25% of our mid-1970s budgets and retaining our existing methods of instruction may have been possible (barely). The further cuts we now must make will mandate a radically different approach.

The Responses We Should Choose

What should we as a group of futures-oriented educators do, if we believe that these predictions for the next 10 years are fairly accurate? Certainly, the implications for our day-to-day activities are staggering. All of education is predicated on

images of the future. Our budgets make assumptions about the
economy; our research is tailored to the future contexts in which
it is to be used; and, when we teach students, we have a vision
of what they need to know given the world in which they will be
growing up. What does it mean for all our daily work if these
fundamental notions about the future that underlie so much of
what we do need to be altered?

When people aren't certain about what's going to happen, or
when the future seems threatening to them, the natural response
is to retreat into a psychological framework in which we say, "I
don't know what's really going to happen, but the safest thing to
assume is that at least some things will stay the same. These
perennial issues are the areas in which I'm going to work; it's
too risky to respond to a mere probability." So all of us spend
our time wrestling with the eternal issues and problems. I think
perennial concerns are crucial and should absorb 70% of our time,
but 30% of what we do needs to be oriented toward resolving the
uncertain future issues outlined above.

In practice, such a stance means that where we can see
things "on the river" that differ from the present, we need
deliberately and explicitly to change current decision-making in
budget, curriculum and instruction. Where the future is
indeterminate (and you'll notice that there are large areas of
the future that I have not attempted to forecast because these
are equivalent to a "dice game"), we need to have the courage to
take a broad spectrum, "shotgun" approach in our educational
strategies. For example, we don't know when micro-computer
software will become useful in teaching reading. Such a breakthrough may be eight years away, or eighteen. But, if we are
making plans that involve classrooms 10 years from now, we'd
better ensure that our plans are flexible enough to incorporate
the potential existence of micro-computer instruction. This may
sound risky, but in fact it is the least speculative stance we
can adopt: to acknowledge and prepare for legitimate
indeterminacy.

Given the conservatism that emerges during troubled times in
education, being future-oriented in planning takes a certain
degree of intellectual and professional fortitude. A parallel
emotional courage is needed to look at an admittedly grim set of
predictions and still believe that a positive future for education is attainable. While I know that the short-term situation
is bleak and fraught with risk, I also feel that the very
difficulties that confront us also present real opportunities for
change and growth. Educational systems are so resistant to
innovation that ideological appeals seem to produce little long-
term fundamental change. However, if times are bad enough,

education will change out of monetary necessity, and we may be able to justify much-needed improvements in the name of stringency that we could never get otherwise.

For such a change strategy to succeed, we must anticipate the challenges that are coming and have ready pragmatic, field-tested, cost-effective innovations. Here the Education Section can play a major role in allowing us to interact among ourselves in devising such a set of models. If we work together to produce a "master plan" for low cost instruction, we may find educators surprisingly willing to adopt it simply because no other options are immediately available. We may be moving from a "river" to an "ocean" in terms of educational futures.

How might we evolve such a new model for instruction when we ourselves may become so pressed for money that even attending a yearly Education Section Conference becomes difficult? Hines and Gerlach have identified a low resources organizational structure which seems quite effective at promoting change: a segmented, polycephalous, ideological network [abbreviated SP(I)N]. SP(I)N organizations are composed of many autonomous, factional groups (hence are resistant to the cooptation, suppression, or immobilization tactics that can be used effectively against large bureaucracies). The decentralization of SP(I)N associations ensures that they are always responsive to the needs of the membership and do not become overly dependent on a particular leader. Overlapping memberships in the factional groups which make up SP(I)Ns keep communication channels open. The ideological bond that members share provides the common motivation and purpose to keep the organization functioning.

The Education Section now has many characteristics of SP(I)N groups. Should the economy become difficult enough, we could choose deliberately to evolve in this direction rather than toward a traditional professional association model. Similar social inventions to SP(I)N can be used, if we are creative and foresighted, to overcome the resistance to organized innovation that a time of malaise presents.

I believe that the 1980s will be a grim period primarily because our society thought that it could get by with second-rate education for most citizens, that a high technology society could be run by a small group of experts and staffed by a large group of people who had very little idea of how anything worked. This assumption was obviously wrong; a complex society requires that every citizen be as intelligent and creative as possible. The costs to our society of not educating one person--in terms of crime, welfare expenditures, and forgone productivity--are far higher than the direct costs of a good education from kinder-

garten through the doctoral level. For this reason, it is vital
that we as educators become proactive rather than reactive in
shaping education's relationship to the rest of society and in
asserting that an essential part of the solution to our problems
lies in a high priority for genuine educational change.

NOTES

1. See Educational Futures: Sourcebook I (Washington, D.C.,
World Future Society, 1979).

2. O.W. Markley, Changing Images of Man (Menlo Park,
Calif.: Stanford Research Institute, 1974).

3. Jim Bowman, et al., The Far Side of the Future (Houston,
Texas: Educational Futures, 1978. Distributed by the World
Future Future Society).

Importance of Future Studies' Perspective in Education and in Society

Edith Weiner

There is a concept receiving more recognition of late called "educated incapacity." It means that an individual can be so well educated in a particular discipline that he or she is unable to recognize three things:

1) the changes that are taking place within that discipline;

2) the changes that are taking place in the external environment that will affect that discipline; and

3) the impacts that discipline is having on the rest of society.

I have never been a strong believer in asking the experts to tell me what will happen 10 years hence in their fields because I think educated incapacity is a real phenomenon. I think back, for example, to the scientific committee that advised Queen Isabella on Columbus's proposal. Absurd, they said. Obviously, ignoring their advice was the best decision she ever made. I also think back to the time in the mid-1800s, when scientists calculated that a "train" running at more than 15 mph would cause the passengers to suffocate and that blood would spurt from their noses and ears. I think back to the first half of this century, when scientists "proved" mathematically that no space ship could ever escape earth's gravity. And I recall Thomas Edison's remarks about how Westinghouse would certainly kill a number of customers if he attempted to install a system of alternating current of any significant size.

And I apply these lessons to the current climate. Time and again I speak to experts in fields like medicine, economics, manpower training and development, corporate management and politics, and I am amazed at the degree to which educated incapacity takes hold in the brightest, even the most innovative, people. And, needless to say, I have found educators and their associates in library sciences, guidance counseling and teacher training to be no exceptions.

Do these comments sound familiar to you?

* "The teacher can never be truly replaced by a machine."
* "A full formal education is necessary for an individual to function as a well-rounded citizen."
* "An education today prepares one for a career tomorrow."

These, and other cliches like them, are becoming meaningless. A bit of a long-range perspective on where our society is moving will help us understand why I say these things.

Technology

Technology is moving us in many interesting directions. It must be remembered that less than a dozen years ago man had not yet been to the moon. And today we are exploring Saturn and beyond, with pictures relayed back almost instantaneously from the depths of space to our living rooms. Ten years ago we never questioned the ability to meet our energy needs. Today we speak of the need to develop solar, geothermal and hydrogen-based energy systems. Ten years ago we played tic-tac-toe with a friend on a scrap of paper. Today we can play this, and even chess, with no one but a computer. Ten years ago music was played on conventional instruments. Today it is combined with electronic synthesizers. Ten years ago we transmitted information over air waves or through massive copper cables. Today we can pass millions of bits of information via laser light through fibers no wider than a hair. Ten years ago we felt that only drugs could immediately alter our blood pressure. Today we know that we can use biofeedback technology to alter our own body functions. Ten years ago television was a one-way communications tool. Now we are moving into an age when we call it interactive. Ten years ago we knew stenography and typing to be the tools of the secretary. Today they are transcription and word processing.

I could go on and on. But the point is an obvious one. If educators are to prepare themselves and their students for the next 10 years, someone's got to have the foresight and the courage to use, adopt, plan for and understand the role technology is playing in our daily work, leisure and learning environments.

Family

Another change has taken place over the past decade of which educators must be fully aware. When we began the 70s it could be safely said that most children in the school system were living with both natural parents and at least one sibling. The father worked, and the mother was home rearing the children. This meant that a basic family acculturation could be taken for granted, as could all the incidentals that related to that: a 9 to 3 school day, homework that the parent could help with, summer vacations, school psychologists who mostly had to deal with the isolated case of a child whose parents were becoming divorced, and families that were able to plan for and save for their children's higher education.

Today's environment is indicative of where tomorrow's school children will be coming from. Consider the following:

* the high incidence of divorce;
* the proportion of mothers in the work force;
* the increasing number of serial marriages--i.e.
    remarriages;
* the growing number of single child families;
* the growth in unwed parenthood;
* the difficulty facing parents regarding the handling of
    inflation.

There is no question that today the child who lives with both natural parents, with a non-working mother and at least one brother or sister, is in a shrinking minority. And as this minority gets smaller, the needs of the remainder of the student population will have to be dealt with more seriously. Year-round schooling, to accommodate working mothers, is a possibility. Flex-time, or shifting hours, for schooling is another. Electronically conducted classes or homework sessions is another. Dealing with the results of home-based emotional turmoil and transitions is another. Alternatives to financing higher education are another. Obviously, monitoring the evolving culture, the socialization process and the needs of today's and tomorrow's families will be critical for educators.

Challenges to Professional Priesthoods

Authority is an interesting phenomenon. It is something which is granted, and is often taken for granted. I'll never forget the episode on Candid Camera where Allan Funt placed a huge sign on the highway outside Maryland which read, "Maryland closed temporarily." It was incredible to see the number of motorists who pulled off the road, asking how long this would last. One was terribly concerned, because his family was in Maryland.

Despite the fact that this same trick can be pulled today with similar results, the impression one gets from surveying the environment is that more and more people are ignoring the signs. There is a greater propensity to challenge authority, whether this be the law or the experts in various disciplines. We call it a "defrocking of the professional priesthoods." Arising from a number of social, technological, economic and political factors too numerous to go into here, suffice it to say that no discipline has escaped the challenge--not doctors, not politicians, not economists, and not even architects. And certainly not educators. This is borne out by lawsuits against schools for failure to educate; people who insist on educating their children at home; the demands for student and community involvement in curriculum design; and the push for greater decentralization of education. It is critical for educators to be tuned into the major forces in society that are sweeping away the priesthoods and seeing professionals as employees rather than authorities.

The Role of Credentialism

In line with the challenge to authority comes the challenge to institutions in general and to the belief that any institution has the answers, let alone the interests of its constituents at heart. While it has always been the case, we now hear more and more talk of self-preservation having a very high priority within institutions. Indeed, in a survey done several years back, the second highest priority corporate presidents saw colleges and universities as having, just below intellectual stimulation of students, was self-preservation as an institution. Preparation of students for a work role in society was listed as the fifth and lowest priority.[1] Thus, it is no surprise to see academic credentialism as a ticket to one's fortune changing in interesting ways. Another recent study, published in the Harvard Business Review several years ago, surveyed corporate managers as to whether they thought the course material offered in M.B.A. programs adequately prepared students for jobs in management. The results were these: managers felt that the course content was of little use to actual management skills, but that the people who came out of the M.B.A. programs were the kind of people they wanted to hire. Thus, in this case, credentialism is viewed as a filter, not as an indicator of skills achieved.

It is critical, therefore, for educators to track, on a long-term basis, what their role in serving society truly is.

Self-preservation is ultimately at stake, because where the formal educational community fails to serve society's needs, the "peripheral" educational community will come along to fill the gaps. Clearly, adult education has been an excellent example. Job changes as a result of technological obsolescence, economic swings, and political shifts in priorities have sent numerous adults back for schooling. So have social pressures that caused adults to want to acquire more knowledge and to meet new people. It was a long time before educators understood the potential in this market for scholastic services. And the market has still not been seriously penetrated or serviced. The corporate sector would rarely, if ever, let go an opportunity of such magnitude. Indeed, the publishing and film companies are attempting to reach some of this market, as are private specialization schools.

Thus, the theaters for formal education and for peripheral education are finding the tastes of the audiences changing, and only by trying new plays and by casting new characters will the seats be filled. The race is on to see whose bill is most attractive, and it will be an interesting race from my point of view. From your viewpoint, it will be an enormous challenge, and one that requires careful and continual tracking of the reviews, the emerging talent, and the changing social tastes over the next decade. Credentialism, like professionalism, will not provide a safe screen to hide behind. If the performance is not there, the public won't be there, either.

The Information Society

To compound the challenge comes the reality of the information explosion which we, as a society, are experiencing. Michael Marien puts it this way:

> Individually and collectively, we know more than any society that has ever existed. We are the scientific and technical leaders of the world. A greater proportion of the American young spend a greater proportion of their formative years in educating institutions than ever before in human history, and we proudly point to the growing portion of our society that is therefore "educated."

> But all this matters little. The only relevant criterion is what we need to know, individually and collectively, to manage the unprecedented complexity that we have created. As the gap between requisite knowledge and knowledge attained grows, we become an increasingly ignorant society.

It is time to ask how our teaching institutions can keep up with the incredible spiraling of information which includes:

* New schools of information. Here I would include new branches of science like neuropsychiatry and computer economics, new branches of management like public affairs, environmental scanning and affirmative action, and new branches of professional services like holistic health delivery.

* New information tools, beyond the <u>idea</u> of the computer, but built on the myriad of computing applications. Here I would include real time interactive learning modes, widespread access to information, the ability to branch information by specific area of interest, and the portability of information programming and accessing hardware.

* The speed with which information is outdated, most notably in the hard sciences, but also in fields like law, education, mental health, economics, and career planning.

* New paradigms in information generally, such as proposals for large information systems to be sold as a public utility, using information as a national resource, and making information the new tool of participatory democracy.

* The skills needed to manage information, to communicate it, to screen it, to develop it, and to capitalize on it.

Teaching institutions will be profoundly affected by all of these considerations, in some instances spearheading the new age, and in others lagging sadly behind.

New Markets for Education

Much has been said lately about the growing adult education field. Perhaps the best way to deal with this is in a social context, an economic context and a technological context.

Within the social context there are two driving forces which reshape the markets for education. One is demography. As age changes occur in the population as a whole, the numbers of pupils at each level in the educational system changes and new accommodations must be made for these. One reason for the growth of adult education is the aging of the population, swelling the numbers of older people and creating new markets for many services. Education is just one of the services impacted. So demography is a critical long-range tracking need of the educational community. The other social force to be considered within a social context is the changing life cycle of individuals. Where once an individual pursued a life course in which adulthood marked a leaving of the educational arena and an entry in family life and work, this no longer is true. Not only is the formation of a family more often postponed today, it is also more often not even elected as an option in the life cycle. And work life has changed dramatically. Early retirement, the desire to pusue second and third careers, and the increasing use of work leaves have all chipped away at the smooth and orderly progression of single, 40-year career paths. In addition, the life cycle of the female has changed significantly, sending many into educational pursuits after the children are grown, as well as the pursuit of more rewarding careers.

Within the economic context, we see a growing desire for people to better themselves later on in life, to get a second chance, or a changed orientation, for purely economic reasons. Thus, the administrative assistant begins going for an M.B.A., or the engineer goes to law school. In addition, economics plays an important role in job shuffling. When governments could afford to hire, civil service was a secure and financially sound field for many. With cutbacks, employees are forced to seek other fields of work. When the economy forces massive lay-offs, many people seek retraining programs. Given the increasing volatility of the economy, massive dislocations and need for re-education are bound to proliferate.

And, within the technological context, we see more and more positions facing technological obsolescence. This means that either refresher courses are constantly needed for various professions in order to keep up with changes in their fields, or that retraining programs for complete career changes are in order.

It is critical, therefore, that the educational institutions keep abreast of the forces creating new markets for education, the types of markets these are likely to be, and how their needs might best be met.

Regulation and Legislation

For many years, the walls of academe had felt immune to the challenges that the business sector was feeling from government edicts. But in recent years, the picture has changed. Now schools, too, are faced with all kinds of regulatory and legislative mandates, from open enrollment to equal opportunity employment to minimum wage for student aids. The bureaucracy has begun to take hold of the hallowed halls of ivy as much as it has encroached on the bricks and mortar of the corporate world. And suddenly, within the past five years, those of us in the corporate community have watched the academics fighting some of the same battles we had fought regarding burdensome, costly and sometimes poorly designed and executed laws and guidelines. Corporations have instituted many forums for watching, monitoring and shaping the legislative and regulatory thrusts which emanate from Washington, from state and local law-making bodies, and from regulatory agencies. The educational institutions will now also have to have the same kind of scanning capacity if they are to keep pace with the flurry of government activities that will impinge upon the future management and well-being of the academic world.

I have discussed briefly some of the fundamental changes taking place that require a futures-oriented approach to educational planning. I've touched on technology, the family, the challenge to authority and credentialism, the information society, changing markets for education, and the regulatory and legislative scene. Now I'd like to focus on a topic that I have studied carefully for a number of years: the Education/Corporation Interface. My audience for this topic has traditionally been the corporate community. I would like you to put yourself in the position of a corporate manager who must judge the role business might play in the educational arena.

Some Factors Affecting the Education/
Corporation Interface

A. The rapid growth of knowledge (estimate of knowledge doubling every four to seven years). This causes most formally acquired education, in the scientific as well as social studies fields, to be outdated a few years after graduation. In order for corporations to keep their technical and professional staffs up to date, new types of continuing education programs must be established to coordinate corporate professionalism with academic curriculum additions and revisions.

B. The rapid growth of technological obsolescence, leading to job loss and transferral. This necessitates training and retraining programs for those persons whose skills and knowledge are pre-empted by technological progress--affecting vocational schools in particular. (Examples include not only the replacement of typesetters by computerized equipment, but also the eventual substitution of computerized programmed learning systems for some teachers.)

C. <u>Massive manpower shifts in an age of uncertainty,
dictated by wide scale demographic, economic and social factors.</u>
The need for greater academic/corporate cooperation in improving
manpower planning and career counseling programs in these times
has been and will continue to be paramount. Past failures in
this area had led to severe displacements of engineers (as a
result of budget cuts in the space/science sector), teachers (as
a result of poor long-range attention to demographic changes
regarding number of children of school age), lawyers (of whom
there is now an overabundance) and doctors (of whom there are too
many specialists and not enough generalists to meet public
needs).

D. <u>The increasingly poor basic reading and mathematical
skills of current high school, and even college, graduates.</u> For
some time, corporations have been faced with the need to
undertake basic remedial education for their clerical level
employees. With costs rising and many corporations facing severe
cutbacks, the antagonism could mount between the corporations,
who need already-educated employees, and the academic sector,
which would be seen as not having fulfilled its job.

E. <u>The irrelevance of formal education to many on-the-job
tasks and responsibilities.</u> This is a growing problem in terms
of public awareness and corporate discomfort. Studies have
shown, for example, that corporate managers who have reviewed
business administration courses find the course content almost
irrelevant to their requirements for their employees. There is
an increasing desire for on-the-job apprenticeships to replace,
at least in part, classroom learning, with academic credit
awarded for these apprenticeships.

F. <u>The spread of underemployment.</u> This situation occurs
when credentialism, or the stress placed on academic degrees and
diplomas, gets out of hand. There will remain, at least in the
next decade, too few jobs for too many overqualified persons.
The result will be doctoral-level individuals filling masters-
level positions, masters-level persons displacing undergraduates,
and high school graduates squeezed out of even the clerical level
positions. The social tension and unrest, as well as the lowered
productivity which will result from disaffection with jobs held,
will begin posing severe problems for the country.

G. <u>Transadulthood.</u> This is the newly emerged portion of
the life cycle which embraces people anywhere between the ages of
17 and 30 who do not know what they want to do with their lives,
and are not yet ready to make any decisions of permanence or
undertake any serious responsibility. Both the corporate and
academic communities will face the challenge of meeting the needs
of, and problems posed by, this evergrowing segment of the
population.

H. <u>The</u> <u>coordination</u> <u>of</u> <u>corporation-developed</u> <u>technology</u> <u>and</u> <u>the</u> <u>world</u> <u>of</u> <u>education</u>. New technologies developed in corporate laboratories range from mini-calculators for the blind to computerized teaching systems for the gifted. The pace of this technological growth is, for all intents and purposes, dependent only upon the speed with which the educational system can absorb it and afford it. Closer coordination of this will be crucial if the technology is to be maximized and the impact on the schooling system is to be beneficial.

I. <u>The</u> <u>economic</u> <u>environment</u> <u>and</u> <u>its</u> <u>impacts</u> <u>on</u> <u>educational</u> <u>funding</u>. In a time of tight purse strings, the educational community will have to do some rethinking of priorities if it continues to seek corporate backing via contributions and co-sponsorship of programs. Frivolous expenditures in social science research, for example, can be viewed by money-tight corporations as irresponsible use of funds. Closer coordination, short of domination by corporate interests, will be vital if private funding is to remain forthcoming.

J. <u>The</u> <u>emergence</u> <u>of</u> <u>new</u> <u>careers</u>. Corporations are increasingly discovering the need for professionals with expertise not developed in formal academic specialities. Examples are "futurists" and trouble shooters in computer abuses. More give-and-take on a regular basis between university deans and corporate officers for just this purpose will become increasingly necessary.

That's my list of areas where the corporate and educational communities need to cooperate in the future. Now let's look to the results of a study of company presidents done in 1973 to see what they had to say regarding new corporate perspectives of education.

Question: In place of a college degree, what credentials would you accept of applicants for management positions?

Answer: Almost two-thirds said they would accept a certificate of competence in a specialized field (similar to an apprenticeship).

Question: Would you favor a partnership between colleges and universities with business and/or the professions in the granting of academic degrees?
Answer: Two-thirds said yes, they would.

Question: What, in your opinion, are the basic skills commonly lacking among today's college graduates?
Answer: Over 60% said English grammar. Over half said oral and written communications. Almost half said spelling.

Question: Would you be willing to have your company cooperate in the operation and administration of a college or university?
Answer: One half said yes.

Question: Do you favor a 12-month academic year?
Answer: Almost two-thirds said yes.

Question: Has your company been approached by members of the academic community for financial support?
Answer: 87.6% said yes.

Question: In your opinion, in which areas do colleges and universities have a responsibility to students?
Answer: Over two-thirds checked the areas of intellectual leadership, development of marketable skills and the granting of degrees.

Question: In your opinion, in which areas do colleges and universities have a responsibility to business?
Answer: About two-thirds said intellectual leadership and development of marketable skills.

Question: In your opinion, in which areas do colleges and universities have a responsibility to society?
Answer: Three-fourths said intellectual leadership and providing a cultural center.[2]

What, then, do we learn from these corporate presidents? Although an admittedly biased group, they view the main failings of the academic community as being in the area of basic oral and written communications. They feel the major responsibility of the academic community is in providing intellectual leadership. And they accept the idea of not only providing financial support to the academic community, but also curricula and administrative cooperation. It is vital, therefore, that the educational community include in its long-range perspective of where it is going, and how it will get there, the perspectives of the corporate community, which will continue to provide funds for and employment of the students who move through the academic institutions of today and tomorrow.

Thus far I have discussed some major environmental factors that will challenge today's educational institution and the world of the education/corporation interface. Throughout these remarks, I've made it clear that it is imperative for those involved in education to identify and track the environmental forces that will affect the future of education.

How Do You Keep Abreast of
These Changes?

There are three basic ways that the education community can keep track of, and be made aware of, emerging issues and developments that can have a significant impact upon you. And, basically, these do not differ from the ways the corporate community undertakes these activities.

The first is via professional organizations. The associations to which you pay dues should be directed by you, the members, to develop long-range issue identification and impact assessment programs. These should be directed to be ongoing, systematic and broad in scope, with periodic feedback to members via newsletters, seminars, conferences and the like.

The second is via your specific community or organization. On a smaller scale, your own affiliate organization, whether it be a school, a community, an agency, or whatever, should set up a long-range issue identification and tracking system that serves your particular organizational needs, and focuses on your own changing markets, regulatory environment, public affairs, employment issues, career opportunities, and so on. This can be done in any number of ways depending upon your resources, your size, and desire to keep pace with the changing times.

The third way is on your own. Basically, each individual has a responsibility for acquainting himself or herself with those forces that could impact upon his or her clients, his or her programs, his or her own career. This can be done by reading a wider variety of publications than one already does, but with a different orientation. Given the fact that those things that could have second and third order impacts upon what you do may not even be the subject of your reading materials, your orientation has to change from the discrete to the integrated.

Let me give some examples of what I mean by this. Suppose you read somewhere that the cost of electronic circuitry is going down. Suppose you read somewhere else that cutbacks in funds to education must come in personnel. And suppose another article speaks to the increasing cost of paper. Putting all three items together, it is not a far jump to the assimilation of more electronic teaching tools in the school system.

Let's take another example. Suppose you read someplace that the leisure industry is the fastest growing segment of the economy. Then you read that inflation is eating away at a family's disposable income. And another article you come across touches on the continuing high number of divorces in the population. All three together speak to the potential for low-cost educational endeavors to serve a leisure market that is compounded by many people seeking to reorient their lives, to meet new people, and to find outlets for their time and energies.

So it is imperative that you begin to look for patterns in what you read and hear and see--patterns that will shape the future of where you are going, what you are doing, whom you are serving, and why you are failing or succeeding.

To sum up, let me say this. There are opportunities in education that are going unattended. There are problems that are being overlooked. There are expectations that are not being met. And there is a whole future out there waiting to be filled. You can either suffer from educated incapacity and not participate in the shaping of that future, or you can recognize the value of far-sightedness and have an impact on that future that will be better for all parties to the educational communities.

NOTES

1. The Gallagher President's Report, Volume IX, No. 23.

2. Ibid.

Social Change and Educational Outcomes:
1980-2000
Harold G. Shane

Social changes of the next two decades--and their educational consequences--will have so great a worldwide impact that they no longer can be considered in the narrow context of a single nation. Because social change greatly transcends national borders, education, too, needs to become more transnational. And because of the overspill of knowledge in a given field of learning, education needs to become much more transdisciplinary than it heretofore has been.

In my opinion, views such as those expressed above have begun to be voiced both more loudly and by more and more people during the past decade. The significance of this growing consensus as to the need for changes in educational practice cannot, however, be measured by the increasing clamor. The significance of worldwide educational change, if it really becomes significant, will reside in and emanate from much more profound insight and from much greater mutual reciprocity than that which most humans previously have shown themselves to be capable. In the pages that follow I shall endeavor to present some dimensions of the problem of coping with recent and probably future developments in the fabrics of world societies, then speculate about a few of the changes which recent writings in the social sciences seem to anticipate as we move into the 80s and the 90s. The final pages of this essay will deal with the educational consequences.

A basic problem in studying social change. At least as reflected in certain major social sciences,[1] the study of social change is vastly complicated not only by the interdisciplinary linkages among these "soft sciences" but by the fact that they have a strong nationalistic flavor. The concept that scholars in political science have of "human rights," for instance, differs in meaning from one country to another. To elaborate on this point, let me point out that certain philosophical premises have become "locked in" in such fields as political science and economics.

The challenge of a multiethnic and polycultural world to the cooperative development of mutually acceptable educational changes is, to say the least, an imposing one. One need only consider the world economic restructuring that is taking place to see how subject to debate certain premises in this field have become.

There also are variations from one nation to another as to just what "education," "schooling," and "learning" should be construed to mean and the extent and nature of the boundaries which lend them their identity. For purposes of this paper, schooling is used to designate planned and organized instruction intended to maintain and to extend a feeling of belonging to a particular human sub-community, plus the values, attitudes, and skills which this group prizes.

Education is broader in meaning and hence includes experiential input that is derived from many sources including out-of-school or paracurricular experiences which are reflected in changed or in new ways of behaving. Learning[2] is even more broad in scope, transcending both schooling and education because of the lifelong input of personal experience and values, knowledge, methods, and skills which are extracted to form a continuum of experiences encountered from the cradle to the grave.

Now that I have suggested some of the complexities involved in discussing social change and educational consequences, let me turn to a sampling of a few of the social developments and dilemmas which seem likely ones during the next 10 to 20 years.

Social Change and Concomitant
  Dilemmas: 1980-2000

Many of the changes in our lives during the future are certain to be caused by carryover from the "crisis of crises"--biophysicist John Platt's apt phrase--which the world has encountered during the past several decades. The components of our multiple problem clusters are too well known to the reader to require elaboration: the breakdown of once-revered values, the disorientation caused by rapid change, the triple shocks of resource depletion, pollution, and exponential population increase, the widespread mistrust of or dissatisfaction with established institutions (government, industry, church, school, the military, labor unions, the corporate community), inflation, nuclear problems, increasingly deadly weaponry, unemployment, and the like.

Reefs and shoal water ahead. A variety of alarming reefs and stretches of shoal waters promise to threaten the human course ahead and also serve to reaffirm the need for the finest navigational skills on the part of world leaders. Because of the limits imposed by space, and because the prospects for turbulence in the 80s and 90s already have been clearly limned by such scholars as Geoffrey Barraclough, W. Jackson Davis, Willis W. Harman, and Lester R. Brown,[3] have chosen not to provide a mere inventory of our probable potential problems in the years ahead but to select a particularly subtle and largely unrecognized threat to global stability. This is the "present shock" created by _experience compression_, a many-sided phenomenon of which I first wrote in 1973.[4]

The unrecognized attack on human reason. All of us alive today, and particularly those persons born since 1940, have been bombarded by a relentless barrage directed at our senses; a predominantly electronic assault on our reason, an assault on the systems of beliefs and values which previously had been established. Television is certainly the most important factor in the sensory bombardment to which we are increasingly exposed.[5] Let me illustrate.

Television, and, to a much lesser extent, other media have a confusing effect on our time sense--on our sense of temporal congruity. On a worldwide scale in no more than 30 minutes televiewers may choose among a Western U. S. range war of the 1880s, a serial based on the Korean War, or a Walt Disney movie-- each interspersed with commercial "messages" hawking deodorants or hair spray, or depicting a family dispute over coffee arbitrated by the taste and aroma of instant coffee. A moment later a storm warning quietly may glide across the screen while a news update concludes with the suggestion that you tune in at ten to hear more of the details of the latest political developments.

Our traditional sense of remoteness is likewise destroyed, and our emotional involvement enhanced, by the instant interlinkages TV creates between, say, the quiet of one's home and the gripping panorama of the smoking ruin of an aircrash on the far side of the world. Geographic coherence is lost in the process.

The sequencing of unrelated events plus the impact of information overload not only confuse the senses, they also reduce the credibility of reality. All of these aural and visual "electronic penetrations" of human reason--frequently penetrations that are hostile to reason--tend to make us so confused as to lead us to disregard valid data and to find it difficult to cope with situations that require prompt, reasoned decisions.

It would appear that our overloaded sensory circuits are left with a predisposition to "irrational" behavior. Patently, such a development creates a danger which threatens to complicate our efforts to react intelligently to social change and to increase the problems and the opportunities for the next 20 years. With this note of caution, let us now consider some likely developments in the global community during these two decades.

Likely Developments in the Social Sciences

An analysis of developments in prospect for the U. S. and for other world societies is complicated by the paradox of increasing transdisciplinary linkages on the one hand and greater in-depth specialization on the other. The phenomenon of composite terms (e.g., biophysics and molecular biology) which suggests broadening horizons, may, in reality, be due to proliferating sub-specialization within special fields of expertise. Whatever the outcome of transdisciplinary trends may be, one generalization seems to be justified. It is increasingly difficult to deal with political science, or economics, or sociology as separate or isolated fields since these and other social sciences are weaving themselves into a seamless web.

Complexity in communication also serves to create problems both in fathoming meaning in fields of expertise other than one's own and in adequately translating concepts in order to identify their significance for education. As Robert M. Hutchins phrased it some 25 years ago,[6] one of the phenomena of our age is that the intelligibility of our messages has declined while the means of communication have improved.

Our lack of a surprise-free future also fogs our vision since most projections in the social sciences assume that there will be no major system breaks as tomorrow's world comes into being. Actually, the surprises have probably equalled the assumed certitudes that served as bases for many past forecasts.

Finally, scholars in the soft sciences, given the same data, do not invariably reach similar conclusions because their values and their viewpoints are so divergent. They range from agnostic to fundamentalist and from egalitarian to elitist. My attempts to review recent trends reflected in the literature were complicated accordingly.

Images of tomorrow in political science. The next decade might well be dubbed "The Uneasy 80s" if one is to judge them in the context of political science. The ten points which follow capture the relatively gloomy panorama portrayed in the literature:

(1) The increased use of essential commodities as the means of economic and political blackmail to the disadvantage of the industrialized Western World and Japan.

(2) Domestic problems are likely to increase as threatened _aspiration_ levels turn into higher _frustration_ levels in Western democracies because their governments have not been able to deal effectively with shortages, inflation, recession, and unemployment.

(3) The likelihood that transnational antagonism and terrorism will not diminish, and could increase, if social conflict becomes an even more conspicuous reality.

(4) For the world of the West there is the possibility that both personal freedom and social welfare policies may have reached a peak, or at least a plateau, after more than 200 years of progress.

(5) Western middle class resentment and frustration stemming from loss of headway in socioeconomic upward mobility may eventuate in radical self-protective political movements designed to replace democracy with an iron police state government.

(6) We have as yet found no way to accommodate the "revolution of rising human aspirations," and the earth's limited carrying capacity and sociopolitical tensions will intensify as an anticipated population increase of between two and three billion occurs in the next two decades.

(7) On the positive side, the increasing prospect of global crises should encourage limited cooperation among potentially hostile nations with incompatible social, political, and economic goals.

(8) During the 20-year interval with which the participants in this World Future Society Education Section Conference predominantly are concerned, no form of global government seems likely to emerge, although regional coalitions--encouraged by necessity--may increase.

(9) The system of specialized agencies and cooperative regional programs developed by the United Nations offers the

best approach yet devised in attacking non-ideological, world-wide problems responsive to applied science and technology.

(10) Those who become the most successful governors of our interconnected planet, 1980-2000, will be peoples whose images of the future most nearly approximate reality and who are least constrained in the vigorous exercise of carefully weighed survival tactics.[7]

In fine, perspectives from the realm of political science suggest that the pressures and turmoil of recent memory are not only likely to continue but could deteriorate further. Certain implications for schooling/education/learning will be noted in the final pages of this essay.

Portentous trends in economics. In a humorous interchange with the writer earlier in the year, economist Kenneth Boulding commented that it was all right to make projections ". . . as long as you don't believe in them too much." A careful reading of current writings in economics also leads one to agree with Walter Heller who advised his fellow economists that we ". . . have been caught with our parameters down."[8]

Whatever the precise economic developments during the Uneasy 80s may prove to be, the consensus among many commentators is that they will tend to be unpleasant. Not nearly distant enough early warning signals suggest continued and perhaps disastrous inflationary trends, enormous personal debt (up from $500 billion to well over $1 trillion in the past eight years), increasingly internecine international competition, the possibility of U. S. government anti-inflationary measures such as drastic cuts in the money supply in circulation (with a severe credit crunch), major cuts in government spending (with worsened unemployment and hardship for the recipients of welfare), and a 100% increase in heating oil and gasoline taxes to produce revenue and reduce demand (with great and unevenly spread hardship). While such Draconian developments are unlikely during an election year, they could--in the relatively near future--become essential moves to avoid the hyperinflation which racked Germany during the years of the Weimar Republic.

The prospect of yet another Great Depression also may haunt the next decade. Unpleasant credence was given to this possibility by Edward Cornish in his recent long and explicit review of the situation (an article stimulated by Jay W. Forrester's 1978 computerized model) in which he notes that, "The economic conditions of today suggest those at the peak of a long-wave cycle: a decline in capital investment, rising unemploy-

ment, a leveling out of labor productivity, and reduced innovation."[9] Among Cornish's other highlighted (and distressing)
points:

> * Even as Americans relaxed in their unprecedented
> postwar prosperity, forces were at work to undermine it.

> * No one knows how much of the U. S. is already owned
> by OPEC nations.

> * In the U. S. today, most households probably are
> both illiquid and in debt: they have very little money
> available in cash or in the bank, and they owe thousands of
> dollars on past purchases.

> * The current energy shortage is sufficiently impor-
> tant that it could be the "trigger" that would touch off the
> depressionary landslide.

> * The training given large numbers of young people
> today is poorly suited to the workplace, [thus] making them,
> in effect, less effective than they would be without their
> formal education.[10]

One other disturbing prospect pertaining to what could be is
described in detail by W. Jackson Davis in The Seventh Year.[11]
Subtitled "Industrial Civilization in Transition," Davis'
thirteen heavily documented chapters present a disturbing
thesis, namely that, in the absence of a substitute for petroleum
as the world's preeminent source of energy, industrial society is
passing its zenith, and in the future there will be less material
affluence for humankind. In his concluding paragraphs the author
proffers hope:

> The turbulent events of the present . . . are . . .
> not the final hour of the human species, but an epochal
> step in its continuing evolution. History now calls on
> us to bid the past farewell without regret, and to open
> our hearts and minds to the new.[12]

Professor Davis' credentials as a professor of psychobiology
lend credence to his conclusions which clearly delineate an
impressive economic problem of the years ahead. In a world of
rising material aspirations, such aspirations can only be met by
growth--and growth, as of 1980 A.D., demands enormous amounts of
energy in a world adding nearly 200,000 mouths to be fed each
day. Growth also has served to create concomitant problems such
as the risks of pollution and the acute problems of nuclear power
sources.

The complexity of our economic prospects were noted by David Rockefeller in a conversation with the writer. Noting that the pace of change will be increasing, he said:

> My own feeling is that people who would limit growth fail to take into account that to diminish poverty--to improve the life of billions of people living at a bare subsistence level--we _have_ to have continued growth.[13]

So there we have the prospect for continued conflict between those who point to the limits of industrial growth and those who see (through the application of science and technology) the growth of limits.

Sociology _and_ _anthropology:_ _the_ _study_ _of_ _the_ _human_ _riddle._ Anthropology, reflecting the idea of a general science of humankind (a creation of the 19th century), and sociology, the study of societies, combine in current writings and trends to remind us that "the riddle is us."[14]

Anthropologists, such as Edward T. Hall in his provocative writings,[15] have reminded us that persons in diverse cultures have eyes and ears that see and hear differently and which respond in diverse ways _to_ _the_ _same_ _audiovisual_ _inputs_. However, there is at present no suitable evidence suggesting how these differences and the misunderstandings they sometimes create can be alleviated with the rapidity that successful living in the future requires.

In the same general way, sociology's scholars have helped us to see the many fragments of our social problem, scattered like the parts of a jigsaw puzzle, without reaching anything remotely resembling a consensus as to how we might begin to put the pieces together.

For use with my university classes, I have found the model (see Figure 1) useful in suggesting the processes of social change. I include it here to suggest how, in practice, humans participate in change processes.[16] The human riddle, however, remains unanswered with respect to _how_ the enormously important "alternative social practices" (see model, box V) shall be selected with due regard so as to serve the interests of justice and of practical considerations with respect to such matters as protecting the environment and resource sharing. Let me illustrate by drawing on both economics and sociology.

As noted in a _Time_ magazine cover story, "To Set the Economy Right,"[17] various measures presumably can be taken to strengthen

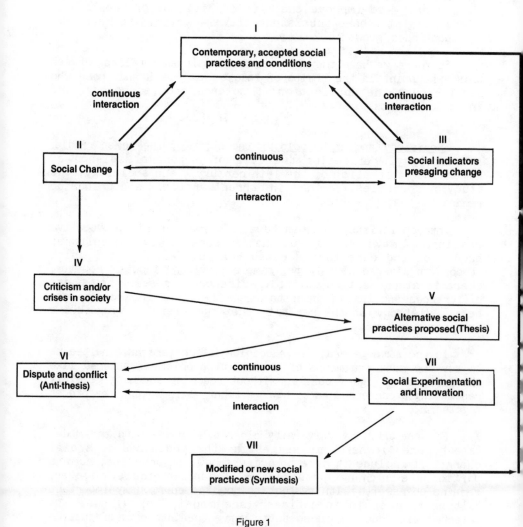

Figure 1

**A Model Illustrating Evolving
Social Change Processes**

SOURCE: Designed by Harold G. Shane, Indiana University, Bloomington.

the U.S. economy in what some scholars believe to be a post-Keynesian era. For example, (1) the money supply can be controlled even more rigorously, (2) production-retarding federal regulations can be eased or rescinded, and (3) government spending could be cut, say, by 10 or 15%.[18] But the cries of protest would be strident (1) lest a recession result from, (2) lest biospheric deterioration be accelerated by, (3) or lest such previous governmental commitments to social and pension programs be kept from serving the welfare of U.S. citizens. Yes, "the riddle is us" and how we conduct ourselves in making the social decisions we will be obliged to reach in the 80s!

Educational Consequences

Trends in contemporary U.S. society suggest a modest number of educational consequences. To summarize, the literature of political science suggests continued turmoil. Sociology posits major transitions and possibly unprecedented transformations if the world's historic industrial cycle should prove to be in its waning years, while economics poses the problem of how the peoples of the world can cope with the present revolution of rising material aspirations when both economic trends and the biosphere are imposing more and more constraints. What do such trends suggest for education?

Some general observations. Several broad recommendations for the improvement of learning through educational changes seem to be justified by present and prospective social changes. For one thing, persons of all ages need to be clearly and accurately informed with respect to what is happening in the real world. In, say, secondary school science, the concept of entropy presented to the learner should be more than an exposure to the second law of thermodynamics. Its nature as a measure of "gone-ness" and its consequences in a closed ecosystem needs to be understood. Greater care also should be exercised in the press and through television in presenting reality.

Even at an early age, learners should be exposed to the concept of alternative choices, as described in the literature, and to the idea that the future can be shaped in desirable ways by wise choices among alternatives. Prudent decisions, learners need to understand, need to be reached (only) after careful examination of the consequences of each alternative that suggests itself.

Finally, educational experiences (particularly those packaged in the form of traditional schooling) need to be improved by structuring them to provide many more opportunities than presently exist for learning how to make reasoned choices among alternatives before these choices become operational. I refer here to developing a respect for expertise in special fields of knowledge, learning to work with others in making group policy decisions, and how to organize in order to achieve worthy mutual goals.

Some specific suggestions for the improvement of learning
In the face of rapid change, and in view of the need for the social decisions which change forces upon us, the following suggestions seem reasonable ones.

(1) Because it tends to undermine temporal congruity and geographic coherence, learners need to have a greater measure of protection for misleading information transmitted by the media.

(2) By more personalized learning, education should increase the differences in the ability of young people to contribute to society. This goal can be approached by re-examining the concept of "equal" opportunity. Since humans are born neither free nor equal, education, including schooling, should be un-equal to improve opportunities for not only the handicapped or deprived but in the best inter-ests of all youth. On a worldwide scale, this is one of the great tasks of the next several decades.

(3) Improved self-images are needed to motivate learners--positive images of what the individual can become in the future--and they are needed by persons of all ages.

(4) Particularly in certain parts of the globe the educational opportunities for women need study and improve-ment or long term problems (food shortages, health prac-tices, mass poverty, illiteracy, etc.) cannot be solved.

(5) The hunt is the teacher in a hunting culture, as anthropologists point out. In societies in transition and perhaps in major transformation, society should be a source of instruction. As Alvin Toffler, among others, has suggested, action and service learning beyond the school campus are important sources of input and personal growth.

(6) Greater heed needs be given to helping persons learn how to learn as we more and more clearly see the need for lifelong education.

(7) Because of the pace of transition, attention should be given to eliminating forms of schooling which lock

young learners into vocational channels where they are misemployed or under-employed. Conversely, the skills prerequisite to sequential changes in employment ought to be encouraged.

(8) Since educational technology is likely to be of continued importance, even more care should be invested in making our software more compatible with the best human values and traditions.

(9) It will not serve the future well if the curriculum indoctrinates learners or if society-as-teacher confines them to past dogma. While we are condemned to re-live the past if we forget it (Santayana's phrase), an intellectually "open" climate is needed for effective 21st century living.

(10) Because of their importance in an often confusing and increasingly complicated world, communication skills (including listening) need to receive even greater re-emphasis than they now receive in either the school curriculum or in the para-curricular learnings which life provides. The importance of the ability to recognize potential doubletalk, ambiguous advertising and invidious propaganda can scarcely be over emphasized.

(11) A better balance should be sought between discussion-discovery (heuristic) type methods and more traditional methods of instruction. There are times when individual learners need to be taught by able teachers since the human heritage cannot be shared if our sole reliance is on group processes.

(12) A general education--a liberating rather than a merely liberal education--has increased in importance if it is construed to mean that the educated person is one continually acquiring a deeper understanding of (1) planetary cultures, (2) a knowledge of threats to the biosphere, (3) an understanding of other humans, and (4) the relationships existing among the first three.

Concluding comment. Two years ago I preserved in print a brief statement of my personal feelings about the human prospect. When I re-read it recently it seemed to provide a suitable close to this venture in speculating about social change and its implications for better tomorrows:

There seems reason to disagree vehemently with those who feel that our long roster of troubles betokens the decline of our species. The challenges which we must meet are not the signs of our decline. Rather, they are the result of our rapid rise from the savagery of the cave to the complex interdependence and mutual need which have come to characterize twentieth century living.

Whether or not our educational agencies will have the vision and the power needed to create educational changes not just for a new century but for life in a new millennium is a moot question. Hopefully, however, by the year 2001 A.D. we will have verified the hope that the fundamental problems now facing us are occurring in the dusk before cockcrow rather than in the gathering gloom of a long twilight.[19]

NOTES

1. E.g., political science, economics, sociology, and the general science of humankind--anthropology.

2. As interpreted in the Club of Rome report, No Limits To Learning: Bridging the Human Gap (London: Pergamon Press, 1979).

3. See bibliography for a representative listing of the "literature of prospective turbulence."

4. In The Educational Significance of the Future (Bloomington, Indiana: Phi Delta Kappa Foundation, 1973), pp. 12-13.

5. For an interpretation of experience compression as both a conceptual description and as a set of techniques for studying the future, see Wilma S. Longstreet and Harold G. Shane, "Educating for the 80's: A Transdisciplinary Approach" (Bloomington, Indiana: School of Education, Indiana University, 1979). 10 pp. (Mimeographed.)

6. In The Conflict in Education (New York: Harper & Bros., 1953).

7. The 10 points are taken from the planned report to the November, 1979 Unesco Symposium in Paris which deals with the evolution of general education content. I have drawn heavily on the views of a valued Indiana University Chair Professor in political science, L. Keith Caldwell, in preparing these statements.

8. In his 1974 presidential address to the American Economics Association.

9. Edward Cornish, "The Great Depression of the 1980s: Could it Really Happen?" The Futurist, 13:353-374, October, 1979.

10. Ibid.

11. W. Jackson Davis, The Seventh Year: Industrial Civilization in Transition (New York: W.W. Norton & Company, 1979).

12. Ibid., p. 283.

13. Cited in Harold G. Shane, Curriculum Change Toward the 21st Century (Washington, D.C.: The NEA, 1977), pp. 151-152.

14. Older readers will probably remember Pogo's immortal phrase: "We have met the enemy and he is us."

15. Among them, The Silent Language (1959), The Hidden Dimension (1966), and currently, Beyond Culture (1976).

16. My model--as many readers will note--was influenced by the pradigms proposed by Thomas S. Kuhn in The Structure of Scientific Revolutions (Chicago: The University of Chicago Press, Second edition, 1970). (Cf. chapters VII-IX)

17. Time, August 27, 1979, pp. 24-25.

18. The increase in government spending is suggested by a 1923 report from Stanley Baldwin, British Chancellor of the Exchequer. Per capita taxation at the time was $80 per year in Great Britain and $26.30 in the U.S. Our military expenditures in 1923 were $251 million (cited in Time, March 3, 1958, p. 9).

19. Curriculum Change Toward the 21st Century, p. 128.

RECOMMENDED READING

Bahm, A.J. The Philosopher's World Model. Westport, Connecticut : Greenwood Press, 1979. 328 pp.

Barraclough, Geoffrey. 'The Coming World Crash," New York Review of Books, 21:20-29, January 23, 1975.

Barraclough, Geoffrey. "The World Economic Struggle," New York Review of Books, 22:23-30, August, 1975.

Boulding, Elise. The Underside of History: A View of Women Through Time. Boulder, Colorado: Westview Press, 1977.

Boulding, Kenneth. From Abundance to Scarcity: Implications for the American Tradition. Columbus, Ohio: Ohio State University Press, 1977.

Brameld, Theodore. The Teacher as World Citizen--A Scenario of the 21st Century. Homewood, Illinois: ETC Publications, 1975.

Brown, Lester R. Resource Trends and Population: A Time for Reassessment. Washington, D.C.: Worldwatch Institute, Paper 29 (May, 1979).

Brown, Lester R. The Twenty-Ninth Day. New York: W. W. Norton and Company, Inc., 1978. 350 pp.

Commoner, Barry. The Politics of Energy. New York: Alfred A. Knopf, Inc., 1979. 101 pp.

Cornish, Edward, et al. The Study of the Future. Washington, D.C.: World Future Society, 1977. 307 pp.

Davis, W. Jackson. The Seventh Year: Industrial Civilization in Transition. New York City: W.W. Norton, 1979.

Ebel, Roland H., et al. "Get Ready for the L-Bomb: A Preliminary Social Assessment of Longevity Technology," Technological Forecasting and Social Change, 13:131-148, February, 1979.

Franko, L. G. and Marilyn J. Seiber. Developing Country Debt. New York: Pergamon Press, 1979.

Hafele, Wolf, and Wolfgang Sassin. "The Global Energy System," Behavioral Science, 24:1699-189, May, 1979.

Heilbroner, Robert. "Second Thoughts on The Human Prospect," Futures, February 19, 1976, pp. 31-40.

Higgins, Ronald. "The Seventh Enemy: The Human Factor in the Global Crisis," The New Ecologist, 9:6-10, January-February, 1979.

Jameson, Kenneth P., and Charles K. Wilber. _Directions in Economic Development_. South Bend, Indiana: University of Notre Dame Press, 1979.

Kohr, Leopold. _The Overdeveloped Nations: The Diseconomies of Scale_. New York: Schoken Books, 1978.

Legum, Colin, _et al_. _Africa in the 1980's: A Continent in Crisis_. New York: McGraw-Hill Book Company, 1979.

Newland, Kathleen. _The Sisterhood of Man_. New York: W. W. Norton, 1979.

Platt, John. "What We Must Do," _Science_, 166:1115-1121, November 28, 1969.

Shane, Harold G. _Curriculum Change Toward the 21st Century_. Washington, D.C.: The National Education Association, 1977.

Shane, Harold G. _The Educational Significance of the Future_. Bloomington, Indiana: Phi Delta Kappa, 1973. 116 pp.

Valaskakis, Kimon, _et al_. _The Conserver Society: A Workable Alternative for the Future_. New York: Harper and Row, 1979.

Planning Changes in Education:
Futuristic Trends and Images

Florence F. Hood

The winds of educational change have been blowing for
several decades, frequently at hurricane force, as public,
private and technological demands for a quality of product
different than that of traditional schools have increased
noticeably. The call for social reform and greater accountability, declining enrollments, private and industrial competition and shifts from formal education are only a few of the
many factors exerting pressures on schools at all levels to
change postures, procedures and programs. Glines has long stated
that if schools are to be significantly better, they must be
significantly different. Further, communities and educators must
begin now, at a much more rapid pace, the transition that will
result in the tremendous potential for change and improvement in
education--through accepting, controlling, and benefiting from
the Electronics Revolution.[1]

While addressing members of the National Association of
State Boards of Education in Williamsburg, Virginia, October 12,
1979, J. Fletcher, a senior policy analyst for the Department of
Health, Education, and Welfare, also declared that public
education must make a radical transformation or become obsolete.
If schools fail to embrace the new technology of computers and
other electronic communication systems, that technology will "put
them out of business." Time after time, new technology has wiped
out old industries.[2]

Bundy concludes that part of the problem in education today
is that we do not have a collective, inspiring vision of the
future. The very core of what holds a culture together is its
myths and images of the future. Thus, in preparing our youth,
indeed, in designing an educational system, what is needed most
is a common view, a vision of the future. It is this kind of

perspective which "gives meaning to the past, instills confidence in the present, and inspires hope that the promises contained in the vision will one day be fulfilled...."[3]

Willers stated that to think about the future is dangerous, but not to do so will be disasterous. Such thought is dangerous because humans now are aware of their capacity to create qualities of human experiences as well as to manipulate them. It will be disasterous if attention is not given to the future because arbitrary cultural drift leaves a society at the mercy of the unknown accidents and social mutations which may be catastrophic. There is a distinct difference in planning for the future and in planning a future.[4]

Statement of Purposes

Based upon the preceding observations and mandates, the major purposes of this paper are, therefore, to:

1. Examine change as it relates to education and educators;

2. Develop an awareness for the need to establish change as a discipline of knowledge in order to help bridge the gap between what is and what should/could be in education;

3. Explore concepts, trends, images and futuristic perceptions of education; and to

4. Establish a foundation for foreseeing and creating changes in educational futures.

Formal education today appears to be for a time and a culture that now does not exist. Though youth and the world are no longer the same, schools remain essentially just as they were at the beginning of the century.[5] The very foundations of education should shift from Band-Aid treatment to integrating planning and systems substitution, finding alternatives to unsatisfactory or outmoded methods. Such education will require participation in systems change among those who are seriously affected by the transformation. Systems are made up of human beings, of people; therefore, as systems change so will people's attitudes, values, beliefs.

Change

The direction is clear that change is the core of "significantly different" schools of the future. Sarason concluded that educators possess limited knowledge about the processes of implementing change.[6]   Bice reported that it may take up to 50 years from the time an educational innovation is introduced until it enjoys widespread use among educators.[7]   A question arises as to whether or not educators can <u>wait</u> for 50 years.   Most authorities are emphatically saying "NO!" How can humans be helped to understand change?

In order to change individual opinions or attitudes, the individual must be willing to accept; this acceptance is often dependent upon incentives which may be in the form of past reinforcements or reinforcement expectations. After an extensive review of the literature on theories of attitude change, Garrison generalized that "A shift in attitude change can be accomplished by providing a logical pattern of facts, gaining participation of the subject in an activity, and to some extent by getting the subject to identify with the opinion of a recognized authority."[8] It was further summarized that at least three major steps showing commonalities are involved in attitude change: (1) recognizing the need for change, (2) incubating the thoughts or time for comparing old beliefs to new information, and (3) changing behavior.

Lippitt, Watson, and Westley commented that no single change can equip a system to meet every problem that arises in the future, unless it is the change from an unwillingness to change to a willingness to change.[9] Desirable changes must be internalized and activated by those affected by the change; they cannot be shaped by outside forces alone. Attitude change does not occur overnight, though a traumatic experience can change a person's attitude suddenly. One who has a negative attitude toward change will be less likely to change than one with no clearly defined attitude, or one who sees change as favorable. Important guidelines for attitude change given by Davis included:

1. The leader must help, by his status, to provide prestige to the group. Those undergoing the change need exposure to people of prestige and credibility.

2. A strong sense of belonging should be developed within the group. There needs to ba a we-feeling or cohesiveness.

3. Changes to be made should be relevant to the tasks to be performed.

4. A clear and well-defined reason for the need for the change should be established with the group to change so that needed pressure for change will be generated.

5. Approval or acceptance by another person or by a particular group is a way of reinforcing attitudes.

6. Information about the needs and plans for change must be disseminated to the group. Communication is a vital element in effecting desired changes.[10]

Consciously or unconsciously, most people resent change and commonly ignore the facts which indicate the need for change. Thus, traditional patterns of conduct are continued. Change requires the acceptance of somethng different and may become a threat to security or even vested interests. One of the most common reasons for not accepting change is that the one who is expected to change does not feel a need for the change. Festinger contends that a felt need to change attitudes or behavior arises or dissonance or dissatisfaction increases; the individual strives for consonance or for a state of equilibrium. Frequently, change agents must create the state of dissonance. When basic values and attitudes are altered, change is usually resisted. This is no less true of institutions than it is of individuals.

Individuals, including leaders and decision makers, may not understand innovative behavior or the processes of change. According to the classic model of innovativeness, only 2.5% of individuals are known as innovators, the first in a group to adopt new ideas. The next 13.5% are labeled early adopters. The next 34% are called early majority, while the following 34% are known as late majority. The last 16% are called laggards, those who are extremely slow in accepting new ideas or in changing behavior. "While most individuals in a social system are looking to the road of change ahead, the laggard has his attention fixed on the rear-view mirror."[11]

Innovators are venturesome, creative, and not afraid to take risks. They are interested in new ideas and thus move from the local circle of peers to broader social relationships. They are usually financially able to absorb losses due to unprofitable innovations. Often they re-invest much of their own personal finances into their professional program. Failures do not threaten them to the degree that other categories are threatened. They appear to be future-oriented.

Laggards are the most localized, possess almost no opinion leadership, and are characterized as traditional. They tend to be suspicious of innovations, innovators, and change agents. The fast-moving world tends to threaten their security and thus, they slow down the innovation-adoption process. They do not want to cause ripples in the stream or rock the boat. They are conser-

vative as a rule. Thus, innovators and laggards are "poles"
apart in their perceptions and behavior. This gap needs to be
closed for changes in education to take place.

Personal and organizational variables affect innovative
behavior. Values, needs, past experiences, open or closed
mindedness, competence, and authoritarianism have been associated
with an individual's rejection or acceptance of new ideas. The
importance of the innovation to the individual may also have an
effect on the degree of acceptance or rejection. Some dimensions
which also influence one's attitude toward the innovation
include: cost, financial and social; returns on the investment,
both short- and long-term; efficiency; perceived risk or clarity
of results and outcomes; complexity, commitment required; ego
involvement; and the likelihood of other innovations following.

Hood concluded that, if programs of planned change regarding
acceptance of emerging professional roles became necessary for
teachers of home economics in Virginia, individualized assistance
provided on a local rather than a statewide level might prove
more beneficial and efficient for teachers as well as for administrative personnel. Thus, greater responsibility for getting
teachers to accept emerging professional roles would fall upon
the local supervisors. However, less than half of the teachers
in the study, which could generalize to the entire population,
perceived their supervisors as a main source of new ideas used in
teaching.[12] This finding suggests that perhaps not all persons
in leadership roles possess positive attitudes toward innovative
ideas or that they may not be innovative. Howsam contended that
in education, where change is desired, administrators and
supervisors favorable to change must be provided; when administrators are seen as obstructing change, or even failing to
encourage desirable change, they should be "retooled or
removed."[13]

Evaluations conducted on efforts of federal change agents to
promote change in local educational practices over the past
decade have raised many serious questions about the usefulness of
federal efforts to promote educational reform. Organizational
climate and motivations of principal actors can play critical
roles in project outcomes. Projects that integrated change in
training with expectations for concomitant classroom behavior
were likely to result in basic change in teacher activities.
Strategies which promoted significant teacher change included
staff training, frequent and regular meetings, and local material
development. The absence of any one of these elements was likely
to reduce the perceived success and the amount of teacher change
on projects. High morale of teachers at a school, the active
support of the superintendent and district officials, and the

teachers' willingness to expend extra effort all increased the
chances of teacher change and perceived success. Attitudes of
administrators tell the staff how seriously they should take the
project objectives.[14]

The impact, rapidity and consequences of change are growing
concerns of society as a whole. Toffler, in Future Shock, noted
that not all people can adequately adjust to the fast pace of
change in culture and society today. Although educators may not
be able to control completely all the activities thrust upon them
by the mandates of change, perhaps they can learn to understand
what is happening and why. Thus, not only will better attitudes
toward change result, but more effective educational systems may
be devised in a shorter time. Chin and Downey suggest that the
concept of change as a basic discipline of knowledge be further
investigated. In such a study theories to tie together testable
propositions, techniques and procedures might be created.[15] Such
courses utilized for in-service or pre-service education might
well be one of the best investments educators could make to help
bridge the gaps between educational change and the future.

Educational Futures

Society today appears to be in a "no man's land" in which
many life styles and philosophies vie for attention. No longer
do we appear to know just what constitutes a good education for
our youth. We cannot define the knowledge, attitudes and skills
which characterize the educated person. The once tried and
unquestionable values, dogmas and idealisms are in a melting
stage of change. This lack of direction is intimately tied to
the cultural and social systems. Bundy as well as others have
differentiated between a superindustrial and a postindustrial
world view. The needs are not the same. Educators must choose
between the two when they are designing programs for the youth of
tomorrow. America must develop a new sense of the future and
what it means to be educated.[16] Fletcher made this same point:
". . . We need to do some very basic fundamental rethinking about
what we mean by public education . . . continuing to do public
education the way we've always done it is a very bad idea at this
point."[17]

Futurists utilize the laws of social behavior to understand
how the present is creating the future. Even though futurists
recognize that schools are slow to change and even resist change,
they see education as society's sole long-term agent for transforming societal practices into teaching/learning systems capable
of creating a bright future. In fact, they advocate looking "on
the far side of the future."[18] Futurists look at the

accelerating rate of change and at its visible products, such as pollution, environmental destruction, the depletion of natural resources, and the widening rich-poor gap. They also record its less visible effects on people such as the threat of nuclear war, stress and coping with sky-rocketing costs, inflation, and a vascillating job market. Bringing their data together, they sketch a picture of what future life might be like.

McHale identified some societal trends which promise to have a substantial impact on education now and in the future. These trends include:

1. A slowing down of the population growth, alleviating some pressure from the numbers game.

2. An aging society as people live longer and the population growth dwindles.

3. A movement from an attitude of material growth to human growth as the economy continues toward lean times.

4. A concern for quality beyond economic utility which denies that more is necessarily better.

5. A shift in human values, aspirations, and expectations which places human beings and the physical environment above material goods, and reflects changes in life styles and models of legitimacy.[19]

Looking at education, Dede observed that presentations given at the First Conference of the Education Section of the World Future Society in Clear Lake City, Texas, reflected growing societal concerns. Some of these trends included: educating beyond school, through a wide range of multimedia and communication systems; focusing education, not on distinct disciplines, but on common problems or in a trans-disciplinary direction; educating a more diverse population, including people of all ages with both short-and long-term goals; promoting a healthy diversity in education by eliminating racism and sexism, while promoting egalitarianism; and moving education toward a transnational, global focus because problems in our part of the world affect, either directly or indirectly, those in other parts of the entire universe. Education and schooling are not the same. These distinctions should be understood by all.[20]

Shane has synthesized the views of 50 distinguished world citizens and educators about America's educational futures 1976-2001. Respondents recognized that not only the United States but the world as a whole is passing through the greatest tidal wave

of transition in history. These panelists agreed that anyone's
problems anywhere had become everyone's problems everywhere, and
that mutually planned interdependence and dynamic reciprocity
could do much to improve relationships in the human community.
Certain points about the future were agreed upon: (1) accelerating change; (2) increased complexity; (3) twilight of the
hydrocarbon era; (4) new concepts of growth; (5) continued
crowding and hunger; (6) third world pressure for equality and a
new economic order; (7) troubled international waters; (8)
welfare, debt, and freedom; (9) a post-extravagant society; (10)
work and leisure; and (11) future-oriented and future-directed
planning.[21]

A logical starting point in reforming education for the
future is in the school itself, according to Silberman.[22] What
should be taught, in what manner, and to what purpose are
judgments to be made in terms of the values of society as well as
the purposes of education. In considering education of the
future, the following information is also critical to education
design: Who will be educated? What will be taught? Where will
education take place? How will education take place? and Who
will educate? The remainder of this paper is organized around
these themes. Projections presented are an accumulation of
research and personal observations, and in no way represents an
exhaustive or all inclusive compilation, but rather a few of the
most obvious trends and images.

Who Will Be Educated?

Current trends indicate, and futurists proclaim, that
education in the future will be from the cradle to the grave;
learning will be lifelong. Research indicates that much more can
be learned before age six than previously thought possible.
Schools will cater to increasingly older students as the pool of
5 to 20 year olds decreases. Obsolescence and change in work
require continued updating of skills and knowledge. Provisions
for more flexible work patterns including entry and exit levels
will provide for a greater mix of work and study. As computers
and other advances in the Electronic Revolution decrease hours of
work and the need for human workers, more leisure time will be
created. Some will have to learn to play and to better use this
"extra" time.

As equity, life-long learning, and adaptation to continuous
change become increasingly vital to societal survival, education
will supply more opportunities for a diversified public. Local,
state, and federal funding will supplement the current expen-

ditures on special groups and minorities including populations such as the handicapped, the incarcerated, the unemployed, and the gifted.

Older generations will learn along side the young, as both generations struggle to cope with the whirlpool of change, rather than drown in the sea of knowledge surrounding them. Many of the best ideas will come from senior citizens who will have the advantage of continual educational renewal, complemented by the richness of their experiences. The utilization of their talents will serve to close gaps created in our alienated family of today, making the aged our mentors in society.

Some scholars have noted that parenting will become recognized as a specific social occupation leading to the professionalization of the family. As parents become educated in techniques of child rearing, much of the education of the young will be returned to the family. It will be necessary for individuals wishing to become parents to receive a license to do so and thereby they will become more responsible for the education and welfare of their own children. Children and parents alike will experience more education in the home with the assistance of electronically equipped machinery such as the spelling, calculating and reading machine.

What Will Be Taught?

In recognizing that education will be serving a diverse population with changing needs, the curriculum of the future will reflect these influences. Home, work, and society at large will provide extensions of the school curriculum while the key word for the school itself will be flexibility. The school curriculum will address such critical issues for global survival as: immigration, mental health, drugs, oceans, water supplies, values, crime, urban development, person abuse, natural resources, sex roles, cultures, satellite living, aquaculture, computer technology, world finance and politics.

Teachers will work with curricula that encourage respect for multi-ethnic, poly-cultural differences; that emphasize achieving a balance between human and environmental needs; that expand the community concerns from a local to a global level; and that identify the dynamics of change. The post-industrial future curriculum will emphasize resourcefulness and self-reliance as adaptive values to change and complexity. Post-industrial education will work toward developing (1) people loyalties; (2) individuality rather than mass conformity; (3) the values of being resourceful and of saving; (4) the desire to lead a simpler, more self-satisfying and self-sufficient life style; (5) a greater understanding of human beings as a part of the total universe; and (6) awareness of environmental, spiritual, and social perspectives in making social and personal decisions.[23]

With some modifications, the goals of future education will not be unlike the "Seven Cardinal Principles of Education," written in 1918.

1. Health. Good physical fitness, improved interpersonal and intercultural attitudes, ability to cope with stress, and an awareness of unhealthy life-styles.

2. Command of Fundamental Processes. In addition to the 3 R's, human relations, communication skills, and the ability to identify knowledge sources and information-processing skills.

3. Worthy Home Membership. Continuing value of the family, but for a greater and stronger affinity group relationship in the future.

4. Vocation. Both secondary and post-secondary vocational training and a good general education with implications for future goals and roles.

5. Civic Education. Understanding of the democratic processes and the development of world citizenship attitudes.

6. Worthy Use of Leisure. The traditional work ethic would give way to new interpretations of work and leisure toward self-fulfillment.

7. Ethical Character. Need to develop ethical character tied to new ethical models and a redefinition of justice and equity.[24]

But schools will not accomplish these goals alone. The entire community will participate; the basic institutions of society will serve as educational resources. Schooling will begin at the cradle with problem prevention education in early childhood, attended to by the family as well as outside agencies, rather than waiting for compensatory education at a later date. Occupational education will transcend vocational training, with workers receiving encouragement for greater versatility. Career guidance will be expanded to a wider range of identification, placement and follow-up services for all ages and ethnic groups.

General and specialized education will be available for young and old alike through computers and telecommunications networks and data bases.

While some futurists sound alarms of doom for the future, others acknowledge that the curriculum of the future will not only adapt to but create alternatives for some of today's problems of peace, energy, agriculture, communications and economics. As space age orientations and solar systems management become more vital in education, a few futurists claim that we will enter an age of abundance in which sources of energy will be hydrogen solar power, nuclear fusion, geothermal power, recycled energy, and wind produced energy. Explorations of these systems by both private and public sources are already in the experimental stages. New crops which need little fertilizer, use salt water, yield high sources of protein, grow in marshes, and produce oil will be discovered or cultivated. All of these developments will become a part of the learning environment of future students.

Where Will Education Take Place?

Since much of vocational training of the future will occur at the place of employment through diverse media and channels, less time will be spent in formal education. Government, business, and industry will provide their own specialized training programs. With the ability to communicate at a distance weakening the monopoly of formal institutions, and the trend toward "clip on" skills and resources (pocket calculators, packaged learning, cassettes, spelling machines) reducing the amount of schooling required to function in society, the home will become more and more the locus of learning and training.

During the day, learning will not be confined to a single place. Some of it will occur in a community library, a museum, a courtroom, or in an industrial setting. Students will be able to study history in the making by pushing a button to tune in a Congressional hearing, see a play on another continent, or visit with Heads of State around the world by means of satellite communications or other electronic systems.

Schools, in a physical sense, will become locations with shifting planes, enclosures, and perspectives. The physical plant will be utilized around the year and possibly, around the clock by various community ventures. Schools will be visual and auditory environments which can engage the learner, enticing and stimulating as well as soothing. Here, learning will be monitored and individualized in a manner that assures that it contributes to the intellectual, social, creative and spiritual awakening of each individual. Alternatives to present schooling locations will include learning centers to develop life coping skills, basic domes, solar greenhouses, and aquaculture farms.[25]

How Will Education Take Place?

Students will experience a highly complex system of assessment and programming over a wide range of intellectual, creative, and other rational capabilities and traits. Learning will be structured in such a way that students will be able to achieve competencies and satisfaction necessary for successful living. This will be done by computer matching of abilities with an array of instructors, environments, and learning programs. Cognitive and affective needs will be identified as the individual _talks_ with the machine. This will be learning on a one-to-one basis which is impossible in schools of today with 25-30 students in a classroom with one teacher. Further, periods of time for learning will vary with the individual.

Advanced technology will produce robots as teachers, for the home and for the classroom.[26] Educational packagers will produce fail-safe teaching materials for differing learning styles and levels of achievement. Students may learn by telecourses, or in a live theater. Thus, individualized instruction will be revitalized, refined, and modified as an instructional strategy of the future. Learning how to learn will become more important than learning given facts or subject matter. Learning how to make decisions which relate directly to life will take priority over learning a set of facts which may soon be forgotten or never used. Teachers will guide, motivate, stimulate, and assist students in selecting their own goals and objectives. Through discussions, suggestions, and raising higher order questions, teachers will cause students to think through the proposals at hand. Teachers will become true facilitators of learning rather than dispensers of knowledge. They will be consultants and mentors. Learning will take place through interactions in conferences, open study, and laboratories; through discussions in small and large group sessions; and through radio and microwave broadcasting, small transistor radios and the cathode ray tube.

Computer systems will perform accurate record keeping. Students may receive immediate feedback to learn of their achievement status at any time. Newspapers will be studied, or read, on the television screens. Due to the extinction of some natural resources, such as wood, paper will be replaced by the electronic screen. Computer assisted learning is already a reality with PLATO (Programmed Logic for Automatic Teaching

Operations), developed in the 1960s at the University of Illinois
with Control Data Corporation. Although machines will never
replace human beings completely, fewer humans will be needed in
the education process. Educators will thus have to change
approaches, and continue to update their understanding of an
increasingly complex delivery system.

Who Will Educate?

No longer can schools afford to be isolated islands,
separate from the home and community. Students of the future are
likely to find that schools resemble the family environment, with
teachers assuming some parental traits and roles like guiding and
encouraging, counseling and listening, while parents are
recognized for the teachers that they are. Local, state, and
federal funding will become more available for preservice early
childhood education, and homes will become individually based
learning centers. Voluntary service, such as workshops, home
visitors, toy-lending libraries, free health and medical services
will aid parents in rearing and educating their own children. As
different use is made of the tax dollar for education, parents
may invest in numerous ways, even electing to educate their own
children at home and in the community rather than sending them to
either private or public school. Travel with parents will
become, then, a vital part of the education of the young.

As distinctions are made between schooling and educating,
community, business and industrial leaders will serve as
educators in their respective places of operation. Elected
political leaders will directly and indirectly educate the total
population. The expanding role of communication media will
replace the old textbook as the primary source of information,
thus reducing the need for basic skills. Calculators will
perform mathematical functions needed to survive in the economic
arena.

Summary

In the present world of accelerating change, global
interaction, shifts in values and aspirations and cultural
diversity, citizens are becoming more aware of their own
potential and needs for self-actualization. Thus, to survive,
present educational institutions will have to change management
systems, curriculum offerings and approaches in the delivery of
education. There exists a great need to redefine what is a good
education for the future. Societal trends continue to have
impact on what is learned, who will be educated, where education
will take place, and how education will proceed.

With all the uncertainly in society today, one truism is certain: Schools as they now exist will become obsolete and extinct if they fail to change to meet the expanding mandates of the Electronic Revolution of the present and of the emerging future.

Individuals and institutions are slow to accept changes especially when they involve personal values, attitudes and beliefs. Federal support to students and schools to promote innovations appears to have little lasting effect. "Even with a massive national effort by ERIC to disseminate information about educational innovations, the problem of how to make users in the public schools aware of educational innovations still persists as one of the major barriers to change."[27]

Peccei, President of the Club of Rome, stated that "This [time] is a turning point in the human venture. Never were there so many children in the world; never was mankind able to influence so decisively their future; and yet, never was this so uncertain."[28] It is imperative that we commit ourselves to an indepth revision of the very foundations of our societies before handing them over to the following generation. All of this calls for change. Peccei states that the most important change must take place within ourselves. We must adjust to different cultures; we must tap human resources yet untapped; we must not neglect human capacity as it is the major asset of humankind at this critical moment.

Yes, to think about the future is dangerous, but not to do so will be disastrous!

NOTES

1. Don Glines, _Educational_ _Futures_ _IV:_ _Updating_ _and_ _Overleaping_ (Millville, Minnesota: Anvil Press, 1979).

2. Stacey Burling, "Schools Urged to 'Modernize,'" _The_ _Virginian_ _Pilot-Ledger_ _Star_ (October 12, 1979), p.A7.

3. Robert F. Bundy, "Social Visions and Educational Futures," _Phi_ _Delta_ _Kappan_ (September, 1976), pp. 85-89.

4. Jack C. Willers, "The Quality of Life in the Seventies and Implications for Vocational Teacher Education," _Changing_ _the_ _Role_ _of_ _Vocational_ _Teacher_ _Education_, eds. Rupert N. Evans and David R. Terry (Bloomington, Ill.: McKnight & McKnight, 1971).

5. H. A. Passow, "Reforming America's High Schools," _Phi_ _Delta_ _Kappan_ 1975, Vol. 56, No. 9, pp. 587-590.

6. Seymour B. Sarason, The Culture of the School and the Problems of Change (Boston: Allyn and Bacon, 1971).

7. Gary R. Bice, Working with Opinion Leaders to Accelerate Change in Vocational Technical Educationl (Columbus, Ohio: The Ohio State University, The Center for Vocational and Technical Education, 1970).

8. Donald H. Garrison, An Evaluatin of Planned Activities to Change Attitudes of Educators and Parents Toward Career Education (Unpublished doctoral dissertation, Texas A & M University, 1974).

9. R. Lippett, J. Watson, and B. Westley, The Dynamics of Planned Change (New York: Harcourt, Brace and world, 1958).

10. J. Clark Davis, "Supplementary Statement: Planning for Changes in Education," Designing Education for the Future No. 3: Planning and Effecting Needed Changes in Education, eds. Edgar L. Morphet and Charles O. Ryan (New York: Citation Press, 1967).

11. Everett M. Rogers and Floyd F. Shoemaker, Communication of Innovations (New York: Free Press, 1971).

12. Florence F. Hood, Change Orientation and Perceptions of Emerging Professional Roles Held by Teachers of Home Economics in Virginia (Unpublished doctoral dissertation, Texas A & M University, 1975).

13. Robert B. Howsam, "Effecting Needed Changes in Education," Designing Education for the Future No 3: Planning and Effecting Needed Changes in Education, eds. Edgar L. Morphet and Charles O. Ryan (New York: Citation Press, 1967).

14. P. Berman and M. W. McLaughlin, "Implementation of Educational Innovation," The Educational Forum, 1976, Vol. 40, No. 3, pp. 345-370.

15. Robert Chin and Loren Downey, "Changing Change: Innovating a Discipline," Second Handbook of Research on Teaching, ed. R. M. W. Travers (Chicago: Rand McNally College Publishing Co., 1973).

16. Robert F. Bundy, loc. cit.

17. Stacey Burling, loc. cit.

18. Jim Bowman, Fred Kierstead, Chris Dede, and John Pulliam, The Far Side of the Future (Houston, Texas: Educational Futures, 1978).

19. John McHale, "Keynote Address," The First Conference of the Education Section of the World Future Society, University of Houston at Clear Lake City, October 20-22, 1978.

20. Chris Dede, "Keynote address," The First Conference of the Education Section of the World Future Society, University of Houston at Clear Lake City, October 20-22, 1978.

21. H. G. Shane, "America's Educational Futures: The Views of 50 Distinguished World Citizens and Educators," The Futurist, 1976, Vol. 10, No. 5, pp. 252-257.

22. Charles Silberman, Crisis in the Classroom: The Remaking of American Education (New York: Vintage Books, 1971).

23. Robert F. Bundy, loc. cit.

24. D. L. Silvernail, "Adapting Education to a Changing World," The Futurist, 1977, Vol. 11, No. 6, pp. 375-376.

25. B. Nourse, Jr., "Students exploring Alternative Life-Styles," Phi Delta Kappan, 1979, Vol. 60, No. 6, pp. 448-451.

26. M. Freeman and G. P. Mulkowsky, "Advanced Interactive Technology: Robots in the Home and Classroom," The Futurist, 1978, Vol. 12, No. 6, pp. 356-361.

27. Donald C. Orlich, "Federal Educational Policy: The Paradox of Innovavation and Centralization," Educational Researcher, Vol. 8, No. 7, pp. 4-9.

28. Aurelio Peccei, "The World We Are Leaving to Our Children," World Future Society Bulletin, 1979, Vol. 13, No. 2, pp. 6-8.

Bridging the Future

William L. Smith

Two quotations or phrases have always intrigued me, and every time I read or hear them my reaction is always the same: I question their validity. The first is, "The more things change, the more they stay the same." The other, attributed to Harry Broudy at the University of Illinois, is, "Ignorance of history is the mother of innovation."

It seems appropriate to me, as a student of history, to address the topic "Bridging the Future" from a contextual framework that embodies the essence of those two statements, and to do so in a manner that reflects both the scholar I would hope to be and the pragmatic practitioner I know I am.

This paper presents three conceptual perspectives. One could simply call them PAST, PRESENT and FUTURE trends, but that is not informative enough, because it would not demonstrate the power of the interdependent relationship of time and events that I hope to show.

I would like you to consider the assumption that we are in a society where, to borrow an idea in a phrase from Wordsworth, "The child is father of the man." We are where we are today because past events had their impact on the attitudes, values, and responses of today's adult and youth population. Another way to say this is, "We are today what we lived through yesterday."

Let me summarize briefly the three conceptual perspectives I shall discuss.

NOTE: Pursuant to 17 USC 105, Dr. Smith's paper is in the public domain.

First, I will examine some of the events of the last four
decades. In this connection, I want to make a disclaimer. In a
few short pages, I cannot do justice to all the historical,
social and economic events of the past forty years. The events
I've chosen to emphasize will merely show that to think about the
future, one must look to the past. Indeed, I can recognize some
recurring patterns, as well as some situational characteristics,
that, once analyzed, can help us think more clearly about
planning for what will occur in the next decade or two.

Second, I shall look at the significant trends occurring in
the 1970s which have impacted on our society in general and
education in particular--events which we may be managing or
mismanaging at present. Again a disclaimer may be necessary. I
have been selective in my choice of events primarily because I
wish to prove my points and establish a reasonable framework
within which to discuss the future. My activities in the federal
Government these last ten years give me the advantage of a
national perspective.

Finally, I shall conclude this paper with some judgments
about the future. Since I lack as much prognosticating power as
I would like to have, I went to the literature to learn what
futurists are saying about the world of tomorrow. Four books
that have influenced my thinking are: The Coming of Post
Industrial Society by Daniel Bell; The Far Side of the Future by
your own colleagues, Bowman, Kierstead, Dede and Pulliam; Small
Is Beautiful by E. F. Schumacher; and Creating Alternative
Futures by Hazel Henderson. These books have given me a valuable
perspective about future priorities.

So much for preamble. To begin, the most important event of
the 1930s was the Great Depression. In my opinion, it was part
of the last truly universal crisis experienced by Americans.
Even those of you who were born after the 1930s are still living
under the government structures, political beliefs and economic
theories developed to overcome and prevent such an economic
collapse from occurring again. For instance, I believe that the
adults who lived through the Depression are overly concerned
about their own economic stability. This is easy to understand
when you stop to consider that at times during the 1930s fully
half of the work force was unemployed for relatively long periods
of time. You may recall the pictures of the soup lines and bread
lines of the time. It was a rare family who did not feel the
hopelessness and despair that unemployment creates. As the
anthropologist Jules Henry points out:

Work binds time.
Work guarantees livelihood.
No work, no livelihood.
Time and fear are set free.

The Roosevelt administration responded to rampant nationwide fear and loss of hope by active intervention in every sector of the economy. Jobs were created through WPA, PWA, TVA, CCC, etc. Youths were paid to stay in high school; artists paid to paint and sculpt; writers paid to write. As a consequence of our acceptance of government intervention in every aspect of our lives, the federal bureaucracy grew to include thousands of bureaus and millions of employees. Today's bureaucracy is a legacy from the Great Depression.

For all the government spending and involvement, the economy stayed depressed throughout the 1930s and during 1940 and 1941. It was World War II that ended the Depression. Our needs and the needs of our allies for armaments put our factories into full production. Unemployment of breadwinners was no longer a major problem. Indeed, we found ourselves encouraging women to join the work force in large numbers.

When Japan bombed Pearl Harbor on December 7, 1941, the entire population rallied around the flag and the defense of Uncle Sam in a furor of patriotism. No sacrifice was too great for our boys "over there." The population accepted, almost willingly, the rationing of sugar, butter, gasoline and other products. The war made people feel they were participating in the fight against tyranny.

World War II, however, was the last major event to rally all of the people around one national cause.

After victory over the Axis in 1945, the return of veterans became another major event that changed the face of America generally and our educational system specifically. With his discharge papers the veteran also was given the G.I. Bill of Rights by a grateful people. Among these "Rights" were generous provisions for subsidizing their schooling and guaranteeing home loans. These provisions markedly changed the course of American life by providing men and women from all strata of society with access to the "good" life. In the past it was rarely possible for the average "Joe" to finish school, let alone own his home. Now the government was saying, "If you want to finish school, or go to college and own your home, we are going to help you. It is your right." The veterans responded. The boom in enrollments in colleges and universities was on, and so was the boom in the housing industry as new communities started springing up all

around the older, overpopulated center cities. Along with going
to school and then owning his home, the veteran wanted to marry
and start a family, and another boom--the "baby boom"--was on.

These events put great demands on all of the other sectors
of the economy to produce the goods and services needed by this
infusion of enthusiasm and the promise of the good life. In sum,
the last five years of the 1940s was a time of rising expectations. After all, Americans were victorious over two terrible
enemies: The Great Depression and Fascism.

The period of the 1950s can be characterized as a decade of
complacency, general optimism and a continuation of rising
expectations. The Great American Machine turned itself away from
war and set about the work of satisfying the insatiable appetite
of Americans for housing and a cornucopia of consumer goods. At
the same time, the babies born from 1946 on were beginning to
turn up at the school house door in every-increasing numbers.
This meant that the new communities had to construct new schools
with more classrooms; and more classrooms meant more teachers;
more teachers meant more teacher educators; and the grandest era
of teacher education in American history was on.

Even the Russians unwittingly conspired to foster the role
of education and teacher education in America. When the Soviets
orbited Sputnik, a great debate about the quality of American
education ensued. A flurry of curriculum revision projects was
started and millions of dollars were poured into the training and
retraining of teachers. A Russian satellite made us heirs of a
curriculum development system and an educational personnel
development system. These systems were created by the National
Defense Education Act (NDEA).

But I have been painting too rosy a picture. Much of what I
describe applies during the 1950s to the white, urban, ever-
increasing middle class. As they moved to their suburban
greenery, they left behind in the older, decaying cities the poor
and the minorities. But the poor and the minorities had also
fought for the good life. They, too, had rising expectations.
But for several reasons, not the least of which was the
continuing racism of white Americans, they were forced to satisfy
themselves with the tailings of the American Dream. And, as the
poet Langston Hughes asked:

What happens to a dream deferred?
Does it dry up like a raisin in the sun,
or fester like a sore and then run?
Does it stink like rotten meat, or
crust and sugar over like a syrupy sweet?

> Maybe it just sags like a heavy load,
> or does it explode?

Not only was Langston Hughes prophetic, but academia had its prophets too. Frank Riessman described the plight of the Culturally Deprived Child. James Conant described "social dynamite" in his book Slums and Suburbs and predicted that "white flight" would ghettoize the poor and minorities, thus putting off dealing with their needs. But the poor and the minorities would not be put off with promises. Black pride swept the country, preached by Martin Luther King, Malcolm X, and others.

The 1960s were going to be the decade of awareness and increasing optimism, when the dream was to be made real. If it meant burning down the ghettos, then so be it. If it meant fighting a war on poverty, then so be it. If it meant pouring millions of dollars into elementary and secondary schools to give the children of the poor a "head start," then so be it. After all, this was the decade of the New Frontier and the Great Society.

In addition to the revolution in the ghettos among the poor and minorities, there was an equally powerful counter-cultural revolution among the young. Born into a world quite different from the one their elders were born into, they valued different things as well. They valued a society of love, peace and social justice. They valued the simple life, these "flower children." They opposed the arbitrary use of power, whether on the college campus or in the White House. Many a university president left office, and indeed, in 1968, a President of the United States decided not to run again for office because of pressures arising from the values of these young people.

The women's liberation movement received its greatest impetus during this period due to the unisexual attitude of the counter-cultural youth. Age was the only criterion that was used for exclusion from leadership roles. Many of these young women, who are executives today, gained valuable skills and experiences in major leadership roles during the counter-culture revolution.

But, for all of the hope and militancy of the 1960s, Americans began to lose some of their faith in the possibility of making the dream real. For one thing, vast sums of money were not producing the anticipated changes. For another, we could not end the war in Vietnam. A small nation of 20 million Asian people would not be defeated by the invincible American war machine with its sophisticated weapons and seemingly endless material resources. As the war dragged on, our society was shaken to its core. Valuable resources were diverted to a war nobody wanted.

The old platitude "Victory with honor!" had a hollow ring.
Finally, the war ended to the relief of almost all Americans.
But Vietnam had put such a burden on our resources that it left
as a legacy a terrible inflationary spiral that seems to threaten
the very core of our economy.

Yet, at the same time, there was also the beginning
involvement of courts, state legislatures, Congress, consumers,
teachers, and community in education decision making--decisions,
which had, historically, been the sole domain of the
professional.

The 1970s have been a decade in which Americans have had to
face up to the traumatic realities of a rapidly changing world--a
world of social pessimism and of very private optimism. For one
thing, there is today the growing belief that money alone will
not change the human condition--it takes people with commitment
and courage. Improving the human condition, we have learned,
also takes patience. This was and is a bitter pill for people to
swallow following the victories of the preceding decades,
especially for people accustomed to instant response and
solutions to technical questions and problems. In the 1970s, we
came to realize that the alleviation of human suffering, want,
deprivation, and discrimination is not an easy goal to attain and
requires vast resources of time, money, and people.

Another reason for social pessimism is the mistrust of
authority that has infected America like a plague. Because of
national scandals such as Watergate and Koreagate, a great many
Americans believe that they know just as much as their leaders.
Presidential failures made cynics of people who had never doubted
before. They doubt not only national leaders, but judges,
doctors, scientists, clergy, attorneys, businessmen, journalists,
teachers, and even futurists. The attitude seems to be, "You
can't trust people in power."

So today, in education for instance, there is a massive
demand for accountability. Taxpayers refuse to tax themselves
based on the word of school officials in whom they have lost
confidence. Although schools may be closed and programs trimmed
to the bare bones, the electorate seems at best reluctant, and at
worst unwilling, to support an enterprise in which they have lost
faith. They seem to be saying, "We have given you millions of
dollars and the children still can't read. What have you done
with our money?"

Classroom teachers are also feeling the consequences of this
mistrust of authority figures. Even school children challenge
the teacher's authority in ways that were unheard of just a

decade ago. Many teachers are seeing that their leadership is something that must be earned and that respect does not automatically come with the teaching certificate. This is hard for teachers to accept. And yet, to survive and to help children learn, teachers must become more responsive, more accepting and more caring.

On the other side, there is a private optimism. Oddly enough, Americans, according to Harris polls, still trust American democracy to work. They still believe that there is opportunity for personal advancement and improvement of life style. Many of the attacks on the social problems started in the 1960s go steadily forward, but without the fanfare. Women's liberation, Affirmative Action, consumer protection, environmental protection, desegregation of public schools are a continuing legacy from the post-war decades. What impact will these events have on our planning of priorities for the future of American education?

Perhaps the over-riding aspect of the past four decades is the scope and rate of change. Profound change has occurred in every aspect of our lives. Here are some selected factors and trends facing education and educators today:

1) Our values and assumptions are challenged on every side in this complex and changing industrial society. We find ourselves questioning what is real and what is relevant. There seems to be an increasingly temporary nature to relationships.

2) An expanded emphasis on accountability forces us to have the ability to demonstrate that we can do what we say we set out to do. This is reflected in debates on competency-based programs, competency testing and minimum competency level performance criteria.

3) There is an increasingly authoritative basis for education decisions to be made by other than traditional decision-makers. Federal and state regulatory agencies, the courts, and legislatures, both state and federal, are forcing interaction between agencies and groups who traditionally have not seen fit to make decisions or to work together. Witness the impact on special education of Public Law 94-142, The Education for All Handicapped Children Act, or the impact of Lau v. Nichols on bilingual education.

4) The limitation of resources has increased competition for the dollar and forced coordination if not collaboration among many. It has forced the question of how one attempts to improve institutions while managing decline.

5) There are shifts in the distribution of population. School enrollment declines, while our population increases and becomes an increasingly older population.

6) There is an upsurge of interest in peer teaching and learning. The focus is on a desire for choice in program or service delivery.

7) The greater focus on the individual recognizes unique growth patterns and the desire to extend the range of human variability while accepting greater diversity.

8) Life style changes and the change in the structure and stability in the family have become an important influence. Changes in mobility and career patterns, and in the use and degree of leisure time have increased our awareness of the process of education occurring outside the schools. This difference between education and schooling raises important political and educational questions.

9) Our society appears to have growing expectations for our schools while at the same time diminished faith in our institutions. This is a trend that is both complex and ironic.

All of these factors and trends are, of course, interrelated. Yet we treat them as independent variables, negating all that we already know about systems theory and its application to schools as formal organizations.

In the winter of 1979, I spent a weekend in the mountains of Colorado at an invitational retreat sponsored by Chris Dede and Dwight Allen. The experience in Colorado had a profound impact upon me.

First, the physical setting, isolated as it was, enabled us to look across, and not up, at Pike's Peak and to reflect upon the beauty and wonder of nature. The cold, thin air turned my thoughts to how overweight and out of shape I really am. But most important for purposes of this paper was the emotional and intellectual stimulation provided in that setting.

I accept the fact that futurists truly believe that the struggle for human survival on this planet has frequently demanded the reconstruction of past experience as a guide for future behavior and the use of some form of extrapolation, going from the general to the detailed, to make judgments about the future.

I like the analogy of two sets of railroad tracks heading side by side in the same direction. The upper track with a pragmatic train makes assumptions about what the future will be, identifies the trends and issues which have caused the macroproblem, describes the problem and outlines scenarios of what the future will hold. The lower track with a normative train makes value assumptions about what the future should be, also identifies critical trends and issues but then proposes alternative solutions and finally outlines scenarios of what the future will hold. Both tracks have different processes which provide different scenarios, yet they are interrelated in that both look at the same critical trends and issues but with a different set of underlying assumptions.

One of the exercises required at the retreat was to speculate on what the world would be like 30 years from now in the year 2010. The more I thought about the future the more inadequate I felt in that group. Since I was clearly the least experienced and the least trained futurist of the eleven people in the room, I was the first to speculate. Broudy's principle, "Ignorance of history is the mother of innovation," has many applications.

Recalling that I had read Orwell's book, 1984, in the 1960s, I extrapolated to 2010. This was my forecast. Society would be: more structured; more prescriptive; more autocratic; more efficient/effective focused; more present-time oriented; more competency based; more up and out in age demarcation; more regulatory-based and more conformity-based.

"That should shock them," I thought to myself smugly. When the session had ended there were only two in this group of eleven who were more optimistic about the future than I had been, and only slightly at that. The grim reality is that there are not many who make a business of thinking about the future, regardless of their assumptions, who feel good about it. While concerned with society and the world, it becomes easy, using the same data, to focus upon education in general and the education of teachers specifically. I think that if we continue as at present, in the education of teachers and the schooling of our children, the future of formal education as we know it is doomed to fail.

What stimuli could make a usually optimistic bureaucrat react in such a pessimistic and uncharacteristic way? Among these was an article in the Sunday, February 18, 1979, Washington Post about the latest Gallup poll. The column was headed "Appeal of Teaching as Career is Down." The article asserted that "No doubt reports of higher teacher unemployment or underemployment have affected the attitudes toward education, but creation of new technologies . . . is also an element in the decline." What the Gallup poll failed to add in that account are: the lost sense of esprit; the sense of dehumanization; the sense of powerlessness; even worse, the lost sense of meaningfulness; and finally, the sense of leaderlessness that pervades the profession. Young people vicariously experience these changes on a daily basis, by watching our behavior as we go about the business of schooling and education.

The irony in this situation is that, while the overall number of college students desiring to enter the profession has dropped 50% in the last five years, it is also dropping at an annual rate of anywhere from 1% to 5% by college class. Yet, there are large numbers of state colleges and universities, still processing a high volume of undergraduate teacher education students, that are proceeding with business as usual and, even worse, fighting to maintain undergraduate education, unaffected by the weight and implications of these data. The fact that these institutions appear either insensitive or unresponsive is bad enough, but the real tragedy is that, among those who are sensitive and aware, there is little evidence that anything is being done at either the undergraduate or graduate level to deal with these phenomena.

Three other examples illustrate the plight in graduate education. John Ryor, the former President of the NEA, was quoted in an article more than a year ago as saying that the profession is losing talented and competent teachers earlier than anticipated because they cannot cope with the abhorrent and emergent values, attitudes and behaviors of our young people in the schools today. Albert Shanker, President of the AFT, was quoted in The New York Times, at about the same time, as saying that the profession is losing talented and competent teachers earlier than anticipated because they can't cope with the structural and organizational constraints imposed on teachers by administrators, supervisors, and the system itself.

Both are true statements, interestingly enough, but that's not where it ends. Elementary/secondary school principals and college directors and deans are either resigning or requesting reassignment to lesser administrative positions for almost the same reasons described above.

There seems to be little evidence that higher education or teacher education or the school system itself has begun to address the problem of stress in schools. Nor has the importance of school climate or the critical impact of George Spindler's accurate description of the changing value structure in our society been addressed. Even more important, this situation has not been faced: the lack of knowledge and skill that teachers, administrators and university faculties have in relating to and interacting with each other--as well as with adults outside the profession (those in the community, for example)--in a manner that reflects tolerance, empathy, understanding and non-threatening behavior. Finally, the need for these groups to feel secure in giving or receiving critical peer critiques of each others' work is a problem whose importance has not been adequately recognized or dealt with.

These are trends and issues that, while still manageable, can be handled now by teacher educators and researchers in a problem-solving context. But to do so educators will have to change their attitude regarding their involvement in such efforts from "because there is a chance to do something" to "because it must be done and we are best equipped to do it."

The Education Daily carried a headline, U.S. HOUSE PANEL HEARS GLOOMY PREDICTION FOR FUTURE OF EDUCATION. It went on to say,

The House Elementary and Secondary Education Subcommittee on April 25, 1979 heard that the prospects for elementary and secondary education are gloomy unless steps are taken to reverse current trends and educators come to grips with new technologies.

"We are aware that things are drastically wrong. We are aware that things need to be changed, but as a society, we are immobilized." Robert Theobald, an education consultant from Arizona, said during a hearing on the future of elementary and secondary education.

Agreeing with Theobald's grim view of the future, Art Lewis, from the University of Florida's College of Education, said, "The future we're drifting into is not the future we want. If the present trends continue, we'll see a weakening of education . . .that could well spell the end of the American dream."

Both Theobald and Lewis said the schools aren't preparing students for the kind of society that is emerging now. "We're educating for a time that is vanished. Kids are bored to tears in schools. Kids get more information from TV and real life than in the classroom," Theobald said.

Lewis added that colleges of education faculties are staffed with former teachers instructing future teachers about the world they taught in 10 or 20 years ago, not about what is happening today. Theobald sees the industrial age coming to an end and this society entering the communications era where information and knowledge are readily available because of technology.

Computers are the wave of the future, and computer literacy will become a new basic skill, the panel predicted. Earl Joseph, who teaches at the University of Minnesota and is a staff scientist and futurist at Sperry-Univac, said that computers will be in wide use in schools and homes by the end of the 1980s.

"Eventually, computerized information appliances could well make obsolete the physical school and office by allowing it to be worn or carried by each of us, as well as students at all education levels," he said.

Joseph added that by the 1990s such computers and their knowledge banks should cost less than what it costs now to travel back and forth to school or the office. "Obviously such a trend, obsoleting geographically located school and office buildings, will have drastic revolutionary and lasting future impacts on business, management, society and education," he said.

University of Florida's Lewis predicted that in the future anyone who can't work with a computer will be handicapped. He said that from his experience, "children learn very rapidly to work with computers; it's the teachers who have difficulty."

Joseph predicted that the increased use of computers will mean "displacement of teachers and other people in education." He said, however, that this does not automatically imply that fewer teachers will be required in the future. What this does mean is that many jobs will be changed in order to deliver more education, at each level, and to implement a lifelong approach to education rather than staying with the "innoculate the youth only scenario."

Taking a different view, Jane Newitt, a Hudson Institute senior professional staff member, said she doesn't see a sudden surge in the use of computers in the future. Instead, the introduction of computer technology in the school will increase at a steady but gradual pace, and it will increase, not decrease jobs for teachers.

These problems are real and with us today as are the demands that education be multicultural, collaborative, and accommodate learning and behavioral problems of all children in the regular classroom.

Like many futurists we use change as the theoretical framework from which to challenge basic assumptions implicit and explicit in industrial-era world culture. We accept the fact that future humans face so severe a revolution that it has implications for intellectual obsolescence and the problem of how to control human destiny.

Many of us base this belief on two factors: the pace of change and the change of scale. In the former case, the pace of change, children will no longer be able to live in the same kind of world, socially and intellectually, that their parents and grandparents did. Today not only does a child face a radical rupture with the past, but he or she must also be trained for an unknown future. Change is occurring and accelerating at a rate beyond human control, and perhaps beyond perception. People have difficulty dealing with changes they do not anticipate.

In the case of change in scale, the way we experience the world is evidenced by the number of persons each one of us knows and the number about whom each of us knows. No biological organism or human institution which undergoes a change in size and a consequent change in scale does so without changing its form or shape. Using the 1971 Carnegie Commission on Higher Education Report on College Enrollment Since 1960, one prognosticator felt there is no further need for research-type universities granting Ph.D.s. The major growth need for the year 2000 would be in community colleges and comprehensive colleges, primarily in metropolitan areas. The conclusion is that, by the year 2000, the United States will become a mass-knowledge society and that the post-industrial period will be characterized by such rapid changes that many time-honored institutions and values will be rendered obsolete.

In our present industrial civilization, the requirements for social conformity are still rather severe, but in the post-industrial phase almost absolute social conformity will be required to preserve the technological basis for survival. It seems clear that a new era (i.e., revolution rather than evolution) representing much more than a mere continuation of technological invention has emerged. Essential components of the phenomenon include computers, systems theory, genetic research, biological/medical discovery, space exploration, worldwide electronic communication and cybernation.

Change in these and related fields is now taking place at a rate which threatens to reach beyond human comprehension. One of the great fears is that we will experience information overload, a psychological breaking point which can cause the mind to shut out new stimuli and refuse to accept new information.

What meaning does this have for us today as we ponder the future priorities in education? Our task will be to shape our institutions to prepare eductional personnel, of one description or another, to educate children for successful participation in a vastly complicated and uncertain future society. We do recognize that a major educational problem for the future will be to provide global learners with learning of sufficient breadth so they can gain some understanding of the forces that are shaping their world. We shall have to remove specialization in schooling, so familiar to us in this industrial society, in order to provide a foundation for comprehension and control of revolutionary change. A good beginning is Penny Damlo's efforts here in Minneapolis to combine theory, forecasting exercises and practicality for high school students to deal with the scientific and psychological implications of the high frontier. But we cannot start with a focus upon children, we must begin with ourselves. We cannot plan this process for tomorrow--we have to begin today. We cannot prepare children to be adaptive and secure when we ourselves are not.

I have often written or said that the 1970s was a period of reality, the 1980s a period of humaness, the 1990s a period of technology and the years 2000 and beyond a period of inter-cultural world communities. My numerologist friends keep forcing me to remember that eight is a critical number and that the 1980s will be disruptive and more technological than I am willing to admit. I firmly believe that we as adults, in the most technological society on the face of this earth, cannot and will not be able to adapt, adopt, accept or utilize the knowledge explosion available to us from technology until we have come to understand and accept ourselves. I disagree with many who feel that dramatic change will occur in the near future which will produce an unstable state, only because I have faith and some small evidence that we as a people are beginning to see beyond the petty turfdom problems of the recent past. We have been forced to see the reality of interdependence, whether it involves energy, world politics, or simply fiscal and human-resource waste. The crisis we are experiencing today will redefine our life patterns.

Although the continuous growth syndrome has and is being changed, and will remain changed for some time to come, forces for change itself are increasing due to economic and

technological changes. We will have to cope with these incresing demands for change, especially in education. Even more important, we are facing a whole new generation of students who look upon education not as a guaranteed vehicle for interesting jobs but as one of several options to an uncertain future. These same students, and the community as well, will have an increasingly major influence on the reshaping of educational priorities. Educators will have to accept this reality on those terms.

The future of public education depends upon our readiness to deal with change and ourselves. In the former it is no longer a question of when but a question of how much. In the latter it is a matter of answering the ontological question of who we are, what we are and how we accept who and what we are.

Education provides the most powerful tool humans possess for bringing about cultural change. While it is still possible to educate people for change, whether we will, in public education, see and accept the challenge really becomes the prime question. It will require all of us working together in what I call win-win situations to build confidence in ourselves and in our system.

This may seem a simplistic notion to many of you. However, I really believe small can be beautiful. If a pebble is tossed into a pond of any size, it forms a ring which expands outward until it dissipates. But if two or more persons toss pebbles into a pond simultaneously, the rings begin to intersect, creating a greater force than can be exerted by a single ring.

That simple analogy conceptually represents the power of interdependence, and it can be used to address any problem however large, however frustrating, in a manageable form that can give us confidence and esprit because we can succeed.

A final point: There are minorities and Third-World people out there who, like it or not, will have a lot to say about the present and future course of events in our society and in world society. They are a force that must be included early in deliberations, in negotiations and in collaborative effort if we accept interdependence. From my observation of the participants at the Education Section's Second Annual Conference, I am compelled to ask myself the questions: "Are people from the Third World disinterested in the future?" "Are they incapable of using data to develop scenarios?" or "Does the World Future Society not see the need for the inclusion of these individuals and groups?"

It may just be that the task of analyzing the future is easier to accomplish with a select few than is the task of shaping the future with the masses involved. This is not meant to be a criticism. It is merely an observation! It forces the last question:

"Is this attitude an affordable one?" It reminds me of the competency-based teacher education movement when, some years ago, the eleven teacher training model development directors, all eminent researchers, turned out to be white males. They had done the research, but when it came time to implement the model, the ethnic and minority school communities refused to accept it until people like themselves were included as experts.

We must accept the leadership role for change within the society. Rather than reflect society, education must therefore be an agent for change, before society can reflect the change necessary to face and plan the future. Wordsworth was so right when he wrote, "The child is father of the man." But unless we come to grips with the responsibility that goes with change we may be bound for the conditions found in the words of the comic strip character Pogo, who said, "We have met the enemy and he is us!"

Section II
Issues and Challenges for the Present and the Future

Section II
Issues and Challenges for the Present
and the Future

Introduction

If the Socratic contention that "the unexamined life is not worth living" were to be paraphrased and applied to futures studies, it might be said that a field of study not critically examined and thoroughly evaluated is not worth pursuing. It is from such analysis and examination that the intellectual tension is generated to make a discipline relevant and useful rather than abstruse and unresponsive to new issues and challenges. Common to all the papers in Section II is a desire to examine critically the field of futures studies as it interfaces with education.

There are numerous issues that need to be examined within the field of futures studies as well as when the futures studies' perspective is applied to education. The papers in this section represent a sampling of such issues, ranging from the ethical, the pedagogical, and the structural to the practical. While it is not always possible to discern answers and solutions to these issues, it is still imperative for futurists and educators to consider such questions.

As often happens with newly emergent fields of inquiry, futures studies is sometimes criticized for its purported failure to generate firm, well-grounded theoretical underpinnings. As a proactive field of work, occasionally accused of being an ideology or a social movement, futures studies is often criticized for its lack of thorough, empirical research into the ramifications of actions taken and choices made by futurists and by individuals guided by futurists. The paper by Thomas Sork raises many of these kinds of questions, albeit in a rather gentle and supportive fashion. After an informative discussion of the research on time perspectives, Sork points out that there are significant cultural and subcultural differences in how time and the future are perceived. While acknowledging that a future focused role image can be quite powerful, Sork questions the unspoken assumption among futurists that future focused time perspective is always desirable or that all individuals are equally capable of developing this perspective.

Although writing about issues in the development of futures studies programs, Michelle Small is also concerned with the progress of individuals in coming to grips with futures studies as a perspective and as a field of academic inquiry. From her experiences as a professor and as a student, Small describes the major problems she feels are encountered by futures studies students. While she does not explicitly discuss the formation of time perspectives as Sork does, Small does identify several deficits common to students who do not flourish in futures studies programs. These deficits center around underdeveloped convergent and divergent thinking processes and may overlap with Sork's contention that some students may not, for cultural or developmental reasons, be capable of accommodating futures studies' perspectives. In addition, there is recognition of uneven rates of and tolerance for change, as have been previously discussed in Section I by Hood and others. With this in mind, is it legitimate to expect that futures studies programs, at whatever level, will be equally beneficial to all students?

Just as the above question may be viewed as heresy by some futurists, the questions about literacy raised by Gayle Hudgens may be viewed by some educators as equally troublesome. Hudgens contends that there is a pressing need to rethink the meaning and future of literacy. Rather than continuing to value without question the "reading and writing" skills so clearly associated with the dominant middle class culture, she asserts that it is necessary to develop a variety of future scenarios from which the most valuable communication skills--whether computer based, electronic, oral, or whatever--can be selected and made available. Implicit in much of what Hudgens says is the notion that the function of literacy is liberation, freeing individuals to be autonomous and to achieve their full potential. The means through which this liberation can occur are many and varied. There is no necessity that literacy be tied solely to formal schooling.

One of the forms of literacy that Hudgens discusses is electronic. This means of communication is central to John Deethardt's discussion of "Education and Electronically Mediated Democracy." In his paper, Deethardt develops images of the future built on forms of democracy not currently possible. But with anticipated changes in the media of communication and in the access points to political decision making, the purposes of education, which Deethardt sees as carried out primarily by schools, will need to be redefined. Deethardt provides a preliminary set of goals for education to accomplish the direct, electronically mediated democracy he envisions. However the transition will not be quick and much remains to be delineated.

Deethardt describes alternative decision making systems and means for citizen participation which would radically alter political institutions. Winifred Warnat focuses on another universal human institution--the family--and discusses family forms expected to become more prevalent and important in the future. It is contended that the family, in whatever format taken, is the initial as well as the most universal setting in which education occurs, a contention generally acceptable to most social scientists and educators. Warnat then goes on to develop the concept of the household school as the prime location for role selection, personality acquisition, value formation, and behavioral patterning. In the household school, as Warnat describes it, each family member, regardless of the type of family, is both teacher and learner. Unlike formal schooling which historically has been separate from "real life" experiences, the family based household school is, as described by Warnat, interactive and experiential as well as cognitively and affectively involving. The intentional, formal use of the family as an agency and a setting for education is not new. In traditional, pre-literate societies, this was the norm, but the transition to modern industrial societies has helped to bring about a separation between family and education. With new technologies that are expected to be a part of the Electronic Revolution (also discussed by Harkins and Joseph, Deethardt, Dede, and others), Warnat expects the family to become increasingly important as an agency for education. Given the important and complex psycho-social dimensions of family life and education within the family, it is imperative that a more sophisticated understanding of the family as a setting for education be developed and that there be more study of and preparation for alternative family forms.

Developing a Future Time Perspective:
Variables of Interest to Educators

Thomas J. Sork

On the surface, the concept "time" appears to be rather straight-forward and unambiguous. It is, some would say, that which is measured with clocks--the measured period during which the experiences of life occur. Yet industrial man's fixation on objective time, as measured by using clocks and other devices for establishing and standardizing the periodicity of events, has resulted in a benign neglect of subjective time: time as experienced by people.

The purpose of this paper is to provide a foundation for exploring the implications that variations in the development of a personal time perspective--more specifically, a future time perspective--have for individuals involved in the enterprise of education. To accomplish this purpose, the following major topics will be addressed sequentially (indicating an expected temporal order of presentation):   (1) the nature of time perspective, (2) the results of selected theoretical and empirical studies of time perspective, and (3) implications of research findings to those involved in education.

The Nature of Time Perspective

In a recent essay on time and a sense of the future, McHale stated that:

> Individuals, cultures, and societies may be modally oriented towards the past, the present or the future. This major orientation has a strong value component which influences the direction of personal and collective actions. Apart from the value placed on time itself, on its duration or on recording its periodicities, the prevailing temporal perspective will determine to a considerable degree how time is invested. Time, space, energy, and other resources may be

allocated, with varying emphasis, to the service of past traditions, to present needs or future prospectives.[1]

But what are the origins of man's temporal perspective? What is it that causes individuals, cultures and societies to develop a primary orientation to the past, present, or the future? Whitrow believes that:

> The psychological origin of the concept of time is. . . to be found in the conscious realization of the distinction between desire and satisfaction. The sense of purpose and associated effort is the ultimate source of the ideas of cause and effect; but it was only by a series of scientific abstractions that man eventually arrived at the concepts of a uniform temporal sequence and a definite causal process.[2]

Once the intellectual bridge was built joining action today with results tomorrow it became necessary for humans to begin ordering their experiences into the three categories of things which have happened (past), things which are happening (present) and things which will happen (future). No longer was the idea of a predestined existence in which random or uncontrollable forces orchestrated the life of the individual the only possible conception of human reality. Realization that some control was possible over life's events may have had a tremendous liberating effect on primitive humans. They were now able to fabricate tools and weapons which could be put to use in acquiring food or defending territory. The cause/effect connection allowed them to become planners. And those who identified important cause/effect relationships (i.e., lunar movements and changes in tides, formation of certain cloud types and precipitation) were given high, almost mystical, status in their social groups because of their ability to make predictions.

But time perspective is clearly a more complex concept than this sequence of development may suggest. Contemporary analysts of the concept have identified a number of discrete dimensions which together provide a much more complete understanding of temporality.

A number of authors including Hultsch and Bortner; Bortner and Hultsch; Kastebaum; Trommsdorff and Lamm; Lamm, Schmidt and Trommsdorff; and O'Rand and Ellis, refer to the concept of extension. This dimension accounts for the size of the time span (usually measured in years) within the consciousness of the individual. It is measured several ways. Frequently individuals are asked to identify a number of important events (past, present, or future) in their lives and to associate a date with each event. Degree of extensionality is then determined by measuring the time interval between the most distant past and future events. Alternatively, if the assessment concerns only the future perspective, extensionality is determined by identifying the most distant future event anticipated by the individual. Another method, which has been used first by LeShan and then by Barndt and Johnson, to assess extensionality is to direct the individual to complete a story for which a standardized "root" is provided. The resulting stories are then analyzed and a scoring system devised to represent the maximum extension of time projected by each subject. The point of maximum extension into the future is referred to as the time horizon.

A second dimension of time perspective identified in the literature is density, which accounts for the perceived eventfulness of time in the person's past, present, and future. Kastenbaum has measured density by asking subjects to list as many events as they could that were likely to occur in their personal future. Lamm, et al have measured density by asking subjects to list, within a prescribed time period, events whose occurrence a person hopes or fears. An index is then developed which allows comparison of density across individuals.

A third dimension is direction or directionality which is intended to assess the relative importance of the past, present, and future. Cottle refers to this dimension as temporal dominance. His measurement technique involves having subjects draw three circles representing the past, present, and future. The relative size of the circle is indicative of the direction of the subjects' temporal orientation. If the largest circle drawn represented the future, then theoretically the subject would exhibit a future directionality. Kastenbaum has done an experimental analysis using the Time Metaphors Test developed by Knapp and Garbutt. This instrument provided subjects with a group of metaphors. Their task was to select the metaphor which most nearly represented what the concept of time meant to them. The subjects' directionality was then determined, based on the selected metaphor.

Little agreement is found in the literature on what other dimensions of time perspective are important. The three enumerated above appear to represent those on which a moderate amount of agreement has been achieved.

Research on Time Perspective

Singer has provided a useful concept to which the findings summarized below can be realted. This concept is the "future-focused role-image" (FFRI) defined as one's self-image projected into the future. Singer presents the FFRI as an important goal toward which educators should work; it is developed concurrently with a future-oriented time perspective. However, as the findings presented below will demonstrate, not everyone is necessarily a candidate for a developed future focused role image.

Age and time perspective. Green has proposed a series of developmental stages which individuals must go through on their way to temporal maturity. Her proposed stages and corresponding age ranges are as follows:

1. Permanence of objects and persons (during year 1)
During this stage the infant comes to accept that people and objects have permanence, that they exist even though they are out of the immediate perceptual range of the child.

2. Clock time (1-3 years)
Children must next adjust to arbitrary time as accounted for with clocks. During this stage the child's patterns of eating and sleeping are governed more by external clock time than by internal subjective time. The child can anticipate adult behavior because both adult and child are using cultural time.

3. Restriction time (3-5 years)
Children of this age find there are times when interests can be safely expanded, and times when it is necessary to stop, obey, and accept a dependent status. Because of this dichotomy of time, the child must learn to tolerate larger and larger periods of frustration.

4. Causal sequences (6-11 years)
At this stage of development the child, through observation and exploration of the environment, identifies causal sequences which produce both positive and negative outcomes. The child begins to realize that doing things in a particular order produces desired results with the least expenditures of effort.

5. Personal time (12-15 years)
Adolescents can see themselves in past time and project their potentialities in the future. They can think about their thoughts. Prior to this stage, the self has been an unconscious cohesive force lacking an overt sense of the

self in time. However, the time perspective, as well as the perception of self, is not projected very far into the future.

6. Mutual time (15-25 years)

"The problem here is the search for intimate compatibility with another person for no other purpose than the complete sharing in time of experience. It may be the mutuality in time of two lovers or of two intimate friends, or the rapport of a younger person with a significant adult. The sense of personal isolation is forever reversed."[3]

7. Alternatives in time (18-25 years)

As individuals enter adulthood they are forced to make choices which will determine the kind of future they will experience. This task calls for an analysis of one's past and an exploration of alternative futures. The future pursued is determined solely by the individual.

8. The uses of time (25-40 years)

"This is the period of greatest convergence between external or objective time and subjective time. One comes to grips with reality, so to speak, by no longer upholding the dichotomy between personal time and clock time. Behavior is brought into line with the consensual validation of group time in order to get things done. Commitment to job, marriage, children and property finally focuses the use of time toward establishing and securing these goals."[4]

9. Reconsidered time (40-50 years)

Evaluation of one's life-to-date takes place at this stage and a decision is made as to whether or not changes in life plan should be made. The now-in-vogue "mid-life crisis" is a consequence of this analysis when the individual decides that a change in life plan is necessary.

10. The fore-shortened future (50-60 years)

During this stage, realization of one's mortality coupled with the rapid passage of subjective time leads the individual to covet what time remains. Emphasis is on achieving unattained goals and conserving, through more efficient use of clock time, the time remaining in one's life. "To disguise the signs of aging often becomes a preoccupation of both sexes, for it comforts the self to avoid recognizing the foreclosure of time."[5]

11. The rich past (beginning at about age 65)

The process of life review requires individuals to recount events of their past and to pass judgment on their actions. Subjective time passes quickly and the focus of attention is on the past.

These problems of time encountered by individuals as they develop show that developing a personal time perspective, of which FFRI is a part, begins at birth and probably does not take full form until the ages of 12-15 years when personal time develops. Further, this theoretical framework, rich in hypotheses, suggests that each stage of development involves a somewhat different orientation to time. Research on time perspective at each stage would seem to require discrete conceptual frameworks and psychometrics.

Studies with adults suggest that directionality favors a future orientation from the twenties to the fifties. "Through the early 50's, people thought that they have made and will continue to make progress. By the early 60's, the past seems better than the present, and the present seems better than the future."[6] Directionality, then, appears to favor a future orientation up to the fifties at which time a shift begins first to equal directionality, and then to a dominance of the past.

Social class and time perspective. LeShan, in one of the pioneering studies relating time orientation to social class, found that the time orientations between lower-class and middle-class 8-11 year olds were significantly different. Children from the middle-class told stories which were more future-oriented than the children from lower-class backgrounds.

In a study designed to compare the temporal outlooks (primarily extention) of lower- and middle-class youth of college age, O'Rand and Ellis found that the middle-class youth had a significantly greater extension of time perspective into the future than did lower-class youth.

Lamm et al reported on both density and extension. They hypothesized that lower-class adolescents would evidence more hopes and fears (density) concerned with private matters than with public matters. In addition they hypothesized that middle-class adolescents have a more widely extended future orientation than do lower-class adolescents. Both hypotheses were confirmed by their research.

These studies suggest that there is indeed an important relationship between social class and time perspective. Consequently, if educators accept the task of assisting youth to develop a FFRI, then youth from lower socioeconomic groups will require more attention than youth from other groups.

Sex and time perspective. Little research has focused specifically on variations in time perspective by sex. Lamm et al reported that males voiced significantly more hopes and fears

(density) than females in the occupational domains while female
adolescents of both lower and middle classes voiced more hopes
and fears in the private domain. Further, lower-class boys had a
more extended future orientation than did lower-class girls.
Bart offers explanations for these findings:

> [F]rom the moment of birth, external and constraining
> forces, many arising from the educational process, have
> shaped us, interacting with and molding our original
> biological sexual identity, to make us into first boys
> and girls and then men and women fitted to be citizens
> of the past. The future is part of the present. Yet
> education sex-types us for obsolete roles by imposing
> sharply different expectations on boys and girls, and
> has reinforced this sex-typing through stereotypes in
> the books students read.[7]

Her challenge to educators seems formidable.

Cultural differences and time perspective. Cross-cultural
studies, limited in number as they are, seem to point to clear
distinctions in time perspectives among various cultures.
Nakamura draws comparisons between Indian and Japanese notions of
time. Indians have developed a static conception of time which
makes it difficult to develop a future time perspective. More
specifically:

> The persistent Indian conception of a transcendent
> reality as more important than the phenomenal world it
> underlies and sustains results in a kind of paralysis
> of the individual's sensitivity to time, if we
> understand "time" to mean the passage and flow of
> specific events in our experience. This paralysis
> manifests itself in a characteristic lack of time con-
> cepts which non-Indians regard as common sense.[8]

Nakamura continues:

> Japanese Buddhism also emphasized the transience
> of the phenomenal world. But the Japanese attitude
> toward this transience is very different from the
> Indian. The Japanese disposition is to lay a greater
> emphasis upon sensible, concrete events, intuitively
> apprehended, than upon universals. It is in direct
> contrast to the characteristic Indian reaction to the
> world of change, which is to reject it in favor of an
> ultimate reality, a transcendent absolute in which the
> mind can find refuge from the ceaseless flux of
> observed phenomena.[9]

Shannon conducted research with Anglo-American, American
Indian, and Mexican American youth from 10-17 years of age.
Expected significant differences were found in the time perspectives (extensionality) between the Anglo-American and other
groups. Shannon explains the differences:

The increase in future orientation for Anglo-
Americans is consistent with previous findings for this
group and reflects the absence of conflict between a
cultural focus on future achievements and the expectations of future reward. A quite different picture
emerges for Indian and Mexican Americans. By
adolescence their growing awareness that members of
disadvantaged subcultures are not likely to realize
substantial reward in the future is in conflict with
the more affluent majority-culture norms of future
orientation. In spite of considerable exposure to
middle-class attitudes toward time they maintain their
present orientation.[10]

Poussaint makes a similar case for the black American child:

In large part, then, a child's image of the future
is a reflection of his socio-economic background, i.e.,
does he belong to the in-group as opposed to the out-
group in the current status hierarchy; is he poor, is
he rich and to what ethnic group does he belong.
Clearly, the future of a slum child will differ vastly
from that of his peer in suburbia. In the United
States, it is undoubtedly the color-caste system that
is the most decisive element in the black child's
perspective on his future life-changes and his self-
image.[11]

Givens studied Navajo temporality and determined that their
temporal orientation (ordering of past, present, and future based
on cultural preferences) was essentially to the present.
Further, "the majority of the Navajo today value the present over
the past and are only beginning to develop a Westernized concept
of the future."[12]

It seems clear from the foregoing that cultural differences
do account for variations in future perspective. But the type of
response educators should make to this realization remains
unclear.

Questions for Further Inquiry

The research findings presented above provoke a number of
important questions which beg the attention of educational

futurists. Indeed, without satisfactory answers to these
questions, the basic assumptions upon which the educational
futures movement has developed may be open to serious conceptual
and theoretical challenge.

1. How much responsibility should educators assume for
assisting learners in developing a futures perspective?

Much research evidence suggests that a futures perspective is
affected by multiple psychological and sociological variables.
In some social groups and cultures the dominant time orientation
is to the past or present rather than to the future. The educational enterprise has accepted responsibility for providing
basic education, discipline, child care, socialization, sex education, and nutritious meals along with other responsibilities.
Is it also education's responsibility to develop a future-
oriented populace? If educators do not accept this responsibility, who will? What are the potential consequences of
continuing to have a small segment of the population (primarily
white, upper-middle class males) dominating the associations,
conferences, and publications dealing with the future?

2. Under what circumstances should educators avoid helping
learners develop a futures perspective?

It seems there are compelling ethical questions which must be
faced by educational futurists. Research suggests that there are
socio-cultural differences in time orientation. Should educators
be attempting to develop future-oriented time perspectives in
individuals who will live in a past- or present-oriented social
system? What are the social-psychological consequences for a
future-oriented person living in a past- or present-oriented
milieu? If the rewards for developing a futures perspective are
culturally-biased, then what right or responsibility do educators
have to foster delayed-gratification, goal-oriented behavior of
those who are least likely to reap the benefits of such behavior?
There appear to be some negative consequences associated with a
futures perspective. How can educators eliminate these
consequences or know when they are destined to occur and thereby
avoid them?

3. What factors are most responsible for retarding the
development of a futures perspective and how can they be
overcome?

Through research the determinants of a futures perspective are
beginning to be identified. As research progresses a predictive
model should emerge which identifies and explains variables

affecting a futures perspective. Clearly some variables will
have much more power in the formula than others. Educators must
face the prospect that some variables may effectively block the
development of a futures perspective, while others, although
providing a formidable barrier, can be overcome using educational
or other means. Deciding when the barrier can be overcome with
education and when it cannot will be an essential question during
the period of scarce resources ahead in the 1980s.

4. What techniques seem to be most effective in promoting
the development of a futures perspective?

Researchers are beginning to report results produced by various
curricula and instructional devices. As with most educational
outcomes there is likely a wide variety of techniques that are
effective in promoting a futures perspective. But as available
resources continue to constrict the range of alternative
approaches which can be used, those techniques found to be most
effective will gain wide acceptance. Until the best techniques
emerge educators must devise strategies based on experience and
sensation from the viscera. Documenting outcomes produced by
such strategies is an important responsibility for all educators.
For without such data it will be quite difficult to determine
which, if any, of the extant techniques are producing the desired
result at least cost.

5. How can the degree of development of a futures
perspective be best assessed?

Futurists extoll the virtues of an orientation to the future.
Yet it is clear from the available literature that considerable
conceptual housecleaning is in order before any agreement is
reached on what it means to have a futures time perspective.
Clearly there are multiple dimensions to the concept of time
orientation and most researchers choose to develop their own
means of measuring it. Such psychometric diversity is important
in any research involving a relatively new concept. But before
research results can be compared and a body of useful knowledge
formulated, some comparability of measurement must be attained.
As more and more researchers struggle with the problem of futures
perspective, the concept will be focused and refined so that all
will eventually use a similar vocabulary and means of
measurement.

Closing Challenge

The reader is now charged with a responsibility.
Educational futurism is in its infancy. If it is to reach its

adolescence with some degree of grace and respectability, a big job lies ahead. Difficult if not embarrassing questions must be asked of this emerging field of study. What evidence exists that its basic assumptions are correct? Is there a clearly developed conceptual and theoretical framework for the field? Are research activities designed to build on one another and thereby produce a validated body of useful knowledge? Is action based on something other than whim or fancy? Is educational futurism here to stay or is it simply another "trendy innovation" which will soon be relegated to the junkheap of discarded social inventions? These and other questions must be addressed if this field is to avoid the criticism that proponents of the field level at so many others: that it is simply an opportunistic special interest group promoting simple solutions to complex problems with neither a rational basis for action nor with clear consideration of consequences.

NOTES

1. John McHale, "Time and the Future Sense," Technological Forecasting and Social Change, Vol. 12, 1978, p. 2.

2. G. J. Whitrow, The Natural Philosophy of Time (London: Thomas Nelson and Sons, 1961), p. 52.

3. H. B. Green, "Temporal Stages in the Development of Self," in J. T. Fraser and N. Lawrence (eds.) The Study of Time II (New York: Springer-Verlag, 1975), p. 7.

4. Ibid., p. 9.

5. Ibid., p. 12.

6. D. F. Hultsch and R. W. Bortner, "Personal Time Perspective in Adulthood: A Time-Sequential Study,": Developmental Psychology, Vol. 10, 1974, pp. 836-837.

7. Pauline Bart, "Why Women See the Future Differently From Men," in A. Toffler (ed.) Learning for Tomorrow: The Role of the Future in Education (New York: Vintage Books, 1974), p. 55.

8. H. Nakamura, "Time in Indian and Japanese Thought," in J. T. Fraser (ed.) The Voices of Time (New York: George Braziller, 1966), p. 80.

9. Ibid., p. 85.

10. L. Shannon, "Development of Time Perspective in Three Cultural Groups: A Cultural Difference or an Expectance Interpretation," Developmental Psychology, Vol. 11, 1975, p. 114.

11. Alvin F. Poussaint, "The Black Child's Image of The Future," in A. Toffler (ed.) Learning for Tomorrow: The Role of the Future in Education (New York: Vintage Books, 1974), p. 57.

12. D. R. Givens, An Analysis of Navajo Temporality (Washington, D.C.: University Press of America, 1977), p. 45.

REFERENCES

Barndt, R.J. and D.M. Johnson. "Time Orientation in Delinquents," Journal of Abnormal and Social Psychology, Vol. 51, 1955, pp. 343-345.

Bart, P.B. "Why Women See the Future Differently From Men." In A.Toffler (Ed.), Learning for Tomorrow: The Role of the Future in Education. New York: Vintage Books, 1974.

Bortner, R.W. and D.F. Hultsch. "Personal Time Perspective in Adulthood," Developmental Psychology, Vol. 7, 1972, pp. 98-103.

Cottle, T.J. Perceiving Time: A Psychological Investigation with Men and Women. New York: John Wiley and Sons, 1976.

Givens, D.R. An Analysis of Navajo Temporality, (Washington, D.C.: University Press of America, 1977.

Green, H.B. "Temporal Stages in the Development of Self." In J.T. Fraser and N. Lawrence (Eds.), The Study of Time II. New York: Springer-Verlag, 1975.

Hultsch, D.F. and R.W. Bortner. "Personal Time Perspective in Adulthood: A Time-Sequential Study," Developmental Psychology, Vol. 10, 1974, pp. 835-837.

Kastenbaum, R. "The Dimensions of Future Time Perspective, an Experimental Analysis," Journal of General Psychology Vol. 65, 1961, pp. 203-218.

Knapp, R.H. and J.T. Garbutt. "Time Imagery and the Achievement Motive," *Journal of Personality*, Vol. 26, 1958, pp. 423-434.

Lamm. H., R.W. Schmidt, and G. Trommsdorff. "Sex and Social Class as Determinants of Future Orientation (Time Perspective) in Adolescents," *Journal of Personality and Social Psychology*, Vol. 34, 1976, pp. 317-326.

LeShan, L.L. "Time Orientation and Social Class," *Journal of Abnormal and Social Psychology*, Vol. 47, 1952, pp. 589-592.

McHale, J. "Time and the Future Sense," *Technological Forecasting and Social Change*, Vol. 12, 1978, pp. 1-12.

Nakamura, H. "Time in Indian and Japanese Thought." In J.T. Fraser (Ed.), *The Voices of Time*. New York: George Braziller, 1966.

O'Rand, A. and R.A. Ellis. "Social Class and Social Time Perspective," *Social Forces*, Vol. 53, pp. 53-62.

Poussaint, A.F. "The Black Child's Image of the Future." In A. Toffler (Ed.), *Learning for Tomorrow: The Role of the Future in Education*. New York: Vintage Books, 1974.

Shannon, L. "Development of Time Perspective in Three Cultural Groups: A Cultural Difference or an Expectance Interpretation," *Developmental Psychology*, Vol. 11, 1975, pp. 114-115.

Singer, B.D. "The Future-Focused role Image." In A. Toffler (Ed.), *Learnining for Tomorrow: The Role of the Future in Education*. New York: Vintage Books, 1974.

Trommsdorff, G. and H. Lamm. "An Analysis of Future Orientation and Some of Its Social Determinants." In J.T. Fraser and N. Lawrence (Eds.), *The Study of Time II*. New York: Springer-Verlag, 1975.

Whitrow, G.J. *The Natural Philosophy of Time*. London: Thomas Nelson and Sons, 1961.

Programs in Higher Problems in Futures Studies Education: Observations Based on Personal Experiences

Michele Geslin Small

In writing this paper, I have used my own experiences as a springboard for discussing what I perceive as significant problems in futures studies programs. The recognition of these problems and the recommendations for solutions grow out of my experiences as director of a futures studies program at a small liberal arts college and as a graduate student in futures studies at a major midwestern university. The catalyst for the preparation of this paper was my participation in a working group on missing components in futurists' education at the 2nd Annual Conference of the World Future Society's Education Section.

One of the problems I perceive in futures studies programs in higher education results from a unique tension between two poles: the nature and needs of the programs and the nature and needs of the students. On one hand there is the nature of the field itself (highly inter-disciplinary, "fuzzy" say the critics) and the needs of futures studies programs: 1) to develop, grow and survive in an academic community faced with dwindling enrollment, limited resources and retrenchment; 2) to establish a sound track record in research so that the field can achieve the respect and recognition it justly deserves; and 3) to serve the students they purport to educate. On the other hand, there are the students attracted to the programs. In this case, I distinguish the students who flourish and do extremely well from those who "flounder" and after a while drop out of the program in total dismay, making comments such as "what am I getting out of this?" or "what am I doing here?"

It seems to me that the students who prosper in the futures studies programs usually seem to be older, and more mature with previous professional experiences. Self-motivated, self-directed and highly competitive, they come to the program with precise and specific goals in mind. In most cases, their interests seem to be best served by benign neglect from their instructors.

In the case of the floundering students, I feel that the problem of incompatibility which arises, stems from the nature of the field and the students' perception and understanding--or misunderstanding--of it. It is highly ironic that the reason why some students choose a futures studies program becomes the reason why they leave it. The attractive feature of the field, namely that it is inter-disciplinary, turns into a fundamental handicap for those students who speak of its "unmanageability," its "lack of structure and organization." In other words, the field and the programs seem to cover everything and nothing.

This paradox, I think, stems from two fundamental weaknesses in the students' educational background: on one hand, for some, the lack of a solid foundation; on the other hand, for most, an inability to synthesize knowledge. This "essential tension" between the convergent and divergent mind which Thomas Kuhn applies to the study of science, has therefore particular relevance to the field of futures studies.[1]

It is important to note that some students have never had a rigorous grounding in a distinct discipline. Their individual temperament might have resisted or avoided the highly traditional and conventional structure of many fields. Attracted by its novelty, they then turn to a futures studies program and perceive its inter-disciplinary quality as a solution to their own disaffection. Tragically enough, it is when they are confronted with the field that their problem becomes more acute and they flounder. What they perceived as their salvation ends up being their downfall.

I believe that in order to tackle the futures studies field which is purposely multidimensional, one has to have acquired previously a rigorous convergent mind trained in the traditional, convergent mode of thinking. In other words, one has to become a "specialist" before one can become a "generalist." The process of mastering knowledge in a particular discipline--to know how we got where we are (historical background), where we are now (current state of the art), to analyze existing research, to apply different methodologies, etc.--cannot but help a student thrive in an inter-disciplinary setting. Because they lack the rigorous training in analysis (convergent thinking), students become unable to make the vital connections which are so significant when one attempts to integrate knowledge.

It is at this point that their original problem is compounded with yet another deficiency common to most students--the inability to synthesize knowledge (divergent thinking). Too often in our system of higher education, it is not until their junior or senior year, if at all, that the students start finally

making some meaningful connections between the different areas
they have been exploring. Their surprise and delight at fitting
together some of the pieces of the proverbial jig-saw puzzle are
somewhat painful in the sense that one wonders why it has
happened so late.

The fault lies with our educational system as it stands now.
If many of the students have received a solid grounding in
logical analysis, very few have been trained to think
holistically. As Edward T. Clark points out, our Western culture
has traditionally used as a starting point for structuring
knowledge, the scientific method whereby one starts with the
smallest self-evident part and proceeds from the parts to
incrementally construct the whole.[2] Yet, as he affirms, "there
is a second starting point from which knowledge can be
structured: The systemic approach begins with the whole in order
to provide a context within which the parts, as they are learned,
can be understood in a different perspective--that is in
relationship to each other and to the whole."[3]

This approach shows exciting promise for the education of
younger generations. Unfortunately, the students being dealt
with in the here and now, even if they take a few courses in
General Systems Theory, cannot compensate for a crucial lack of
years of training in synthesis. Faced with a field which deals
with a multiplicity of areas of knowledge in which they have not
necessarily been trained, incapable of integrating all those
seemingly disparate elements, they experience panic and disap-
pointment.

This leads me to the next point in the long list of reasons
why students flounder in futures studies programs. The first one
is the problem of stress, common to all students but particularly
acute in futures studies programs. The lack of training for
integration that has been mentioned before is exacerbated by the
multiplicity of areas under consideration (each with its unique
concepts and specific jargon), the massive amount of potentially
pertinent information available, and the poor, dispersed and
uneven resources at the human, physical, psychological or
conceptual level. In this context, the adaptive resources of
some students are taxed beyond limits.

As if intellectual stress were not enough for the students
who are supposed to impose their own logic on an inchoate and
semi-amorphous field, emotionally they are constantly put in the
defensive position of having to justify their presence in the
program to their somewhat contemptuous peers. Or they are put in
the frustrating position of attempting to define "in one or two
sentences" what futures studies is all about, to a half-
condescending, half-bemused audience.

The whole picture which emerges from the combination of all these factors is one of helplessness--real and perceived--and a total sense of isolation. It is paradoxical that such a multidisciplinary field as futures studies could engender such a sense of alienation in its students. The reason might lie in the fact that the field, because it is so complex and related to everything, does not touch base with anything. This is in marked contrast to other traditional disciplines where, for example, a student in biology can find much support among his peers in zoology, botany, ethology . . ., because the areas are so closely related and the concerns are common. In contrast, there seems to be very little cohesiveness among students in futures studies programs due to the wide diversity of backgrounds and areas of interest and the lack of time. There is so much to learn in so little time; so much to integrate with so little preparation--a feeling well illustrated in the notion of "futures burn-out."

Finally, looming ahead is the uncertainty of "fitting somewhere" and finding a job in a society which does not recognize futurists as professionals and where the job market is tight even for those who have been trained in the most established and recognized disciplines.

The awareness of the reasons why some students abandon futures studies programs, heightens one's perception of the problem but does not solve it. As I have stated before, the essential conflict resides not only in the nature of the field and the students' perception of it, but also in the needs of the programs on one hand and those of the students on the other.

If the futures studies field were well established, well respected, and a well funded discipline in higher education, the problem might be different. But, as many researchers have pointed out, the field is still in its infancy, still in the process of defining itself, and futures programs are few and far between. Merely tolerated with benign condescension by practicioners of some of the more traditional disciplines, these programs are beleaguered by numerous attacks from more and more vociferous critics who show only contempt for this "wooly minded nonsense."

Because they are so new, futures studies programs also suffer from the lack of traditional prestige, usually associated with the humanities, or the blind, unconditional respect paid to the "hard sciences." Who has heard of futures studies? Yet, at the same time, the very real constraints which affect all academic disciplines today must be faced. Enrollment is crucial, especially in the eyes of those in power who play the "numbers game." Quantity is the order of the day and becomes a sine qua non.

Finally, futures studies programs are still in the process of trying to establish a sound track record, especially in the area of research, in order to alleviate some of the bitter criticisms and further the growth and development of the field.

I am now back to the core of the problem: a tension between the needs of the futures studies programs if they want to survive, grow and establish thmselves, and the programs' commitment to students and their individual needs.

Concerned as we are to insure the existence and development of the field, we might be tempted to succumb to the superficially appealing but fallacious rationalization that futures studies programs need exclusively, first rate students: those highly motivated, highly creative, self-directed learners who are endowed with a solid convergent foundation and gifted with unique divergent capabilities.

Should we then advocate a serious screening in order to "winnow the chaff and keep the grain?"

This position is not only insultingly arrogant but fundamentally erroneous and unrealistic. The students being talked about here are exceptional and the case could be made that all disciplines need and want such students. Moreover, in order to insure the long-term goal of the quality and reputation of the field, the short-term survival of the programs could be jeopardized. Enrollment would decline, which would be tantamount to political suicide.

Thirdly, students are needed to teach and prepare the next generation. Because we live in a society which is more and more specialized and unidirectional, we **must** train people to broaden their horizons so that they can function in our very complex technological world, in which every problem is intricately connected with other areas. Systemic, divergent thinking is a necessity, if we want, as a society, to meet the challenging times we are facing and their implications for the 21st century.

Failing to adequately prepare students would be a tragic example of short-sightedness; without troops, one cannot win a battle. Last but not least, such attitude would negate the avowed educational mission: to train men and women not only to function in a complex world, but to have a desire to contribute to the solution of its many problems.

At the same time, the signals given from the larger environment of futures studies programs--the higher education context--are clear. This is not the time to go the route of

"more and bigger" as was done in the past and request more teaching personnel, counselors, equipment, etc. . . . Obviously it is necessary to try to solve the problem, not by adding new cards to the deck as it were, but by reshuffling the existing ones. Consequently, what I propose to do, to make students happier and more successful, is to re-think the context and implement changes within the boundaries of existing physical and human resources. My proposal, therefore, has direct implications for the faculty of futures studies programs in their advising and counseling duties, as well as for the older graduate students already involved in the program.

To the faculty I recommend the adoption of a "triage" system. I am very aware that the concept of "triage" carries ruthless connotations if we consider its application in the treatment of casualties or its use in the solution of the world food problem. My use of the word will be, I hope, a softer and kinder one. Since "triage" means to sort out through the means of a classification system, I propose to divide the students who enroll in futures studies programs into three categories, after careful scrutiny of their educational records and recommendations and a thoughtful assessment of each individual's interview.

1) The first group is made up of those exceptional students who would do well in any field. The unique combination of convergent and divergent thinking they are endowed with will make them prime candidates for the futures studies program. Yet, instead of catering to them, as seems to be generally the case, they should be left to their own devices. A judicious blend of timely appreciation and appropriate positive reinforcement will launch them on new tracks towards new goals and new visions, without hampering their creativity by forcing them to conform to the standard mold.

Allowed and able to capitalize on their individual disciplinary backgrounds, whether they be in the "hard sciences," the social sciences, the arts, or the humanities, these students will be the ones who will make the greatest contributions to the research and development of the field.

2) The second group stands on the other extreme of the spectrum. They will be those who, for various reasons, personal, educational or both, could not function at all in a highly inter- disciplinary setting. Dragging them along would be a disservice to them as well as to the program. They should be carefully advised so that they can find an area more appropriate to their needs, one in which they can learn, grow and achieve to the extent of their capabilities. The motto "let each become what he is capable of being" certainly applies here and every effort should be made to help such students reach this goal.

3) This group, which will form the majority of futures studies students, deserves the faculty's best efforts. The standard advising procedure adopted in other disciplines, whereby students have little choice but to take a prescribed and sequential series of courses which ultimately will lead to the mastery of the subject, cannot apply in futures studies programs. We are not in the position, nor should we ever attempt, to "crank out" futurists.

Special attention should be given to each student and his or her particular background. Made aware of their individual strengths and weaknesses, students should be carefully guided to tailor the particular program which best fits their needs. For some, it will mean courses in different methodologies; for others, it might mean courses in other disciplines to remedy some basic deficiency. But whatever the case, the utmost flexibility to adapt to each individual situation should be combined with the utmost vigilance to make certain that students, at all times, know and understand why they are here, what they are doing, and where they are going.

This will be a time-consuming proposition. Yet, futures studies programs, because they are so new, and not yet besieged by hordes of students--a blessing in disguise--can and should take the time to nurture each of their students.

This proposal puts a heavy burden on the shoulders of the faculty of futures studies programs. Not only are many of them stretched thin between their responsibilities in teaching, research, advising, administration, and committee work, but also, the most careful initial advising that I have just recommended will not automatically spell success unless the problems of lack of skills and resources, information overload, stress management, lack of support and professional self-concept are also dealt with.

It is at this point that I propose to tap a seldom used source of energy--the students themselves. By capitalizing on the unlimited talent resource of the students already involved in the program, I propose to build a truly caring and synergistic environment where new students can flourish instead of flounder and where all involved can benefit.

Granted, some of this is already happening in some futures programs, but it is rather spontaneous, unorganized, irregular and concerns only a few select students who are not necessarily those who have the most problems.

In the academic area, I would like to suggest, for example, weekly seminars where a more experienced student would meet with a group of one to five newer students. These sessions could go many ways depending on the needs of any particular group. On one hand, the students could discuss some of the concepts found in the readings or presented in class; hone and refine their own perceptions by contact with others' views; exchange ideas, suggest some sources pertinent to the area at hand, etc. On the other hand, the students could also provide each other with some meaningful tutoring in the area of skills, be they in communication (by reading and giving each other a critique of their papers, on content as well as form), or in other areas such as statistics, computer science, etc.

The result would be truly synergistic in the sense that all could benefit from the exposure to a wide diversity of backgrounds the opportunity of receiving input from an audience, and the change of sharpening their own ideas in the process of sharing them.

The benefits of such an experiment would also go far beyond the realm of academics. Everyone knows that a student is in the best position to understand the needs and problems of other students, be they as trivial as mere information to get things done (e.g., library, registration . . .) or as fundamental as the need of being with people who share the same goals and are enthusiastic about the same things. The peer support system, thus generated, would definitely help alleviate the problems of stress, information management and alienation, help maintain high physical and intellectual activity levels while insuring psychic equilibrium, and in the long run give the student population a strong "esprit de corps" much needed in the beleaguered futures studies programs.

Finally, to build a strong professional self-concept, students, with the help and guidance of the faculty, could organize and participate in colloquia, attend regional, national and international conferences, work on the staff of a professional journal (or create their own), etc. These "real life" experiences would certainly provide meaningful professional contacts and develop self-confidence and poise with regard to stress-producing requirements such as participation in seminars, oral examinations and presentations at professional meetings.

Two objections could be raised to this proposal: those of time and management. To the first objection I will simply reply that "one makes time" if the reward is worth it. In the case of the present state of futures studies programs, I believe it is. To the second, I trust individual programs to develop and implement this idea to their own satisfaction, in accord with their own context. In some cases advanced students could be financially renumerated by making their contributions part of a teaching assistantship, for example. Other programs might select to give credit to advanced students on the basis that such "practical training" is vital to those who will eventually hold positions in public education or in public life.

The mechanisms to insure accountability could also be worked out under some contractual agreement between faculty and students whereby the students would keep track of the number and length of their meetings and turn in some report that would be "gradable" by the instructor.

Where there is a will, there is a way. When the necessity and the urgency of helping the students who flounder in futures studies programs becomes evident, the "how to" questions can easily be resolved contextually, as long as imagination and goodwill prevail.

The problems that futures studies programs experience today are very real. I hope that this modest proposal will spur others to reflect on these questions, generate some solutions, and share their ideas. Only by creative action will we avoid the disaffection mentioned earlier, help the field grow to its next stage of development, increase our numbers, serve students, and since students are the link with the next generation, meet our moral obligations to humankind.

NOTES

1. Thomas S. Kuhn, The Essential Tension: Selected Studies in Scientific Tradition and Change (Chicago: The University of Chicago Press, 1977), pp. 225-239.

2. Edward T. Clark, "Systemic Thinking: A New Mode of Educational Thought," Education Tomorrow, IV, 5, 1979, p. 1.

3. Ibid.

Is Literacy Passe in a Pushbutton World?

A. Gayle Hudgens

When Robert Theobald proclaimed that "literacy is not such a bright idea any more"[1] he offered a cast-iron believable case for an elitism which could, in the ideological climate of the electronic age, be taken as self-evident. The notion that literacy skills are obsolete in an advanced industrial society increasingly dependent on nonprint media and telecommunications is, given the _prima facie_ evidence, untenable, even pernicious. With more than 50 million adults in the United States eligible for literacy training, the argument can indeed be made that we are wasting our time, money, and energy on basic skill programs that are expensive, often ineffective, and reach only two to four percent of the target population.[2] Others have argued that we are not asking the necessary questions about whose literacy it is that we are developing, why it is being taught to this target group in this particular way, and what its real or latent functions are in the industrial complex with respect to manpower needs.[3]

The _problematique illetre_ is particularly complex not only because of disagreements such as these, but also because no standard definition of literacy exists.[4] Without getting into that polemic which involves disputes ranging from reading grade levels to what it means to be a fully functioning human being, we can safely say that persons dependent on non-print media are perceived to need less developed literacy skills. Other persons, however, may be interested in community development, for example, and they may have information needs which can be resolved only through print media.

At one time or another in the growing debate over what central skills will be needed for future survival, the following elements have been cited: reading comprehension; computational literacy (or numeracy); problem-solving; economic progress; coping skills and the extension of one's emotional and intellectual range; and the avoidance of welfare, crime, and

depression. Obviously, if these are important components in the
literacy arena, a need for analyzing and developing a wise literacy policy for the future is evident.

This essay addresses the need for rethinking the future of
literacy. The first portion considers the historical background
and touchstones of literacy, global dimensions, and some philosophical issues surrounding evolving literacy requirements. Part
II is a guide for brainstorming the literacy issue for developing
a position statement with policy implications. The methodology
is derived from Leys' "deliberative questions."[5]

Part I

Advancing literacy in the countryside by educating the
masses to transcend their everyday realities, like changing
reality in the scientific realm, has had a variety of consequences on the pattern of world events over time. Jefferson and
his cohorts properly linked literacy with enlightened citizenship
and self-government. In later centuries literacy came to mean
earning power and upward social mobility. Without literacy,
people could not easily raise their economic and social expectations. But ironically, without expectations they possessed no
incentive to learn to read, as Eugene Genovese so aptly put it:

> The obstacles did not all concern fatigue, limited
> cultural horizons, a lack of books and paper or of an
> available tutor. Beyond all these lurked another.
> Mrs. Kemble suggested to the son of a literate
> plantation slave that he ask his father to teach him to
> read. He answered "with a look and manner that went to
> my very heart, 'Missus, what for me learn to read? Me
> have no prospect.'"[6]

Historically, oppressed minorities (frequently constituted
of culturally and linguistically different groups) often have
been caught in this ironic, no prospect circumstance. Intimately
tied to social and economic issues, the literacy bind has rested
in the dead center of the struggle between the haves and the
have-nots. Several examples drawn from social history illustrate
the intensity of this conflict.

For centuries the Catholic Church denied the "ignorant and
the impressionable" access to the scriptures by restricting
education to certain classes of people.[7] Kuczysnki, in his Rise
of the Working Class, quotes a president of the Royal Society who
spoke out against literacy for the common people in fearful terms:

> However specious in theory the project might be, of
> giving education to the labouring classes of the poor,
> it would in effect be found to be prejudicial to their
> morals and happiness; it would teach them to despise
> their lot in life, instead of making them good servants
> in agriculture, and other laborious employments to
> which their rank in society has destined them; instead
> of teaching them subordination it would render them
> fractious and refractory .... It would enable them
> to read seditious pamphlets....[8]

The Nat Turner revolt represents a classic example of the
knowledge-is-power struggle and it stimulated reactionary and
repressive legislation and local restrictions in the South: "in
some places it became a crime merely to sell writing materials to
slaves."[9]

To transform the marginalized peasant in Brazil through
literacy meant to transform the social reality of the 1960s so
radically that the creator of the method and theory of "pedagogy
of the oppressed"—Paulo Freire—was imprisoned and later exiled.
For his success in stamping out illiteracy simultaneously raised
the consciousness of the masses, a condition that starkly
conflicted with the military regime, one of whose aims was to
protect the interest of the mainstream literate ruling class.[10]

In other political contexts and in other times, however, the
elimination of illiteracy has been viewed as essential to
governments whose priorities were of a different kind. During
the early thirties in the Soviet Union, for example, when radical
social and economic restructuring was occurring, literacy
development was one of the Soviet government's primary thrusts.[11]
The United States, through public and private policies and fiscal
and programmatic action, has committed itself explicitly to
educational equity and literacy acquisition for all members of
its society.   Through its enormous allocations of grants to
individual students, the U.S. has recognized the need for
financial aid for minorities in particular.   A variety of
government grants for research and new programs have recognized
the right of every citizen in the land to read.   Nevertheless, in
1975, the U.S. Office of Education reported that 23 million
Americans between the ages of 18 and 65 could not read or write
well enough (beyond the fifth-grade level) to function adequately
in our modern technological society.   A Ford Foundation report,
more recently, has suggested that the target population for a
massive literacy campaign ranges between 54 and 64 million.[12]

If the ninth grade reading level were to be adopted as the
Navy standard, over 25% of the recruits who enter the Navy would
require some form of reading remediation.[13]   The Senate Select

Committee on Equal Educational Opportunity frequently receives devastating testimony on illiteracy discrepancies vis a vis ethnic breakdown. For example, a Chicano leader lamented gross educational inequities: ". . . the Mexican American has (a lower) educational level than either black or Anglo, the highest dropout rate, and the highest illiteracy rate."[14] And in a summary report of the Adult Performance Level Project, Northcutt et al reported that comparing competing levels of competency by ethnic groups showed a great difference between whites and all minority groups:

> While 16% of the Whites are estimated to be functionally incompetent, about 44% of the Blacks and 56% of the Spanish-surname groups are estimated to be so. Here, as with other variables that have been discussed, the differences are probably due to the relatively lower levels of income, education, job status, and job opportunity found among minority groups in this country.[15]

Northcutt's study and others like it have been criticized because the results were based on batteries of tests which purported to assess achievement in reading, but there was "no check to find out whether lack of reading skill or lack of specific knowledge" (or general cultural knowledge) was the prime reason for lack of correct performance on test items.[16] In other words, they may have been measuring the ability and willingness to be a "middle-class American."[17]

The United Nations Educational, Scientific and Cultural Organization has also discovered that culturally there are many different kinds of reading and literacy problems. In a report entitled Women, Education, Equality: A Decade of Experiment,[18] in which programs in the Upper Volta, Nepal, and Chile are discussed, the editors emphasize that societal factors often hamper needed educational change. From a global perspective, then, literacy development poses a complex set of problems. After a 10-year crusade against illiteracy, UNESCO in 1976 issued a report acknowledging that their own valiant effort was a dismal failure. World-wide illiteracy had actually increased!

No matter what labels one chooses--barely literate, functionally illiterate, functionally incompetent--effective performance in advanced industrial societies is highly dependent on reading skills, the key tools for the acquisition of survival knowledge in modern civilization.[19] For people to function adequately at the everyday level of reality and for larger suprasystems to solve the cluster of world-wide problems growing at an exponential rate--what the Club of Rome has called the problematique humaine--sub-issues such as functional illiteracy must be mastered or else global "disparities may drive mankind over the brink into final destruction."[20] And we all will be left with little prospect.

Paulo Freire's conviction that man gains prospect--and dignity--through the process of conscientação (the ability to think beyond one's immediate environment) suggests that all persons must become active participants in analyzing their world and in changing the conditions of their lives, whether those conditions relate to their family, community, or job.[21] Since job-related literacy demands are important in an advanced industrial society like the United States, recent government-funded research projects on adult functional literacy have tended to emphasize the nature of reading tasks rather than an individual's skill level measured by standardized but possibly culturally-biased tests.[22] Successful performance on reading tasks "imposed by an external agent" has taken precedence over generic skills.[23] Qualitatively measured, competencies may be equal, but performance is what counts in getting ahead, in upward social mobility, and in increasing life's options.

Whether job-related literacy skills, at one end of the spectrum, should become the primary goal of policy-directed research is a volatile question. At the other end are some educational futurists who maintain that funding basic skill development makes no sense at all in a computerized world. Somewhere in between these polar views lies Freire's notion of conscientação. At this stage, perhaps a contemplative discussion can enlighten those concerned about policy formation for adult literacy development.

In the twilight years of the 20th century an appropriate and timely question is, "Regardless of ethnicity, social class, cultural background, age or sex, what are the literacy demands on a fully-functioning person?" The answer to that question would entail a misty excursion into numerous disciplines. Risking oversimplification, it can be said with reasonable certainty that a fully functioning individual needs a secure economic base from which to move beyond a basic survival/subsistence level. Maslow's hierarchy of needs provides a useful model since it encompasses not only the needs for job-related skills, but also suggests implicitly that one cannot move beyond his/her immediate experience until one has satisfied those basic economic needs. Given this expanded viewpoint, then, literacy studied strictly as a job-related task-demand seems a sterile approach. If one of our goals is to enable people to go beyond their immediate experience and enlarge their scope of the world, both temporally and spatially, then certainly literacy demands will go far beyond merely being able to read instructions for doing a job or for learning how to do a job.

From a macroview analysis, however, the task of literacy development is characterized by cobwebbed dynamics. National policy formation based on a model of human and knowledge capital growth promises to have a significant impact on long-run educational investment in general, and literacy development in particular.[24] The so-called enlightenment function of social research, in a world fast becoming more dependent on electronic media than on the printed word, likewise fosters beneficial possibilities.[25] At the same time, the changed economic reality has made the economic rewards of a postsecondary education specious at best, and a number of critics are presently questioning the benefits and exposing the limitations of traditional literacy.

Erich Fromm, for example, after living in Mexico for a number of years observed that:

> People who are illiterate or who write little have memories far superior to the fluently literate inhabitants of the industrialized countries. Among other facts, this suggests that literacy is by no means the blessing it is advertised to be, especially when people use it merely to read material that impoverishes their capacity to experience and to imagine.[26]

Fromm's observation seems to be especially true of literacy acquired through formal institutional channels. It appears that formal education, as known in the past, will have to make greater investments in efficiency and in quality of training to meet the critical demands of a rapidly changing society, demands which will entail innovative and imaginative individual social members.

Freire has provided a provocative orientation for literacy in nonformal settings and what doors it can and should open. In his reflections and interpretations upon the relevance of Paulo Freire for American adult education, London has remarked that:

> The crucial modern need to gain more influence and control over our lives has been frustrated by the growth of bureaucracy; the development of technicism and large-scale organizations and institutions; an accelerating gap in capital resources and income between the industrial and developing societies; and the increasing tendency to view man mechanistically as an object.[27]

Freire's vision, in London's opinion, contains a potential contribution for encouraging alienated adults within the U.S. society to pursue schooling and literacy.[28] Through consciousness-raising efforts such Americans might become

> . . . aware of the variety of forces--economic, political, social and psychological--that are affecting their lives. . . . The awakening of consciousness is necessary so people cannot only critically analyze their world and thus attain freedom, but also become aware of their own dignity as human beings.[29]

Freire describes the basic aim of education as liberation-- that is, liberation from object-status, from submergence in a morass which Freire calls the state of "primary consciousness." In this state, man is "submerged by reality and his interests center on the most vegetative aspects of his life."[30] Freire's method for raising consciousness is dialogue. Basically, dialogue is an encounter between men mediated by the world. Its purpose is the pursuit of truth; its substance is a liberating act of creation. Freire's concept of dialogue implies a humanistic, an "optimistic" view of the world: the belief that any man, if freed from fear and the "internalization" of oppression (hence the title of his most famous work, Pedagogy of the Oppressed, 1970), can add "his meaningful and unique contribution to the collective effort of all men to humanize the world."[31] Implicit in Freire's conceptualization of dialogue is equal participation--between teacher and student. The forces motivating dialogue and its necessary components and conditions are love, humility, and intense faith in man's vocation to realize his fullest humanity, hope, and critical thinking--not accepting the extremes of either the political left or right. Dialogue for Freire is education; "Without dialogue there is no communication and without communication there can be no true education."[32]

Realistically, in order to initiate the type of consciousness-raising that Freire describes, it would be necessary to allow wide-spread grassroots discussion of sensitive sociopolitical and economic issues. Asher DeLeon, longtime UNESCO administrator on educational issues, believes that the problems of illiteracy are more or less institutionalized sociopolitical problems.[33] DeLeon believes that formal education, in its time-bound, place-bound context, systematically excludes the majority of people and is merely a microcosm of society at large. As such, formal schooling cannot be expected to change problems in literacy or general educational competence.

Because of widespread skepticism concerning the
effectiveness of schooling, numerous educational leaders have
been prompted to question whether institutions should be
investing so much on basic skill development. Might it be
futile? Will basic literacy skills even be necessary in the
future?

Literacy as we know it today (ability to read, write and
compute) may be unnecessary by the 21st century, or perhaps even
earlier. We have already mentioned the stance of Robert
Theobald. Peter Wagshal, Director of the University of Massachusetts' Futures Studies Program, has written that electronic media
(audio, visual, and computer) are rapidly replacing print media,
and hence, back-to-basics approaches fail to acknowledge this new
reality. Wagshal puts it tersely:

> The 'basics,' in short, have always had something to do
> with knowledge, communication, and maybe even wisdom,
> and we have always assumed that the ability to read,
> write and compute were necessary prerequisites for
> achieving those ends.[34]

The passivity of print media and the exclusivity of use by
the affluent elite are two long-time flaws which will supposedly
be corrected by the electronic revolution in information/
communication:

> A book is inherently passive: you can ask it all the
> questions you want, but it simply cannot respond. . . .
> How much more would we know of Freud's thought and work
> if we had videotapes of his therapy sessions instead of
> only his books?[35]

Knowledge via electronic media will soon "be everyone's
property, rather than being restricted--as it currently is--to
the minority who can afford the luxury of reading and writing."[36]
Wagshal suggests that if there is to be a return to the basics,
there should be less emphasis on the 3Rs and more emphasis on the
goals they were intended to implement: "for every indication
suggests that 21st century America can be a society in which
knowledge, ability, and wisdom are exceedingly wide-spread in a
population that is substantially illiterate."[37]

Critical questions with respect to investments in literacy
development relate to job-related literacy demands (basic to an
individual's survival needs) versus the types of literacy and
basic skills required in our advanced industrial society. Other
critical questions relate to non-print knowledge sources
(fundamental to policy issues surrounding the future of

schooling) versus equal opportunity to expand the scale of thinking which cuts across socioeconomic and ethnic divisions while maintaining pluralism (essential for maintaining a culturally democratic society).

The general decline of basic skills and increased numbers of adult semiliterates across the nation indicate we have reached the watershed for resolving these critical issues. The unexamined assumption that job-related literacy provides sufficient incentive to motivate adult semiliterates to learn to read seems to be a dangerous pivot on which to balance the future of literacy planning and policy design. This may possibly be one of the reasons, qualitatively, literacy skills in this country have failed to be upgraded. The paradox of dual rejection makes progress all the more difficult. This is especially true when the assumption is made that semiliterate "pariahs" should want to assimilate into the mainstream middle class. When minorities reject this option, trainers and researchers imbued with Anglo middle class values often reject their charges as incapable, hopeless, and noncompetitive. This is the point where assimilation versus pluralism emerges as a policy issue in the literacy arena. Do we design programs that attempt to assimilate culturally different adults into mainstream middle class modes of existence, or do we encourage cultural pluralism and humanism? In the future will we be more dependent on oral (spoken) and nonverbal communication via sound tapes and picture phones than on verbal/reading skills? Is there a possible relationship between the decline in SAT scores and our evolving literacy requirements? What are the qualitative differences between learning via television and learning through books and other printed matter? What kinds of communication skills will be most valued in the future? Where should educators place the emphasis during the next two decades?

Outraged by the unconscionable cost of welfare and crime to both society and the individual, Jesse Jackson aptly and eloquently expressed to the 66th Texas Legislature his opinions about the emphasis of future education:

> In many parts of the nation illiteracy is high because investment is low . . . . Education does cost and ignorance costs even more. Education does cost. If one went to any state university in this nation, The University of Texas, UCLA, LSU, any state university in this nation, on a four-year academic scholarship, it would cost less than $20,000. If one went to a penitentiary for four years, on a four-year penitentiary scholarship for the same four years, it would cost between $50,000 and $126,000. Education and

employment cost less than ignorance and incarceration.
It's a critical choice for the nation. Schools at
their worst are better than jails at their best.[38]

It's a critical choice for the world as well. We have an
opportunity to develop a policy--a positive statement--on the
Future of Literacy. We have a chance to help the "information
poor in America" learn "which formal channels to tap in order to
respond to his needs."[39]   Since the "information poor," like the
semi-literate,

- Watches many hours of television daily (but not public
  TV), seldom reads newspapers and magazines and never reads
  books;

- Does not see his problems as information needs;

- Is not a very active information seeker, even when he does
  undertake a search;

- May lean heavily on formal channels of information if it
  becomes apparent that the informal channels are inadequate
  and if his needs are strongly felt;

- Is locked into an informal information network that is
  deficient in the information that is ordinarily available
  to the rest of society;[40]

a policy that recognizes the heritage of literacy for enriching
one's information needs is essential unless we are willing to
risk a world in which canned information--Newspeak vintage--comes
off the home computer in measured mediocre doses.

A number of questions have ben posed, many of them
representative of contradictions. Perhaps we should now ask what
implications for central skills can be gleaned from exploring the
question of how life will change in the next two decades. We
haven't yet asked what the workplace will be like. Will
productivity be more or less important in the future? What kinds
of recompense can be expected? Compensation, promotion,
participation, selectivity? Will civil liberties on the job
become more of an issue as Mills suggests?[41]   "How will the
society change between now and the year 2000--in the ways people
work, live, behave, communicate with one another, and govern
themselves?"[42] What implications do these expected changes have
for developing a new literacy policy?

Part II

Do the questions we raised in the first portion of this essay move us closer to a wise literacy policy for the future? Probably not. What are some analytical questions we can ask of a policy on literacy needs of the future? To develop a framework for recommending wise action through a position paper stating policy concerns surrounding central skills needed for future survival, I propose that we use Wayne A. R. Leys' model of "deliberative questions."[43] It was Leys' conviction that to demand that "philosophical ideas sanction a policy, without investigating the local facts, is to expect someone to judge without knowing the alternatives." Beyond bare alternatives, he required that one ask what standards, what loyalties, and what interests were involved in a policy decision. To save us from blind trial and error he recommended that we look at precedents, effects on happiness, motives, consistency with principle(s), loyalties, and to be aware of prejudices. He called attention to value-blindness by warning that we must look for value considerations that others forget. But, perhaps most important, he insisted that we ask this question: WHAT ARE THE RIGHT QUESTIONS TO POSE?

If the heritage is wiser than some of the heirs, then perhaps at this stage it would be wise to look backwards into the wisdom of the past and consider one of Leys' 10 alternative models.[44] Which method of deliberation is best? Leys sugges-ted that community interest would best be served by the Utilitarian, Casuistry, or Moral Idealism approaches. For a brainstorming exercise, let us attempt to deliberate using the Utilitarianism approach devised by Bentham, and outlined for us by Leys.

The "right" question to pose first according to this model is: WHAT ARE THE PROBABLE CONSEQUENCES OF ALTERNATIVE PROPOSALS? First, we have to know what the alternatives are. Then we can list their consequences. An outline of a brainstorming session might look something like this:

A. 1st alternative:
   To stress the 3Rs as custom seems to dictate.

   Consequences:
   i. inadequate solution for coping in today's and tomorrow's world. (We could quote authorities here such as Maslow or Nader, for example.)

   ii. the Sabertooth Curriculum Syndrome.

   iii. (some additional consequences should be added).

B. 2nd alternative:
    Literacy is passe; we must reconstruct education to
    teach the use of non-print media, problem-solving
    skills, oracy, computer/calculator use.

Consequences:
  i. Brave New World/1984/Newspeak; only elite would be
     able to read; automaton masses conform to mediocrity
     and homogeneity.

  ii.(some additional consequences shouldbe added).

C. 3rd alternative:
    Combine the two (A and B above) in quality and
    intensity

Consequences:
  i. best of all possible worlds?

  ii. (some additional consequences should be added).

After we have thoroughly explored the first question, the
second question is: WHICH POLICY WILL RESULT IN THE GREATET
POSSIBLE HAPPINESS OF THE GREATEST NUMBER? "B" might result in
"happiness of the greatest number," depending on the definition
of happiness. "C" of course is the ideal, if sufficient funding
could be found for applying it to the masses.

The third question is HOW DO THE ALTERNATIVES COMPARE IN THE
INTENSITY, DURATION, CERTAINTY, PROPINQUITY, FECUNDITY, PURITY,
AND EXTENT OF PLEASURES AND PAINS? (Oh, for the rebirth of
Benthamite language!) We might draw a graph and through
hypothetical consensus decide how the alternatives compare:

Figure 1

Of Pleasures/Pains		3Rs	Non-print	Both
	Intensity	much pain	latent pain	pleasure/pain =
	Duration	lengthy	lengthy	?
	Certainty	quite	uncertain	probable
	Propinquity	?	?	not overmuch
	Fecundity	?	limited	probable
	Purity	simple	simple	complex
	Extent	much pain	"bliss"	mixed

The fourth question Bentham would ask is WHAT PROPOSED ACTIONS ARE PROTECTED FROM A SCRUTINY OF PROBABLE CONSEQUENCES BY SACROSANCT PHRASES? One answer will likely differ from the next, but a good guess is that the last alternative (C) will probably provide the most protection.

WHAT IS THE FACTUAL EVIDENCE FOR ASSERTIONS ABOUT BENEFITS AND DISADVANTAGES? It might be suggested that SAT scores would rise, a perceived benefit. A possible disadvantage might be the need to renorm IQ tests.

These questions are only a beginning point. An updated set of core questions is being used in a National Institute of Education funded project on literacy development at The University of Texas at Austin:

- What problem(s) might be related to the literacy dilemma?

- What evidence can we seek to support _and_ refute this idea?

- Can this data be gathered, and, if so, how?

- If this idea is refuted, what further questions would we ask?

- If a hypothesis is supported, what policy changes would be recommended to ameliorate the problem?

- How would we support this recommendation (i.e., why do we

It is conceivable that such questions might raise all sorts of specters. If, for example, one of the participants is an avid reader of The Futurist, he/she might suggest that if the Kondratieff Cycle is on target for these seemingly different times, what we ought to be teaching in our schools is self-sufficiency—how to grow our own food, how to forage wild strawberries—not the basics![46]

Another individual might raise the specter of future competition between employer expectations and corporate demands which will be balancing new technological developments with uncertainties about the economy, deregulation of product markets, diversification, and liquidity/credit conundrums.[47]

The central idea of using deliberative questions, however, is to afford the opportunity of raising specters in order to anticipate various future scenarios of what the most valued communication skills will be and thereby develop a wise literacy policy for the challenges of the 1980s and beyond.

NOTES

1. At the 1st Annual Conference of the Education Section of the World Future Society, Houston, Texas, October, 1978.

2. Carman St. John Hunter and David Harman, Adult Illiteracy in the United States, A Report to the Ford Foundation (New York: McGraw-Hill, 1979).

3. Michael W. Apple and Philip Wexler, "Cultural Capital and Educational Transmissions: An Essay on Basil Bernstein, Class, Codes and Control: Vol. III--Towards a Theory of Educational Transmissions," Educational Theory, 28 (Winter 1978), p. 35.

4. S. D. Roueche and A. G. Hudgens, A Report on a Theory and Method for the Study of Literacy Development in Community Colleges. Submitted to the National Institute of Education, Contract No. 400-78-0060, September 1979, The University of Texas, Austin, Texas.

5. Wayne A. R. Leys, Ethics for Policy Decisions: The Art of Asking Deliberative Questions (Westport, Connecticut: Greenwood Press, 1952, rpt. 1968).

6. Eugene D. Genovese, Roll, Jordan, Roll: The World the Slaves Made (New York: Vintage Books, 1976, rpt. 1972), p. 566.

7. Justo Sierra, The Political Evolution of the Mexican People (Austin, Texas: The University of Texas, 1948, rpt. 1969), and Leopoldo Zea, The Latin-American Mind (Norman: University of Oklahoma Press, 1949, rpt. 1970).

8. Jurgen Kuczynski, The Rise of the Working Class, Trans. C. T. A. Ray (New York: McGraw-Hill, 1967).

9. Genovese, p. 562.

10. Gayle Hudgens-Watson, "Our Monster in Brazil--It All Began with 'Brother Sam,'" The Nation (January 15, 1977), pp. 51-56.

11. A.R. Luria, Cognitive Development--Its Social and Cultural Foundations (Cambridge, Massachusetts: Harvard University Press, 1976).

12. Hunter and Harman, op. cit.

13. T. M. Duffy, J. D. Carter, J. D. Fletcher, and E. G. Aiken, "Language Skills: A Prospectus for the Naval Service," Navy Personnel Research and Development Center Special Report 76-3, October 1975.

14. Yearbook of Equal Educational Opportunity, 1975-76, First Edition (Chicago: Marquis Academic Media, Marquis Who's Who, Inc., 1975), p. 46.

15. Norvell Northcutt, et al, Adult Functional Competency: A Summary (Austin: The University of Texas at Austin, Division of Extension, Industrial and Business Training Bureau, March 1975), p. 8.

16. Thomas G. Sticht, "The Acquisition of Literacy by Children and Adults," a paper prepared for the Delaware Symposium on Curriculum, Instruction, and Learning: The Acquisition of Reading, 2nd, University of Delaware, June 1975.

17. Toward Holistic Literacy in College Teaching. Forthcoming. Media Systems, a division of Harcourt, Brace, Jovanovich; and Hunter and Harman, op. cit.

18. UNESCO, Women, Education, Equality: A Decade of Experiment (Paris: UNESCO, 1975).

19. Sticht, op. cit.

20. Mihajlo Mesarovic and Eduard Pestel, Mankind at the Turning Point: The Second Report to the Club of Rome (New York: Dutton, 1974).

21. Paulo Freire, Pedagogy of the Oppressed (New York: Seabury Press, 1970); and P. Freire, Pedagogy in Process: The Letters to Guinea-Bissau (New York: Seabury Press, 1978).

22. Sticht, op. cit.

23. Ibid., p. 4.

24. Richard B. Freman, "Investment in Human Capital and Knowledge," Capital for Productivity and Jobs (The American Assembly, Columbia University), (Englewood Cliffs, N.J.: Prentice Hall, 1977, pp. 96-123.

25. Carol H. Weiss, "Research for Policy's Sake: The Enlightenment Function of Social Research," Policy Analysis, 3, No. 4 (Fall 1977), pp. 531-45.

26. Erich Fromm, _To Have or To Be?_ (London: ABACUS, 1976, rpt. 1979), p. 41.

27. Jack London, "Reflections Upon the Relevance of Paulo Freire for American Adult Education," in _Paulo Freire: A Revolutionary Dilemma for the Adult Educator_, ed. Stanley Brabowski (Syracuse, N.Y.: Syracuse University Publications, 1972), p. 23.

28. Ibid., p. 25.

29. Ibid., p. 26.

30. International Institute for Adult Literacy Methods, _Paulo Freire, Literacy Through Conscientization_, ed. J. W. Ryan (Teheran, Iran: International Institute for Adult Literacy Methods, 1974), p. iii.

31. Ibid.

32. Freire, 1970, p. 81.

33. Asher Deleon, "Adult Education as a Corrective to the Failure of Formal Education," _Prospects, 8_, No. 2 (1978), pp. 169-76.

34. Peter H. Wagshal, "Illiterates with Doctorates: The Future of Education in an Electronic Age," _The Futurist, 12_, No. 4 (August 1978), p. 243.

35. Ibid.

36. Ibid., p. 244.

37. Ibid.

38. Jesse Jackson, Address before the 66th Texas Legislature, Regular Session, March 27, 1979, pp. 1023-24.

39. Thomas Childers, _The Information Poor in America_ (Metuchen, N.J.: Scarecrow Press, 1975).

40. Ibid., p. 42-43.

41. D. Quinn Mills, "Human Resources in the 1980s," _Harvard Business Review, 57_, No. 4 (July-August, 1979), pp. 154-162.

42. The College Board, _Future Directions for a Learning Society_ (New York: College Entrance Examination Board, 1978), p. 12.

43. Leys, op. cit.

44. The ten systems Leys analyzed were Utilitarianism (Bentham), Casuistry, Moral Idealism (Plato and Kant), Stoicism (Epictetus and Spinoza), Aristotle's Golden Mean, The Ethics of Psychologists (Hobbes and Butler), the Historical "Logic" of Hegel, the Historical "Logic" of Marx, Dewey's Instrumental Thinking, and Semantic Analysis.

45. Research Associate Jane Morris developed this set of questions for the Texas project on literacy development.

46. Edward Cornish, "The Great Depression of the 1980s: Could It Really Happen?" The Futurist, 13, No. 5 (October 1979), pp. 353-380; and Ralph Hamil, "Is the Wave of the Future a Kondratieff?" The Futurist, 13, No. 5 (October 1979), pp. 381-384.

47. Mills, op. cit.

* * *

This article is based in part on work performed by Dr. Hudgens as staff member and Associate Director of the Project on Literacy Development at the University of Texas at Austin, pursuant to Contract No. 400-78-0060 of the National Institute of Education, specifically, its Teaching and Learning/Reading and Language Groups. It does not, however, necessarily reflect the views of that agency, and is not here printed at the expense of the Federal government.

Education and Electronically Mediated Democracy

John F. Deethardt

Introduction to Democracy and Electronics

I can foresee three types of democracy which could replace our present form of government. Our present form of <u>represen-tative democracy</u> has really become "an autocracy, in which all decisions save one are taken by the autocrat, and the only decision left to the people is the occasional choice of autocrat."[1]

The first alternative is a <u>digital democracy</u>.[2] The major promise of cable television, in the near-term future (one to five years)[3] is for electronic opinion polling with instantaneous results. Such polling would be a technological supplement to our elective autocracy. A congressman's access to the mood of the constituency on any issue could certainly be improved.

The second type of democracy now in the dreaming stage for sometime in the middle-range future (five to 20 years) is the <u>demographic democracy</u>, whose chief philosopher is Phil Jacklin, a philosophy professor in California. "What is needed," he says, "are objective formulae whereby spokesmen who are demonstrably representative of substantial and/or concerned groups can be identified."[4] He believes direct democracy is impossible, but democracy which makes information accessible, giving access to media and providing for access to audiences, is possible in a representative form. This form is not to be confused with the present oligarchic form of republicanism.

The third type of democracy I can foresee in the long-range future (20 to 50 years) is the pure, electronically mediated democracy, the <u>direct democracy</u> which Jacklin feels is impossible. Direct democracy would be a substantial change from the status quo, as would Jacklin's demographic democracy. One major philosopher of direct democracy is J.R. Lucas of Oxford University. He bases the definition of democracy on decision-making procedures. He asks three key questions of who makes the decision, how the decision is made, and in what frame of mind it is made. Decision-making is more democratic if most of the population makes the decision, if decisions are reached by discussion, criticism and compromise, and if the decision made is concerned with the interests of all.[5] Jacklin's principle of diversity in representation satisfies some questions of justice in allowing most interested factions to be heard, but Lucas' principles cover more questions of both liberty and justice. Jacklin constructs a system of participant priorities among party-centered spokesmen, issue-centered spokesmen, and special messages.[6] Lucas is not as constructive as Jacklin in inventing ways of applying democratic theory to society. It is the purpose of this program to consider social inventions that will satisfy the needs of citizens in a democracy for liberty, justice and communication in decision-making. If we can first invent an embodiment of those principles, then we must, second, consider what training and educational needs will enhance the actualization of that embodiment of principles.

John Platt, surveying the crises which lie ahead of us, concludes that we need catalytic analyses to interpret those crises and the use of television to disseminate information and foster debate.[7] His analysis points at the power of television and the significant consciousness-raising in such individual work as that of Rachel Carson, Ralph Nader, and Paul Ehrlich, but he stops short of naming one factor that nearly all analyses leave out. Listing world problems and pointing to the availability of media of communication for consciousness-raising quite often omits the pragmatics of political communication which will do the work of raising political consciousness.

My argument is that our national economic habits are more important to us than political processes. In television, free speech is subordinated to profitable speech.[8] In general, I find lip service is given to our political ideals, but covert, if not overt, implicit, if not explicit, condemnation of our civil liberties is expressed when economic interests enter the picture. If the Bill of Rights were put to a vote today, the provisions would likely be defeated. Edgar Friedenberg says:

> This seems to me a fundamental point. Liberty is an
> ideological item or set of items, and it is none the
> worse for that. But when it gets cross-grained to the
> economy and the power structure, it usually doesn't
> survive--and it certainly doesn't grow and bear fruit.[9]

The need for the Fourteenth Amendment seems to escape Frieden-berg, for nowhere, he says, does the Constitution show discrim-

ination in purveying rights to race or sex groups. There is no
sexist language in the U.S. Constitution which would indicate
that certain groups would be excluded from its provisions, yet
discrimination has continued unabated, requiring new constitutional constraints on those who would discriminate; even the
judiciary has perpetuated discrimination. Friedenberg concludes
that "the answer, like the explanation of continued racial
and sexual discrimination, surely lies in the social and economic
utility of such discrimination."[10] The continued development of
the higher mental processes in representing in a public forum the
causes of those who would be excluded for economic reasons will
be stultified in our present political system, because "the most
powerful media are commercial and business-oriented."[11] So the
economically more powerful can make decisions that will keep the
economically less powerful from participating and thus from
developing their own larger awareness. The growth of those who
do the excluding is also stunted by lack of awareness of the
views of those they exclude. Henry Steele Commager sees the
ascendance of economic considerations as a danger to democracy.
In a televised interview, he analyzed it thus:

> . . .if other democracies can abolish poverty or
> abolish ghettoes, it's a certain kind of economic
> system. Perhaps it's this extraordinary combination
> that Tocqueville saw of a social-political democracy
> with economic individualism which will not allow the
> social democracy to move into the arena of public
> health in the full scale, to move into the arena of
> public housing on a full scale.[12]

Commager says we are on the verge of a great revolution in which
the judicial system, the least democratic structure in
government, reverses the effects of that economic imbalance,
putting political considerations ahead of economic. He asks the
question of our ultimate problem: How do we make social equality
compatible with economic inequality?

Education and the Electronic Society

Education has been imbedded in the political system,
depending on tax monies for its existence and being guided by
elected policy-forming boards or appointed officials. Business
and industrial educational programs are imbedded in the economic
system and have a different set of funding facts and policy
controls. Lately, however, higher education is becoming more and
more involved with the economic sector through grants from
business and industry. Serious questions about the relationship
are being raised. John Kenneth Galbraith says:

> Colleges and universities can serve the needs of the
> techno-structure and reinforce the goals of the indus-
> trial system. . . . It will be the consequence of a
> purely passive response by educators to the development
> of the industrial system. . . . Or the colleges and
> universities can strongly assert the values and goals
> of educated men--those that serve not the production of
> goods and associated planning but the intellectual and
> artistic development of man.[13]

A large part of any radical change in the offing will be, in the
light of what Galbraith says, the reassertion of educational and
political values over economic considerations, and the change
will not be easy.

Our national habits of economic individualism are becoming
stronger every year, and education is escaping into the
industrial sector where it will find a more generous funding
base, or if the economic agents do not want the takeover of
educational institutions, they will at least keep it in a
compromised, subordinate position, where they can control its
potentially threatening activity. One student asked in a column
of my university's newspaper, "Why do so many accounting
professors miss so many classes?" The director of the accounting
program answered, saying that contacts with the industry have
increased five times the amount of grants contributions,
established more points of entry into business for graduates,
made more loan monies available for education expenses, and
provided relevant, up-to-date experiences in the field for
professors. Now that makes a lot of practical sense. The mass
communications department makes the same arguments, as do
chemistry, petroleum and all other engineering entities,
agriculture, home economics, law, medicine, and so on.
Vocationalism will cause education to follow where the economic
system leads. The deliberative processes in government have also
followed the leads of powerful lobbies in business and industry,
as we are well aware. Relative to this, J.R. Lucas, referring to
the actions of lobbyists and campaign contributors, says, "Even
to this day, admirers of the United States of America, are
somewhat embarrassed by the explicitly bargaining approach that
legislators bring to bear on the discharge of their functions."[14]

The influence on the media of communication is the main
theme here, because social inventions for the establishment of an
improved democratic system will rely heavily on the mass medium
of television. One critic states:

> The existing value system, propped as it is on the
> commercial and exploitative drives to profit and

control, nullifies the potential of all new developments. . . . New developments will be undermined if
old values direct what we do with what we learn.[15]

Another analyst and critic says that the blandness infecting our
views of political activity, discussion, debate, especially in
the mass media, is a direct result of the overriding commercial
interests of media owners.[16]

I believe that the development of the consumer under the
economic priorities of the so-called industrial age will be
supplanted by the intense development of citizenship under the
political priorities of the coming communications age. That is
how I view the next transformation in humankind. Values, habits
and institutions will be changing as this political consciousness
evolves. Acceleration in history is the manifestation of the
onset of a mutation in the evolution of consciousness in which
political awareness is inherent. We then will have come from the
dictum of Louis XIV, "L'Etat, c'est moi!" to the realization that
"L'Etat, c'est nous!"

More and more television programs are picking up the
participatory-interactive notion of political dialogue. "60
Minutes" has ended with a "Point-Counterpoint" feature. The
"MacNeil-Lehrer Report" usually places antagonistic forces in
intense juxtaposition. "The Advocates" airs expert opinions on
two sides of important issues. One "Advocates" program showcased
QUBE, the instantaneous digital response system in Ohio. Johnny
Carson has developed the character of Floyd R. Turbo as a
travesty of the citizen communicator, but the Committee for Open
Media has had some successes in San Francisco and elsewhere in
the country with the institution of "Free-Speech Messages."[17]
These examples of focused and intensified dialogue may be
harbingers of intentful, systemic institutions characteristic of
the learning society to come in the communications age. Omar
Khayyam Moore, who invented the talking typewriter which teaches
two- and three-year olds to read and write and which could
revolutionize education from the earliest years on, has the
credibility to instruct us in the meaning of the learning
society:

We assume that the shift from a performance to a
learning society calls for a thoroughgoing transformation of our educational institutions--their administration, their curricula, and their methods of
instruction. Education must give priority to the
acquisition of a flexible set of highly abstract
conceptual tools. . . . What is required is the
inculcation of a deep, dynamic, conceptual grasp of

> fundamental matters--mere technical virtuosity within a
> fixed frame of reference is not only insufficient, but
> it can be a positive barrier to growth. Only symbolic
> skills of the highest abstractness, the greatest
> generality, are of utility in coping with radical
> change.[18]

In that statement, Moore foresees a revolution in which the
generalist takes over where the specialist ruled; the symbolic
skills comprise the chief tools of the development of mentation,
and the transformation needs to be systemic. The interactional
use of television to educate citizens will animate the learning
society. Malcolm Moos believes we can use the new instruments
technology has given us to create the learning society. "Its
object," he says, "would be to raise every man and woman and
every community to the highest level of citizenship attainable.
In such a society the role of educational institutions would be
to provide for what is notably missing from them today, and that
is the interaction of minds."[19] Moos continues by saying, "Man's
true profession then, . . .from the first democracy to today has
been community building--which is really politics. . . . We must
invent new methods of encouraging voter participation. . . .[20]

We have on the one hand, the choice of proceeding as we
always have, with ad hoc adaptations which "view the present
reality as the only constant," catering to the conservatism of
the business system, and handling the problem in any fashion that
results in survival for the then-existing situation.[21] On the
other hand, the choice is to plan the creation of a system of
direct democracy mediating the sounds and sights of developing
minds by the speed of light in a communicating, learning society.
Rather than view the coming period of economic retrenchment as a
loss of conspicuous consumption and of a high "standard" of
living, we should view what is happening to us as an ascent to a
new plateau on our historical learning curve with unprecedented
vistas whose impact no amount of prescience can calculate.

Some Design Features

If some plausible lines of reasoning that lead to the
eventual creation of a direct democracy can be seen, then we
should reflect on some features in the design of a creation. The
direct, electronically mediated democracy is political influence
bubbling up from the bottom of the pot rather than trickling down
from the top. The social invention of community forums and human
networks is essential at the first level. At the decentralized,
local level, politics is more issue oriented. An elective
autocracy, our representative democracy, is focused primarily on
personalities. In its present form, we elect a good person with
some general issue-identification and then trust that person to

make decisions for us. An issue-oriented democracy would end the
practice of solo speeches by candidates and institute direct
clash in debate among proponents on the issues. A new direct-
democracy party starting up today would air the conflicts within
its own membership on all important issues of the day. All of
the needs and plans requisite for decision-making on any or all
social problems would be carried to the public, not by one
person, but by a multitude of persons; personalities, contrary to
present practice, would not be a major issue. The chief
executive would not be a father figure but a functionary, as
would the senators and representatives, who would not legislate
but collate. Public education on social problems and solutions
should carry over into a more active interest in public service
by full-time, but temporary public servants.

The problem of the bureaucracy is brought about by making
government a machine to be run rather than a joint enterprise in
which we are all involved to some extent.[22] Currently, elected
autocrats make general policy decisions and then turn over the
job of practical working to unelected officials, thus insulating
themselves from the practical details of policies and alienating
the public from their government. In turning government over to
autocrats as a public trust, citizens are removed from overseeing
decisions and their impact on daily life. Most people do not
identify with the implementations carried out by bureaucrats and
the atmosphere is clouded with frustration and doubt. "A
decision publicly arrived at is better understood and likely,
therefore, to be better carried out."[23]

Each community is more than likely a microcosm of all
important devisions on any given question. The product of a
community forum will be a series of videotaped discussions on
topics such as crime, nuclear power, foreign policy, taxation,
etc. The videotapes of a community forum should be exchanged
with those of other communities. Community functionaries sent to
the national capitol would be _issue_ representatives who would
reflect the whole spectrum of opinion and engage in attempts to
build a better national consensus from the roots up. Involvement
of all citizens in the community forum is the basis for
establishing policy at the national level; the propositions
formulated at the national level in a conference of issue
representatives will be listed for a national referendum. Then
the digital democracy is useful, after discussion is complete, in
reducing the complexity of millions of responses. This is the
only road that leads from autocracy and ad hocracy to direct
democracy. "Only a complicated system can accommodate our
differing requirements for a political system. . . ."[24] National
fucntionaries can be made more accountable as collators of
community thinking since the tasks assigned to them are clearly

specified by the results of the community forum process. The
issue representative on crime would be a temporary bureaucrat in
public service to the justice department, and he or she would
confer with other community representatives to translate the
forum results into propositions for the national referendum.
These bureaucrats would have a sunset clause in the terms of
their service. The propositions would include essential details
of operations having stated impacts on everyday life in plain
language. The result is this: nearly everybody decides nearly
everything.

Intermediate levels of consensus-building procedures should
be designed to embrace regional associations of communities. One
issue representative would go forward to the next highest level
of conference and one representative would report back to the
originating community. Thus feedforward and feedback would
provide the continual attentiveness to communal concerns. Making
decisions takes time, and representation would be involved on a
temporary but full-time basis. This system would increase the
competence of representation, in that issue competence would be
requisite for representing the community to the regional and
national meetings. If the citizen education objectives set for
the community forum are adequately met, other citizens would be
equally qualified to act as issue representatives in subsequent
phases of decision-making, and continuity would be assured.

The national referenda will settle the issues finally for a
time. They will be the culmination of the process that began in
the communities some months before. In a direct democracy, the
referenda will probably be taking place every month. If the
forum process at the community level has achieved its objectives
of wide participation, apathy in the referenda process will be
low. Nobody need disown decisions made through this process.
The digital technology of taking referenda are not hard to
imagine in a wired nation with two-way, interactive technology,
and I'm not worried that a direct democracy cannot be engineered.
I am more concerned with the behavioral engineering problems, and
that is why I put the achievement of a direct democracy in a
long-range future (20 to 50 years).

Education for Direct Democracy

Education for the direct, electronically mediated democracy
will need to (1) build political self-concepts; (2) clarify
people's political values; (3) increase cognitive complexity and
tolerance for ambiguity in people; (4) develop in people skills
in the functions of public communication; (5) adapt people to the
inevitability of communication apprehension in moving into

significant impersonal relationships; (6) train critical listeners and viewers; (7) provide interaction and media experiences, and so forth. Education must redefine its mission, its methods and instructional models to develop people emotionally, behaviorally and intellectually ready for participation. Education for communicative participation must be civilized, politicized, globalized and futurized. A civilized communicator will show that he or she has evolved from an awareness of self to a general awareness of impersonal relations. Politicized communication has evolved from the realities of private communication serving economic and interpersonal ends to the realities of communication in human networks and mediated expression as a means for enlarging the social context of influence, liberty and justice. Globalized communication shows the effects of a trained appreciation for the complexity of the code/relationship matrix of communication barriers. Finally, in futurized communication, there are manifestations that the speaker has an enlarged time perspective, an extra-temporal awareness of inevitabilities, a supra-individual consciousness, and a clarified teleology. I have tried to be constructive about our future political relationships, which, for better or for worse, depend on the schools in the final analysis.

NOTES

1. J.R. Lucas, Democracy and Participation (Baltimore: Penguin Books, 1975), p. 184.

2. Peg Key, "Policy Issues in Interactive Cable Television," Journal of Communication, 28 (Spring, 1978), p. 206.

3. Earl C. Joseph, "What Is Future Time?" Futurist (August, 1974), p. 173. His categories will be used throughout.

4. Phil Jacklin, "Representative Diversity," Journal of Communication, 28 (Spring, 1978), p. 87.

5. J.R. Lucas, op. cit., p. 10.

6. Duplicated materials obtained from Phil Jacklin. Also, Phil Jacklin, "Access to the Media: A New Fairness Doctrine," The Center Magazine, 8 (May/June, 1975), p. 49.

7. John Platt, "The Future of Social Crises," The Futurist, 9 (October, 1975), p. 267.

8. Ronald D. Brunner and Kan Chen, "Is Cable the Answer?" _Journal of Communication_, 28 (Spring, 1973), p. 84.

9. Edgar Z. Friedenberg, "Our Class-Biased Bill of Rights," _Civil Liberties Review_, 3 (October/November, 1976), p. 70.

10. Ibid.

11. Jacklin, "Access to the Media," p. 48.

12. "Democracy in America: A Conversation with Henry Steele Commager," _Bill Moyers' Journal_, 411 (April 16, 1979), transcript p. 13.

13. Quoted in John D. Pulliam and Jim R. Bowman, _Educational Futurism in Pursuance of Survival_ (Norman: University of Oklahoma Press, 1974), p. 75.

14. J.R. Lucas, op. cit., p. 34.

15. Barry N. Schwartz, ed., _Human Connection and the New Media_ (Englewood Cliffs: Prentice-Hall, 1973), p. 3.

16. Jerome A. Barron, _Freedom of the Press for Whom? The Right of Access to the Mass Media_ (Bloomington: Indiana University Press, 1973), p. 84.

17. William Hanks and Peter Langini, "Television Access: A Pittsburgh Experiment," _Journal of Broadcasting_, 28 (Summer, 1974), pp. 293-297.

18. Omar Khayyam Moore and Alan Ross Anderson, "Some Principles for the Design of Clarifying Educational Environments," _Handbook of Socialization Theory and Research_, ed. David A. Goslin (Chicago: Rand McNally and Co., 1969), p. 584.

19. Malcolm Moos, "Citizenship as a Profession," _Vital Speeches of the day_, 1975, p. 251.

20. Ibid., p. 252.

21. Robert Boguslaw, _The New Utopians: A Study of System Design and Social Change_ (Englewood Cliffs: Prentice-Hall, 1965), pp. 21-22.

22. R.J. Lucas, op. cit., p. 78.

23. Ibid., p. 141.

24. Ibid., p. 247.

Future Families as Household School Institutions

Winifred I. Warnat

In a 1979 New York Times editorial, Colin Greer, executive editor of Social Policy, pointed out that the debate on the family is as strong and as lively as ever. According to him, the debate falls into two camps--(1) the people who are worried about the family, and (2) the others who are worried about those who worry about the family. He goes on to present five views on the family:

1. The family is decaying--the traditional nuclear family is falling apart, a sure sign of impending disaster;

2. The family is evolving--it continues to develop in order to keep up with the times;

3. The family is not changing much at all--the crisis being faced by the family is seen as simply a form of inter-generational conflict;

4. There are changes in the family--it is undergoing a natural process--as society changes so, too, does the family;

5. The family is in retreat--it is an oppressive force fighting the power of the human potential movement, and being beaten back by the positive and progressive forces freed in our emerging post-industrial society.[1]

My position tends to be a combination of the views that the family is changing and the family is evolving. The family remains a constant element over one's entire life span. Whether we like it or not, from birth until death, each and every one of us has membership in some form of family.

Current Status of the American Family

To provide an overview of what has been happening to the American family, Paul Glick, Census Bureau expert, presented the following statistics in his 1979 report, The Future of the American Family:

* 77% of American families are nuclear, with 16% of that group made up of remarried families;

* 10% are single-parent households, usually headed by women;

* 10% are persons living alone;

* 1% are made up of heterosexual, unmarried couples;

* 2% are in other kinds of living arrangements.

That means that approximately 61% of American families at present, represent the traditional nuclear form, while 39% represent alternative forms of family. Glick's report also revealed that:

* one divorce occurs for every two marriages;

* the divorce rate has doubled between 1965 and 1975;

* the average number of children per family dropped from the peak of 3.7 in 1957 to the current 1.8 per family;

* since 1960, there has been a 100% increase in single-parent families;

* one of every two children under 18 has a working mother;

* one out of three school-age children lives in a home headed by only one parent;

* more than one half of all mothers with school-age children work outside the home;

* the number of households headed by women has increased by more than one third in this decade;

* finally, 45% of American infants born last year will live part of their lives with only one parent before they reach the age of 18.[2]

In the May 15, 1978 issue of <u>Newsweek</u> there was a special report titled "Saving the American Family." In terms of marriage probabilities, the report stated that of all adults in the United States:

* 96% will marry;

* 38% of those will divorce;

* 79% of those will remarry; and

* 74% of those will divorce again.[3]

In the same report, University of Massachusetts sociologist Alice S. Rossi stated:

> What was defined a decade ago as "deviant," is today labeled "variant" in order to suggest that there is a healthy, experimental quality to current social explorations "beyond monogamy" or "beyond the nuclear family."[4]

<u>Family Circle</u> magazine, in its September 1, 1978 issue, contained a special report, "What's Happening to Marriage and the Family in America?" in which it was pointed out that:

* one out of six families no longer has both a husband and a wife;

* nearly half of all American families have no children under 18 years of age;

* in only one third of husband-wife families is the husband the sole wage earner;

* one marriage in four involves a man who has been divorced and even more include a woman who has been divorced;

* the divorce rate is distinctly higher at the low-income level;

* women who work and can be financially self-sufficient are three times more likely to become divorced.

The report also identified four areas of significant change between spouses in marriages and families today: (1) increased egalitarianism, (2) more role sharing, (3) greater sexual freedom, and (4) more opportunity for personal growth.[5]

Although diverse in approach and audiences addressed, all three of these reports hold in common the fact that the American family is neither dying nor seriously ailing. Each reinforces the belief that the family is evolving and is being adapted to a rapidly changing society. They also concur that, in these new and varied forms of family, some are certainly more difficult to manage, some are fraught with additional responsibilities and unique problems, while others remain clearly lacking as viable forms of family.

Families of the Future

With that overview of the current status of the American family, the groundwork has been laid to explore the likely forms of family that will be dominant in the future. Three current trends--postponement of marriage, lower birth rates, and increased numbers of women in the work force--are considered to be major contributors to future families. Each of these trends is likely to be buoyed even further during this period of what may turn out to be prolonged and increased economic austerity. In keeping with those trends and reinforced by them as well, three family styles have already surfaced and are beginning to burgeon. They are (1) the single-parent family, (2) the reconstituted family, and (3) the no-kin family. It is within the context of these three variant family forms that the concept of the household school will be applied.

First of all it might be helpful if each of us took a look at our own personal family membership. In my own life time, as a daughter I have been a member of a traditional nuclear family, a single-parent family, and now a reconstituted family. As an independent adult, I have been a wife in a reconstituted family, and now a member of a no-kin family. Most of us have the benefit of personal experience in more than one type of family structure. However, we tend to be oblivious to the diversity, and the contributions to our learning.

Before discussing the three types of future families, it should be mentioned that, in the very recent past, considerable stigma was attached to anyone who opted for one of these three variant forms. Such castigation has not totally disappeared; society still prefers that people marry or remarry. According to the late Margaret Mead, "We're in a terribly overmarried society because we can't think of any other way for anybody to live, except in matrimony as couples."[6] Research on these variant forms of family is also sadly lacking, especially since most research continues to interpret these forms as aberrant and adversely compares them to the traditional nuclear family. Even though we know that these new forms of family may indeed be more complex and more difficult to manage, we do not know whether they are weaker or worse structures than those to which they are being compared.

The Single-Parent Family. Basically, the single-parent family focuses upon two populations--unwed mothers and separated or divorced parents who have not remarried. Such parents must serve as breadwinners, as well as play roles of both mother and father. Even though the single-parent family is the most difficult of the three forms of future families, it is the most rapidly growing one and will continue to be so. This family style, more than any other, has brought to light the need for quality child care services as well as the inequities of the traditional parental roles in raising children. As we approach the 21st century, American society will make great strides toward recognizing and accepting the single-parent family as a healthy part of the family norm. This change will be most apparent in the formal education arena where an increasing number of educators will either come from single-parent families or be the head of one themselves.

The Reconstituted Family. The basis for the reconstituted family is remarriage with one or both mates bringing at least one child from a previous marriage into this new family arrangement. Although the reconstituted family is the most acceptable future family form based on current societal norms, it is the most complex due to its intricate family relationships between parent and child, stepparents and stepchildren. The reconstituted family structure will continue to grow, partially as the result of our longer and healthier life span, and partially as the result of its social acceptability. Not improbable is the expansion of serial monogamy to the extent that it will not be considered unusual for a person to be married three and even four times over a life time. Out of necessity, formal education will need to make appropriate adjustments in interpreting family life and in the preparation of students for marriage and parenting.

The No-Kin Family. The no-kin family refers to the surrogate family in which the single person, who has no relatives near or who chooses to live totally separate from them, assumes membership. This is usually a group of friends or co-workers bound together by a mutual caring. Of the three forms of future families, least is known about this one, yet it is one that also will continue to grow. The postponement of marriage has already proven to be a major contributing factor, with widowhood at the other end of the life span being another significant factor. Clearly functioning as part of a family unit is reinforced by the no-kin family as it addresses a universal need to affiliate with

others on an intimate familial basis. There is much to be
learned from this family style which may provide the greatest
opportunity to determine those factors which contribute to or
hinder functioning as lone individuals in society.

Why are these three forms of family increasing? Primarily
because all three are adaptations of the family structure in
response to an increasingly complex society--a society that
places greater and greater demands on the individual. Because of
their interactive nature, the single-parent family, the
reconstituted family, and the no-kin family provide the
individual with special communication and socialization skills
beyond the scope of the traditional nuclear family. Also,
through each form a family member is able to develop greater
adaptation to stress in a manner that is positive rather than
negative. Finally, each of these three future families
encompasses a unique learning environment in which family members
nurture and cultivate their sense of personal worth, their
sensitivity to others, and the means of expressing themselves to
their associates, whoever they may be.

The Family as Educator

The underlying premise of this essay is that the family, in
all of its variant forms, is society's primary education
institution. While only peripheral attempts have been made to
address this notion, some worthwhile considerations have evolved.
One of the more explicit works to consider the educational
functioning of the family is Jane Hope Leichter's The Family as
Educator in which it is pointed out that, of the vast research
conducted on the family as educator, the educative process or
processes used have been ignored. In fact, research places
primary emphasis on the cognitive aspects of familial education.
It is Leichter's contention that there is a critical need to
understand more fully the processes of education within the
family, and to view those processes in the context of multiple
and ever-changing relationships within the family. According to
Leichter, the concepts of socialization, enculturation, and
development are potential vehicles for examining the ever-
changing educational encounters between individuals and their
family environments.[7]

Earl Schaefer, noted developmental psychologist, also
recognizes the family as the major educational institution. He
sees children, as well as parents, as teachers and urges that
children be motivated and trained to teach one another. He views
education, with its various forms of teaching and learning, as a
major component of the entire life experience. His perspective

focuses upon the development and utilization of the educational
function of the family as a valuable resource, beneficial to both
the formal education and social service arenas. Schaefer
identifies ten characteristics of family interaction between
parents and children, contending that the cumulative effect of
these characteristics and the family's care of children provides
the foundation for the educational process followed by the
family.[8]

In "The Family: A School for Living," educational researcher James Garbarino presents a child-oriented view based on the
way the interdependence of families, regardless of their structure, affects personal education. His concern is with the
ecology of the family; the way the family as a social system is
grounded in a network of institutions and values that shape the
conditions in which family members develop. Garbarino points out
that American families act as educators through two processes.
The first process is modeling, which involves observing behavior
and then copying it. The second process is interaction style, in
which families either initiate and maintain effective relationships or fail to do so. Garbarino goes on to identify two
factors that influence the successful functioning of these two
processes. They are (1) the degree to which families model
socially representative and valued patterns of behavior in their
lasting relationships, and (2) the competence and mental health
of the family members themselves.[9]

The implications of these perspectives for future families
center around the willingness and ability to obtain a better
understanding of how the family functions as a primary education
institution. The groundwork has been done; the need to pursue
this is obvious., The power of the family to influence the
development of each of its members will remain paramount. The
single-parent family, the reconstituted family, and the no-kin
family possess unique capacities for adaptation to change, as
well as constructive responses to stressful living environments.
Through the household school, these unique capacities and
constructive responses can be further realized and actualized.

The Household School

Every family is a household school; and in the household
school, each family member functions as both educator and
learner. Its environment encompasses the conditions, including
the social and cultural circumstances, that directly influence
the family structure and its specific, individual membership.
Learning activities conducted in the household school concentrate
on three approaches--observation, imitation, and experience.

While both cognitive and affective learning take place in the family, the household school contributes more to affective learning than any other education institution. Whether the family is single-parent, reconstituted, no-kin, or traditional nuclear, the environment in which the household school operates is a major determinant influencing learning capacities and functioning, especially in the affective dimensions. Within this environment, affective learning concentrates on individuality and on the socialization process. In this context, affective learning encompasses the development of attitudes, feelings, values, and beliefs as expressed through behavior.

Household School Tasks. The primary function of the household school is the education of its members, which involves four major tasks that serve to develop each family member's human understanding and insight, coping capacity, and ability to adjust to change.

1. The first task is Role Selection--identifying, preparing for, and performing the varied and numerous life roles each assumes as a family member throughout the life span. Each family member acts out a variety of roles that demand unique sets of expectations, responsibilities, and skills. At any given time, a family member must be prepared to perform simultaneously any number of roles. Role selection encompasses recognizing role expectations, observing others operating in a given role, and being motivated to function in a certain fashion. Each of the three future families addresses some unique aspects of role selection. For example, the single-parent family includes the roles of a parent and a single; the reconstituted family the roles of natural parent and stepparent; and the no-kin family the role of parent-child surrogate.

2. The second task is Personality Acquisition--recognizing and expressing personal feelings and attitudes about self and relationships to others. All humans experience innumerable life events which promote a broad range of emotional responses. Those responses require adjustments in the expression of attitudes and feelings which have been triggered. Through the household school, a determination is made by family members of the appropriateness of the response. Personality acquisition involves making note of how emotions are expressed, what the reactions to those expressions are, and then deciding which ones are most in keeping with one's sense of self and beliefs about others' perceptions. In terms of personality acquisition, a dichotomy of choices is common to the three families of the future. This ambivalence is exemplified in the single-parent family by the dichotomy between parenting and dating; in the reconstituted family it is between the fairness and affection

expressed toward natural children and that expressed toward stepchildren; and in the no-kin family it is evident in the desire to be alone while also desiring to be with others.

3. The third task is Value Formation--acknowledging and following the values and beliefs endorsed and adhered to by the family. Every family has a special system of values and beliefs that provides members with the basic criteria for deciding good from bad, right from wrong, and truth from untruth. Within the family, each member is expected to abide by this system of implicit rules and regulations. In the operation of the household school, the interpretation of and rationale for the value and belief system are provided by the membership, which also functions as both judge and jury to any family member who does not comply. Value formation takes into account recognizing the system, and accepting, rejecting, or modifying it as changing life circumstances are accommodated. Because of their break with tradition, the three future families challenge this task most. For instance, in the single-parent family, the traditions of the two-parent family are, of necessity, rejected and new alternative traditions are established. In the reconstituted family, while the traditions of the two-parent family are not discarded, they are dramatically modified and expanded. And in the no-kin family, an entirely new set of traditions emerges that reflects the diversity of its membership--each person contributing an aspect from his or her own personal set of prior traditions.

4. Finally the fourth task is Behavioral Patterning-- discovering, choosing, and practicing personal behaviors through interaction with the people encountered in the family environment. Determining the appropriateness or inappropriate- ness of actions is a dominant and fundamental aspect of the family. Many of the patterns of behavior that are seen, imita- ted, and ultimately used are those initially presented by other family members. Based upon the individual actions and reactions of each of its members to given circumstances and emotions, the household school is a learning laboratory that provides participants with a number of models for molding behavior. Behavioral patterning encompasses noticing how others act, being cognizant of the kind of response there is to the act, and then determining whether or not it is suitable. For the three families of the future, unlearning and new learning are signif- icant aspects in addressing this task. In the single-parent family, for example, it is necessary to unlearn the mutually- dependent relationship between marriage partners and learn anew the total independence of being without a partner. In the reconstituted family, it is necessary to unlearn the delimiting perspective of family development through the birth of children and learn anew about the more diverse ready-made family. In the

no-kin family it is necessary to unlearn loneliness and learn anew the kinship of closeness to others who are not related in any way.

The Learning Process. The household school, which contributes to the development of a personal management system, operates on an experientially-based learning mode. It serves to improve functioning--primarily in the affective, but also in the cognitive domains--as individuals within and without the immediate family environment. All family members are continuously experiencing and living through the dynamics of the four major tasks of the household school. These four tasks are addressed through a five-step sequential process. Each step relates to definition, cultivation, and orchestration of roles, attitudes, feelings, values, beliefs, or behaviors. The sequential steps include:

Step One: Identification--observing how family members act and react;

Step Two: Selection--choosing what appears to be appropriate and compatible with one's sense of self;

Step Three: Performance--acting out one's selections to find those that fit, and discarding those that do not;

Step Four: Modification--practicing one's performance and making changes to accommodate personal interpretation, and;

Step Five: Adoption--completing modification as the action becomes a part of self.

This process applies to each life event experienced, which in turn addresses at least one of the four household school tasks. A life event is an episode one experiences, such as a party, an automobile accident, childbirth, being fired, a vacation, graduation, or the end of a romance. Actually, life events can be classified as learning lessons, many occurring within the framework of the household school.

As families of the future continue to evolve, the learning process of the household school will remain constant with its family members becoming more and more tuned in to it. Contributing to this increasing level of awareness will be expanding knowledge about the psycho-social functioning of the human being as well as the ability to apply that knowledge to household school operations.

Implications for Policy and Practice

To determine what implications future families as household schools have for policy and practice, some sense of the present situation is needed. There currently exists a flurry of interest in and study of the American family, as there has been during this entire decade. However recognition of the importance of the family as an avowed educational institution has certainly been negligible. The family's educational functioning is still interpreted on the basis of cognitive learning and the socialization of children. In that regard parents are the teachers (in keeping with a formal education orientation). The buzz words for how the family functions as educator are "parenting," "parent involvement," and "parent education," with an occasional notation also given to "family life education." In any other form the family is totally disregarded as the invaluable resource it can be to formal social institutions, especially education.

Instead, the family is constantly being attacked and is said to be disintegrating. This is best exemplified by the recent endorsements of the U.S. President. In his address to the National Advisory Committee of the White House Conference on Families in 1979, President Carter stated that the family was part of the national crisis in confidence that Americans were facing. He went on to say, "Without question, the American family is in trouble."[10] The "International Year of the Child" is being classified by all reports as a dismal failure in its attempts to accomplish anything of significance for the benefit of children. To aid the ailing American family, President Carter established in October 1979, an office on Families in the U.S. Department of Health, Education, and Welfare (HEW). Add to this the futile attempts to pass child care legislation to help families with working parents and the narrowly focused federal benevolence involving some 331 federal programs supposedly designed to help families. This is indeed a dismal picture of how the notion of the dying American family has been perpetuated. It certainly does appear that as children have been used as scapegoats for much of this century, the same treatment is now also going to be afforded the American family. Nonetheless, the family will remain the strongest social institution as it continues to adapt successfully to the social, economic, political, educational, and technological changes and traumas impacting on society.

In their significant work, Family Policy: Government and Families in Fourteen Countries, Sheila B. Kamerman and Alfred J. Kahn revealed to what extent the United States lags in helping its families.[11] Their study showed that: (1) all but the United States offer family allowances to supplement parental earnings when children are present; (2) all but the United States have maternity benefits and leaves of 14 weeks to nine months providing the opportunity for parents to develop strong relationships with their infants before returning to work; and (3) all but the United States have special housing allowances or priorities for families with children. The United States is unique in only one aspect of government help--the Aid to Families With Dependent Children Welfare Program which helps support mothers with no income who remain at home to care for their children.

The most comprehensive effort at analyzing federal legislation as it relates to family policy in the United States is that being conducted by the Family Impact Seminar of the Institute for Educational Leadership at George Washington University in Washington, D.C. Through its delvings, it has discovered 268 federal programs that have potential for direct impact on families. One hundred and nineteen of those programs emanate from HEW and concentrate on poor families. One hundred and forty nine programs related to families are administered outside of HEW and also tend to concentrate on poor families, but are not limited exclusively to them. Some of the other departments involved with such programs include Housing and Urban Development, Labor, Interior, Justice, Treasury, and Transportation.[12] Thus far, the work of the Family Impact Seminar provides evidence that the family is viewed, in the political arena, from a deficit perspective; that federal legislation and programs distort the family picture through their emphasis on the poor; and that, at best, there are only cursory and occasional efforts being made to establish any kind of healthy and constructive policy to benefit all American families.

In spite of all that, the family is not dying. It simply cannot, since it is with all of us from birth onward. But it is changing and evolving into more complex forms, in keeping with the increasing complexity of society. Unfortunately, the negativism being promulgated does have significant impact on the development and establishment of future policies and practices related to the family. Mary Jo Bane, Harvard Professor and author of Here to Stay, cogently analyzes the unlikelihood that the United States would develop an explicit family policy.[13] She points out that mere mention of families in our political arena generates heated controversy. She states, "Far from being an attractive slogan . . . 'Family Policy' has become a red flag."[14] As a result, until there is some sort of consensus on its merits, it is highly improbable that the United States as a nation will be able to rally around a family policy that addresses all American families. Regardless of whether or not a formal family policy is adopted, family remains at the core of

social policy. And with the emergence and dominance of family
types of the future--single-parent, reconstituted, and no-kin--
the family's prominence as the single most influential dynamic
impacting upon social policy will continue to escalate into the
21st century.

While there is growing consensus on the inevitability of a
rapidly approaching period of crisis of national and global
proportions, we must proceed with extreme caution so that we do
not wallow in the mood of pessimism that is presently so
pervasive. Without disregarding the trying times ahead, a level
of optimism must be sustained to take us beyond the crisis to a
new sense of social and personal well-being. The family is the
major vehicle for doing so.

NOTES

1. "Once Again the 'Family Question'," New York Times,
October 14, 1979, p. E19.

2. Paul C. Glick, "The Future of the American Family,"
Current Population Reports: Special Studies (Washington, D.C.:
U.S. Department of Commerce, Bureau of Census, January, 1979).

3. "Saving the Family," Newsweek, May 15, 1978, pp. 63-90.

4. Ibid., p. 67.

5. Bernice and Morton Hunt, "What's Happening to Marriage
and the Family in America?" Family Circle, September 1, 1978,
pp. FC1-FC8.

6. "The Future Revised," Wall Street Journal, March 18,
1976, p. 1.

7. Hope Jensin Leichter, ed., The Family as Educator (New
York: Teachers College, Columbia University, 1974).

8. Earl S. Schaefer, "The Family and the Educational
Process," in Families of the Future (Ames, Iowa: Iowa State
University Press, 1972), pp. 26-45.

9. James Garbarino, "The Family: A School for Living," National Elementary School Principal, Vol. 55 (May, 1976), pp. 66-70.

10. President Carter's address to the National Advisory Committee on the White House Conference on Families, July 27, 1979.

11. Sheila B. Kamerman, and Alfred J. Kahn, eds., Family Policy: Government and Families in Fourteen Countries (New York: Columbia University Press, 1978).

12. Sidney A. Johnson, III, and Theodora J. Oomes, "Is Government Helping or Hurting Families?" Forum (Spring/Summer, 1979).

13. Mary Jo Bane, Review of Family Policy: Government and Families in Fourteen Countries, by Sheila Kamerman and Alfred Kahn. Harvard Educational Review, Vol. 49, No. 3 (August, 1979), pp. 390-393.

14. Ibid, p. 392.

For Further Reading on the Household School

Winifred I. Warnat, "The Household School as Life-Span Learning Center," in The Family in Post-Industrial Society, ed. David P. Snyder (Boulder, Colorado: Westview Press, 1979).

Winifred I. Warnat, "The Household School Perspective Applied to Parenting and Competency-Based Education," Journal of Adult Literacy and Basic Education, Vol. 3, No. 3 (Fall, 1979), pp. 234-240.

Section III
Theory and Visions for the Present and the Future

Section III
Theory and Visions for the Present and the Future

INTRODUCTION

Theoretical treatises and visionary thinking are necessary components in any discipline, but they are particularly crucial in a field as new and unorthodox as futures studies. It is from such discussions and thinking that the boundaries of a field are clarified, commitment to the field is re-examined, new adherents are brought into the fold, and the disenchanted are provided a justification for disavowal and departure. It is from such discourses that practitioners learn, voluntarily or not, to think the unthinkable. For a field as multi-faceted as futures studies, it is from such theoretical and visionary dialogues and papers that the legitimacy of varied world views and approaches is reaffirmed. Pluralism may be acknowledged as desirable and even encouraged.

The range in visionary, theoretical papers is great, from the perfunctorily formal but academically sound to those that encourage flights of intellectual fancy. If such papers are in fact conveying unfamiliar vistas and are describing new theoretical models, they ought to provoke reaction and even controversy. It is our expectation as editors that the four papers included in this section will do just that.

Based only on a cursory examination of the titles, the papers in Section III would seem to be dissimilar. Other than the overlap suggested by the references to feminism and women, what could possibly be the commonality among papers entitled "Education and Its Transformations," "Futuristic World Views: Modern Physics and Feminism," "Ethnotronics and Human Learning Futures," and "Women And Children As Builders Of the Future"? Despite the seeming lack of a shared focus, the papers selected for inclusion in this section have in common threads of metaphorical thinking and allegorical imagery which may help the reader to think about what has been considered, up to this point,

the unthinkable and the unthought. All of these papers have
moments where the authors have engaged in the types of
speculations and flights of imagination which "free up" the heart
as well as the mind. Moreover there is in all of these papers a
willingness to acknowledge and legitimize more than one world
view or approach. In addition to encouraging serious discussion
of new possibilities and paradigms, an acceptance of pluralism
may be fostered.

In "Education and Its Transformations," Jean Houston
discusses education in terms of the capacities and potentialities
inherent in individuals. She is concerned that education, for
too long, has supported itself on short term successes and long
term failures. For many years, formal education has been
fragmented, reductionistic, and authoritarian. Houston contends
that we must "move from isolated, topical treatment of curriculum
issues to comprehensive curriculum renewal for total education."
This will, of course, require a rethinking of the purposes of
education and of the nature of learners as well as a re-
examination, using an holistic model, of the processes of
education. To better understand the range of capacities humans
possess, Houston strongly recommends cross cultural inquiries.
From such inquiries and from neurophysiological studies, it is
apparent that there are many different modes of knowing, most of
which have not previously been part of school based education.

Different modes of knowing and alternative world views are
of prime concern to Gerri Perreault and form the bases of her
observations about potential changes in higher education.
Perreault discusses, quite eloquently, modern physics and
feminism, two seemingly disparate areas, and describes them as
futuristic world views that may produce important transformations
in contemporary world views. In addition to contrasting
classical physics with modern physics and patriarchy with
feminism, Perreault presents a rather appealing case for the
similarity of emphases and the subsequent world views of modern
physics and feminism. It is her contention that recognition and
acceptance of these alternative world views would precipitate
many changes in higher education. These changes would include an
emphasis on the interconnectedness and interdependence of people
and the planet, a linking of education to experience, a balance
of rational and intuitive ways of knowing, and recognition of the
inseparability of the knower and the known.

Even though they are starting with different theoretical
concerns than Houston and Perreault, Arthur Harkins and Earl
Joseph are no less visionary in their paper "Ethnotronics and
Human Learning Futures." They are concerned with the interface
between humans, components of human cultures, and computer based

technologies. Their view of education and of learning, albeit implicit, is much broader than schools and institutional settings. They envision readily available, convivial, computer based technologies designed to amplify and to assist individuals and groups in daily activities. While the future that Harkins and Joseph envision is technocentric, it has a humanistic quality in that the emphasis is on human enhancement. Presented in a rather assertive, non-critical tone, there is the implication that the future they project is inevitable. This not an unusual quality in utopist, visionary works.

Rather than looking, as Harkins and Joseph do, to human generated technologies as sources of change in the future, Eleonora Masini looks to the many individuals whom she believes have the capacity to store and nurture the seeds of change. In her paper, Masini focuses on two such groups of individuals-- women and children--and describes their capabilities as builders of the future. She contends that these capabilities grow out of "a union of rationality with intuition and emotion," a union also valued by Houston, Perreault, and others. In addition Masini sees women and children as storehouses of the seeds of change and of a better future because they are, for the most part, outside the mainstream of the social system and outside the loci of power.

Education and Its Transformations

Jean Houston

We are in the time of the darkness before the awakening. We are living in the last quarter of the 20th century with the end of the millennium coming up as a major construct in our lives. And the end of the millennium warrants far more serious concern and challenge than do the fears and fancies which accrue around the fin de siecle.

The age in which we live is shivering amidst the tremors of ontological breakdown. The moral mandates; the structural givens; the standard brand governments, religions, economics; the very consensual reality is breaking down. The underlying fabric of life is changing as is the process by which we organized our reality and thought that we knew who, why and where we were. The world by which we understood ourselves, a world which began in its essential mandates 2000 years ago with certain premises about man, God, reality, and the moral and metaphysical order, and which in terms of our existential lives began about 300 years ago with the scientific revolution, is a world that no longer works, whose lease has run out, whose paradigms are eroding, and that no longer provides us with the means and reference points by which we understand ourselves. We are not unlike the cartoon cat who runs off the cliff and keeps on running, treading air over the abyss before he discovers his predicament.

There is a lag between the end of an age and the discovery of that end. We are the children of the lag, the people of the time of parenthesis. Then, to add powerfully to this, is the fact that we are Americans, and that means a great deal, for we are probably the oldest modern nation on earth. By that I mean that we were the first to move through the consequences of the industrial revolution, the urban revolution, the cross-ethnic revolution, the democratic revolution, the materialistic revolution, the atomic revolution, the outer space revolution, and now, the inner space revolution. We are an old people in terms of the expectations of the modern world. We are fast becoming post-moderns.

Despite the awakening pulsations of the third millennium A.D., we are gravely threatened by problems peculiar to the time of lag, problems having to do with the lack of a story and the lack of depth and vision in an age of frenetic activity.

We look about us and see a growing wasteland with its hazards of mass destruction through nuclear and biological weapons; its threats to privacy and freedoms; its growing overpopulation and exacerbated unemployment; its increasing air, noise, and land pollution and depletion of the earth's resources; its information overload and vulnerability to collapse and breakdown; its dehumanization of ordinary work; its proliferation of institutional megastructures which have left us with a vast chasm between public and private life so that the political order has become detached from the values and realities of individual life, and the individual gives neither moral sanction nor legitimacy to the political order.

We are all aware of a governmental disunity so pervasive and pummeled by so many special interest groups that no coalition of interests is apparently strong enough to set priorities for the overall public good, to effect reforms that have wide public support, to root out inefficiency and corruption, and to inspire confidence in political leadership or in leadership of any kind.

Previously in America, coalitions used to be forged by the political parties, but look around you. The party as we have known it is over. The voracious rise of special interest groups is especially distressful because of the way it has separated so many levels of government and so many levels of education. Legislators can afford to become paranoid about the separation because that is their job. Educators cannot become so paranoid for their tasks involve the growth and resolution of human beings.

And yet we desperately need a global sensibility. We are not regional people any more. If any of you have ever lived in a very small town, you know what small-town consciousness is like. Most of you are probably cosmopolitans. I suggest to you the equation that the village human is to the cosmopolitan human as the cosmopolitan human is to the planetary human. We are about to become planetary people. We are at a time of emerging and converging global sensibility, except that we have neither the psychology nor the education to know what to do with it. The irony is that the majority of Americans still live under balkanized local governments, regional rivalries, and warring layers of government which prevent the establishment of needed national policies, much less international ones.

You have only to read the newspaper or watch the news to know that part of the urgent task of our time is that of challenging the now defunct political imagination which has hitherto organized around stratified bureaucracies, empires, and nation states and in which people only intermittently communicated with each other.

Now that we are in an age of frightening interdependence, the old territorial imperatives must give way to the necessities of a mutually shared planet. The knowledge that we have entered into a planetary community, with its binding together of peoples, compels an organic vision of what must be done to achieve an ecology of cultures, races, and sensibilities.

As a professional in human behavioral research, I have discovered that if you want to explore the full range of human potentials, you cannot look at just one kind of person or culture. Most of the human potentials of our planet have been manifested by different races, cultures, and societies around the world. It is only in cross-cultural inquiry that one discovers the genius of a human being. No longer can a single society try to overwhelm all others with a presumed "rightness" of its religious, economic, or political ideology. We need the full complement of known and unknown human capacities in order to respond to the enormous problems and complexities of our time. And it is only in the tapestry of cultures that we begin to gain any notion of the range and variety of these capacities.

Right now, most thinking about complex problems is linear, analytical, and hierarchical. The whole world is at hand, everything in the planetary existence is resonant with everything else, and yet we keep on plodding along as if everything were separate, doing one thing at a time, and inevitably failing. Part of the mess we are in is that we are using 19th century ways of thinking and learning in a third-millennium world. In such a world things must be learned in multimodal ways because everything is resonant with everything else. This is heterarchical thinking, a thinking and learning style in which one becomes aware of many patterns at the same time, as well as of the pattern that connects them together. Hierarchical thinking which persists in linear analytic discrete modes of knowing is a crippling atavism which distorts and inhibits the learning process. Many educators suspect this but are prevented by school bureaucracies from doing anything about it.

The extraordinary range and dimensions of human knowings and experience, both personal and cross-cultural, are not being used to solve the problems with which we have to deal today. What happens, both in government and education, is that we apply a

patchwork quilt of Band-Aids to solve critical problems. We
observe, for example, a great number of complex short-term
solutions to social and economic problems. We also perceive the
long-term failure of those brilliant solutions because of their
psychologically simplistic bases. Here is a brief but revealing
portrait of the great successes of our culture and of the long-
term problems resulting from that success:

Success: Reducing infant and adult mortality rates.
Result of Excessive Success: Regional overpopulation
and problems of the aged. We do not know what to do
with so many old people. They have great genius to
give us, but we have not yet understood the genius of
the elderly.

Success: Highly developed science and technology.
Result of Excessive Success: Hazards of mass destruction
from nuclear and biological weapons, threats to privacy
and freedom, surveillance technology, bioengineering.

Success: Machine replacement of manual and routine labor.
Result of Excessive Success: Exacerbated unemployment.

Success: Advances in communication and transportation.
Result of Excessive Success: Increasing air noise and
land pollution, information overload, vulnerability of a
complex society, and breakdown. Disruption of human and
biological rhythms.

Success: Efficient production systems.
Results of Excessive Success: Dehumanization of ordinary
work. Efficient rather than effective education.

Success: Affluence and material growth.
Result of Excessive Success: Increased per capital consumption of energy and goods leading to pollution and
the depletion of the earth's resources.

Success: Satisfaction of basic needs.
Result of Excessive Success: Worldwide revolution of
rising expectations and rebellion against non-meaningful
work.

Success: Expanded power of human choice.
Result of Excessive Success: Increasing gap between the
have and have-not nations, frustration of the revolution of
of rising expectations, exploitation, and growing pockets
of famine and poverty.[1]

What we see in this chart is the enactment on the field of history of the story of the <u>Sorcerer's</u> <u>Apprentice</u>. The apprentice, understanding almost nothing of the subtle dynamics of the powers he is dealing with, and of himself in relation to these powers, is overwhelmed by his evocation of the automated brooms. When he says the magic word, the broom starts to multiply itself, and before long a battalion of brooms are pushing rivers of water through the castle. He is nearly done in by the sheer excess of his success as the brooms and pails of water flood the castle in their mindless mania for cleaning and efficiency.

What was lacking in the success of the apprentice and of western technology is a sense of the vital ecology that links inner and outer worlds. The dominant social paradigm of a reality perceived in largely economic and technological terms is deficient, and it is bound only by the objective external dimension of things. It contains, therefore, no internal limiting factor. The external environment is strictly limited in its resources so each solution yields ten new problems, and our successes become world-eroding failures. Our response is always to stay in a state of crisis reaction--which is why one National Geographic Society television special commented that the human race should be put on the list of endangered species along with the elk and the caribou.

Education is characterized by the same kind of patterning. So much of educational planning and decision making has been primarily one of making crisis decisions. Suddenly a school is overcrowded. Suddenly district enrollment dramatically falls. Suddenly test scores are too low. Suddenly the elected board wants a new superintendent. Suddenly something must be done for the mentally gifted. Suddenly a group of parents are angry about the new bus routes. Everything runs on a crisis mentality, and the poor administrators scurry to put out existing fires before the next one erupts, and the needed revision of education goes by the boards.

Expanding federal curriculum efforts modeled on this emergency approach have institutionalized a crisis mentality. New emergencies have led to a rapid proliferation of subject-oriented projects and the emergence of a patchwork curriculum at the precollegiate level. These programs now include drug abuse education, ethnic studies education, metric education, environmental education, moral education, consumer education, driver education, sex education, global education, economic education, leadership education, health education, energy education, and nutrition education. The present federal effort in the area of curriculum leaves out the essential dimension of any balanced curriculum, the fusion or integration of the topical material into an interdisciplinary instructional program. The present Band-Aid approach diverts attention and scares resources away from what is really needed in educational reform: basic education with contemporary social concerns presented in a dynamically integrated way so that students learn to read, write, and compute and become aware of the planetary process. We have to move from isolated, topical treatment of curriculum issues to comprehensive curriculum renewal for total education.

There have been wonderful attempts to revise education. In the 1960s, extensive revision was attempted, but in such a piecemeal manner that all those successful, innovative programs died. Remember how, during the 1960s, innovation in education was the byword? Hundreds of conferences were conducted. The Kettering Foundation sponsored a network of innovative activities. Millions of dollars were expended. Educators traveled throughout the United States to visit model programs, and the literature was filled with success stories and change processes. For a while it was one successful fad after the other. Do you know what happened? Everything worked, and practically nothing failed.

Everything worked because the great innovations of the 1960s were patterned after the successful experimentation of the 1930s. They tried to change from efficiency to effectiveness. They tried to improve with solid scientific data the affective, psychomotor, and cognitive development of children. Wonderful efforts of team teaching, flexible scheduling, and individualized learning helped many students. Many better programs were developed. Now, this is important: those programs had been developed by and large in the university by innovative educators who then went with their assistants to put them into the schools. As long as that educator was there, it was wonderful; and it worked. But after the innovative leader or program director went back to Harvard or Stanford, the majority of the programs reverted to more conventional approaches or settled into middle-of-the-road compromises that tried to satisfy everybody and satisfied no one.

What we have seen in education is exactly the same pattern of breakdown that we have seen in every arena of society. Education and the process of educating is a total integral, contextual situation which includes students, teachers, parents, administration, and environment. The context, the pattern that connects, was not served by hotshot educators who come in from a university. Innovation does not work out of context. It has to be worked in relation to the whole educational system. Unless something grows as part of the organism as a whole, there will be nothing but fragments. Educators, as the recipients of fragments, are open to a lot of attack--which is why we have the kinds of attacks that are being seen today.

Why is it that Johnny cannot read, spell, or, most importantly, balance his checkbook? How could he? How could he when his education is so fragmented? A fragmentation in government or in education is a fragmentation of mind.

The liberal programs failed because they were not involved in the pattern that connects. No one has ever really looked at what it means to educate an entire society contextually. Why? Because the richness of the human, psychological, and educational processes has been ignored and derided during the recent reign of quantity. The popular absorption in the prodigies of technology not only inhibited the development of a mentality attuned to more subtle inward understandings of reality and social process, but it also encouraged a dangerous interface and modeling of human personality with mechanistic forms. These forms are fine for machines. They do not work for human beings. When human beings become secondary to the so-called efficiency of a given system they almost invariably fail in large numbers.

Look what we did. We took a European system that was intended to educate an elite and which was itself based upon an archaic understanding of the nature of intelligence. We then took this same system and tried to educate everybody and create a mass elite. In so doing, we created a mass failure rate such as the world has never known. Never before, at least as measured by tests, has there been so much failure on the part of so many people. Before long, the failing people or people who perceive themselves as failures will begin to create a failing culture, a failing nation, and a failing civilization. The response to failure in the schools has been to add programs, not to rethink education and get everybody to win--which from my perspective, and from what we are now beginning to discover about the mind and brain, is very possible. The human brain is incredibly overendowed. We use about 10% of our physical capacity and far less of our mental capacity. With a holistic integral education it is quite possible that many students can learn to use a much greater range of their innate capacity. But this assumes that there are many different kinds of intelligence and different ways of educating that intelligence.

Educational transformation is the time for waking up. It is enormously significant that the current crisis in consciousness, the loss of a sense of reality felt by so many, the destruction and disillusionment with education, and the rising tides of alienation occur concomitantly with the ecological destruction of the planet by technological means. We are forced into the awareness that we are not encapsulated bags of skin dragging around dreary little egos. Rather, a human being is an organism-environment.

If we are to survive, we have no choice but to reverse the ecological, technological, and linear-analytic plunder. That will mean discovering forms of consciousness and fulfillment and forms of human energy and learning apart from those of consumption, control, aggrandizement, pass-the-test, and manipulation. Clearly, the human race is about to take some major growth steps. We have evolved physically and culturally to have a remarkably fine psycho-social instrument. Now the time has come for that instrument to work, explore, and create with levels and capacities of existence that hitherto have remained more mythical than real.

What is happening is very interesting. At a time when we are experiencing a loss of hope in the social domain, the vision of what human beings can be has never been more remarkable. We are living at the beginning of the golden age of brain, mind, and body research. We may well be standing, with regard to the understanding of our brain, where Einstein stood in the year 1904 when he discovered the special theory of relativity that helped accomplish the great revolution in physics. The new explorations and current advances in brain, mind, and body research are increasingly allowing us to view and probe the capacities of human beings and gradually to learn how to use these capacities much more productively.

For the first time in human history people may become what they are--fully human. Not that this planet has not seen thousands of richly actualized human beings before. Obviously it has, but only with the random individual and never, as far as we know, with great numbers of humankind. The potentials of the human being could be actualized and democratized. We may be in the time of the opening up of the ecology of inner space to humanity at large--because the problem of human survival, when you come right down to it, may no longer be that of discovering new economic or political solutions but rather one of a growth of the qualities of mind and body of a human race. That should be education's concern.

Most of us have been raised to have the experiential intake and the faculties of a much more limited and bounded culture. We have not educated our brains, bodies, and our conscious receptors to take in the enormous amounts of information and multiple levels of knowing that we need for modern decision-making. In some ways we are still being educated in the family, by the environment, and in the schools for the demands of about 1825, not for the 21st century. We have a 19th century psychology whose paranoid insularities and aggressions are trigger happy with the 20th century technology. It is all going to burst very fast. The ecological and the technological crises may force us to do the work on ourselves that we avoided for too many centuries. We use but a fraction of our capacities and live as crippled, distorted versions of who we are.

This came home to me in a remarkable experience I once had. I live not far from a leading center on the East Coast for mentally retarded people. Every year, the center puts on a show, generally a musical comedy such as <u>Oklahoma</u>, <u>Carousel</u>, or <u>Fiddler on the Roof</u>. All the parts are played by the mentally retarded patients. I went the year they put on <u>Fiddler on the Roof</u>. You could tell that the people in the chorus were retarded, but you could not tell about the principals. The man who played Tevye was so magnificent, so full of high drama, rhythm, and theatrical brilliance that I turned to my friend, and said, "What a fake, what a fake! He is an out-of-work, off-Broadway actor who is using these mentally retarded people as a showcase for himself. Isn't that terrible!" My friend said, "No, Jean. It says in the program that he is one of the patients." I replied with great disdain, "Listen, I am the professional. I know. He is a fake. Or else he's a doctor who should have been an actor."

After the show, we went backstage to meet the man who played Tevye. I went up to him and said, "Hi, you were very good. What was the last show you did off Broadway?" He stared at me mutely and continued to do so as I plied him with more questions. Finally, I was so shocked at my own tactlessness that I shocked myself into doing the right thing. I grabbed his hands, and I began to dance and sing to the music of <u>Fiddler</u>: "My name is Jean Houston, and I certainly loved your show . . ." His eyes leaped into knowing, and he grinned at me as he said, "My name is Aaron Schwartz, and I am glad you found me out . . ." Then he began to tell me about his life and demand, in his singing, that I tell him about mine. He did it in rhyme. I was too dumb and couldn't keep up the rhyme. As he sang he told me that when he was singing and dancing he knew who he really was, for when he sang and danced he found himself. He went on and on and on. He told me that when he was as others were, it was as if a curtain fell in front of his mind. When he was singing and dancing, however, the world moved into meaning.

The story of Aaron Schwartz is also our own story. There are many different modes of knowing. He happened to have minimal brain damage, but in music he used other areas of the brain in which different kinds of connections occurred. This is true of so many of us. There is an innate genius in all of us, but we have to find the pattern that connects.

What would happen to human beings and to society generally if we could recover as well as discover the use of our own potential? Much in the new scientific research and the vision of the possible human is predictive of the increase and its consequences. It points to capacities which we all have and which have been demonstrated in the laboratory with thousands of research subjects. These capacities are then learned, integrated into daily life, and even applied constructively to the improvement of many social programs from those that have to do with enhancing educational programs, teaching "non-learners," rehabilitating ex-prisoners, and even greatly restoring and extending the physical and mental capacities of the elderly.

I have been involved with the creation and implementation of such programs for some time now, and for the last 14 years at the Foundation for Mind Research have found that the human capacity is a vast and inexhaustible resource. We have discovered, for example, that most people given opportunity and education can realize more of their potentials in varying degrees. Their bodies can be psychophysically rehabilitated and a more optimal physical functioning achieved. As the body's capacities are extended so are its capacities for awareness, the ability to move and to sense enhanced; cognitive and feeling functions improve also, for the extensive changes in the brain's motor cortex which must precede changes in the muscular system affect adjacent brain areas as well. Thus we find that owing to the close proximity to the motor cortex of the brain structures dealing with thought and feeling, and tendencies of processes in the brain tissue to diffuse and spread to neighboring tissues, the changes in the motor cortex will have parallel effects on thinking and feeling.

In our applications of these methods to education and the rehabilitation of the elderly, we have found that these movement exercises frequently result in enhanced capacities in learning, remembering, and problem solving. We find throughout our work that if you wish to extend the capacities of the mind, you must at the same time extend the capacities of the body which is the instrument of that mind.

In other areas of our work, people learn to think in images as well as in words, to practice in subjective time the rehearsal of skills, and to experience the acceleration of thought processes. They can learn to think kinesthetically with their whole body, they can experience cross-sensing, the self-regulation of pleasure and pain and acquire voluntary control over some of the autonomic functions by means of biofeedback and autogenic training. As an exciting extension to this kind of research we find that subjects can be taught to speak to their own brains directly, so entering into conscious orchestration of mood, attitude, learning, and creativity.

In our laboratory individuals are enabled to experience the extensive range of consciousness. Most of us exist with regard to the dimensions of consciousness as if we were inhabiting only the attic of ourselves, with the first, second, third, and fourth floors, and the basement going uninhabited and remaining unconscious. When we begin to take up residence in these other realms of ourselves, when we extend the domain of consciousness, the pragmatic effects are numerous. People can learn how to work with dream content, how to better concentrate and how to remember more effectively. There is a tapping of the creative process and an experiencing of those levels of the self where one's personal existential life finds analogies with universal constructs and broader formulations.

To evoke and work with these capacities is to restore the ecological balance between inner and outer worlds. It is to gain a wider use of the self, a larger measure of self-knowing. It is also to move beyond the conditionings and cul de sacs of our present environment and problems and to bring individuals into very different relationships in their world.

The extensions of learning are grounded in the extended use of our sensory perceptions. By the time we reach maturity, for most of us our sensorium is a shrunken, crippled version of what it could be. As people grow older in our culture, they undergo a progressive diminishment of sensory acuity and sensory knowing. They become progressively less able to see, to touch, and otherwise to utilize their senses. This loss would seem to be attributable in part to our verbalizing, conceptualizing mental processes and not just to impairment by age. In many hunting and tribal societies, for example, it is the adult and not the child who evinces the most acute and orchestral balance of his senses. In our own culture we have the evidence of professionals who have to keep up a certain sensory acuity for the sake of their art-- the musician's ear, the artist's eye, the perfumer's nose. The blunting of perception has led me to formulate Houston's law: concept louses up percept.

Conceptualization, of course, is essential to the continuance of culture--it sustains the very fabric of civilization. But civilization, as the patriarch Sigmund Freud has warned us, has its profound discontents. In societies where sensory experience is depreciated as a cultural norm (so that one can put most of one's energies into mastering the environment), the body itself suffers attendant harpies--the neuroses, obesities, aggressions, and even the widespread deathwish which seems to characterize much of psyche and history in the 20th century. Is it worth seeing as through a glass darkly, or touching as if one were wearing gloves, or hearing as if through wads of conceptual cotton-wool? Such simple matters may be the stuff out of which historical catastrophies are made.

Now there is a great deal that can be done to regain sensory acuity in one's adult years. Part of it is just paying attention. I think the establishment of preventive educational programs calls for more public decisions. Education for children, especially for small children, should in part be education in sense perception--education in enhancing and intensifying the senses and the child's awareness of a physical state of being so he or she can keep a good body. This is not just to give people good health and sensory acuity. It is to make them much more alert. Ironically, conceptualization is grounded in a refinement of perception.

With the enhancement of sensory and perceptual knowledge, with the recovery of imaginal and symbolic structures, the child learns the virtuoso capacities of brain and body and his mind grows in kind. Ironically, conceptualization in its finest forms is grounded in a refinement of perceptualization. In our research we find quite simply that there is a real equation between the ability to entertain and sustain complex thinking processes and the richness of the person's sensory and kinesthetic awareness.

We have explored dozens of cases of high actualizing intelligence, of people who use their intelligence for creative accomplishment. The great majority of them we found were stimulated as children with rich sensory and arts-related experiences.

Perhaps the most intelligent and sensitive person I have ever known also had the greatest subtlety of sensory refinement. Her name was Margaret Mead and she was far richer and more interesting than the person represented by her public image, remarkable as that was. She thought more, felt more, gave more, and got more out of life than virtually anyone I had ever met. In knowing Margaret Mead, I was experiencing a new style of human being, a new way of being human.

With her cooperation, I eventually began a formal study of Margaret Mead, especially of her thinking and perceptual processes. This study, which lasted five years, until her death in 1978, is especially germane to our consideration of the education and preparation of the possible human. Her early years particularly tell us much about the important effects of sensory and aesthetic styles of learning on cognitive development.

She was born in Philadelphia in 1901 into a family of educators. Her father Edward Mead was a brilliant, rather eccentric economist and professor. Her mother Emily Fogg Mead was a sociologist much involved in causes and community projects. Her grandmother Martha Ramsay Mead--one of the principal influences in her life--was a strong-minded, innovative school teacher. After kindergarten, Margaret was periodically educated at home because her family had thought so much about education that they disapproved of formal schooling. Her mother gave her poetry to memorize; her grandmother dispensed hardy maxims for her to take to heart while her hair was being brushed. She learned basketry, carpentry, weaving, wood carving, and other manual skills requiring fine eye-to-muscle coordination (in which she surpassed nearly everyone else we have tested).

Following a suggestion of William James, her mother exposed her to numerous sensory stimuli when she was still an infant-- colors, textures, pictures of great works of art, and masterpieces of music, including an ancient Greek hymn to Apollo retained in the Byzantine church. She was encouraged to use all her senses in any kind of activity, even the most abstract ones. Dualisms were discouraged; she was trained to accept the unity of mind and body, thinking and feeling. If you ask Western people where "I" exists, many point to their foreheads. If you asked Margaret Mead that question, she responded matter-of-factly, "Why, all over me, of course."

Given this base of rich sensibility, Margaret acquired an unusual ability to store memories and learn abstract material rapidly. When a sensorium is as consciously developed to the extent that it was in young Margaret, then the child and the adult she becomes has more conscious use of proprioceptors, more "hooks and eyes" as it were to catch and keep the incoming information, and then relate it to other information stored in the sensorium. Nor was she limited to five senses. Throughout her life she kept up her childhood capacity for synesthesia (cross-sensing) which most children have by then lost because it is discouraged. A synesthete can hear color and see sound, taste time and touch aromas. Here is a classic exchange with a natural synesthete:

Me: Margaret, what does this room taste like?

Margaret: Something in which spices were put last week.

Me: What do you hear in Bob's face?

Margaret: I guess . . . a symphony.

Me: What is the touch of my voice?

Margaret: Your voice is a brush. It's a brush that's made of very non-bristling material so it isn't like a brush made of pig's bristles, but it isn't as soft as the kind of silk brush that you use to do a baby's hair. It's somewhere in between.

Me: Not nylon, I hope!

Margaret: No, not nylon! It's something live.

Her kinesthetic sense was also developed early and sustained throughout her life so that as an anthropologist, she has the physical empathy to understand, through body sensing, the special skills of primitive cultures. She could feel a complex fishing procedure in her bones and sinews, sense an intricate dance as a kinesthetic rhythm in her muscle fibers. Photographs of her in the field reveal her assuming some of the sensibility of the cultures she is observing. She appears soft in Arapesh, tense in Manus, unfocused and "away" in Bali.

Grandmother Mead insisted that she learn how to do entire procedures from beginning to end, so she learned not only how to weave, but also how to build a loom. Throughout her life whenever she began or joined a project, she invariably followed it through to its natural conclusion (which made for an extraordinary number of projects in progress at any given time).

In contrast, other people often dilute their actions and decisions by employing what I call "the switch." In this technological phenomenon, human behavior becomes observer bound, abstracted from social responsibility, and with no sense of the need to follow through the organic sequencing of a process. One begins to lose the sense of how to guide the beginnings, middles, and ends of things. At the Foundation for Mind Research we have tried to remedy this by helping many schools develop a rich arts-related curriculum in which children learn to think from a much larger sensory and neurological base. For according to current theory the left hemisphere is the site of analysis and sequential learning including verbal and mathematical skills, while the right is the site of visual and spatial abilities. The entire spectrum of intelligence--thinking, learning, adaptation, problem-solving, re-constructing, creativity--is at its best the result of the cooperation of both hemispheres working together and informing each other. The neurological dominance of one

hemisphere over the other could only diminish the nature and
capacity of this intelligence. Thus there is great need for
educational programs that develop both sides of the brain, that
evoke both reason and imagination, thinking and feeling, concept
and percept, abstraction and immediate concrete experience, words
and images, body and mind.

In the arts-related curriculum which we have developed,
children very early become capable of using many different kinds
of materials and methods with success. The child is taught how
to work with clay, with glazing, with block printing, paper
mache, tissue collage, weaving, batiks, as well as more complex
uses of chalks and paints. In learning these things, he also has
to learn in a tangible and expressive way many of the mathematical principles which he will need to carry out his work:
principles of design, line, form, color, texture and structure.
Measurement and fractions are learned naturally and with ease as
the child constructs his art work. In order to weave, he has to
learn something about the making of grids and this he does with
far less pain and confusion than if he learned about grids in an
abstract context. Since learning is occurring with both right
and left hemispheric functions, the child tends to bring much
more of himself to any learning situation. Thus he does not
fail, and children educated in this way as measured by standard
tests are routinely scoring one to four grade levels above
normal.[2] Also, since arts-related education involves the child
in entire cycles of any process, these children, like the young
Margaret Mead, become far more resourceful and responsible in
initiating, carrying out and completing other kinds of projects
with which they involve themselves.

To return to the early education of Margaret Mead, we learn
that Grandmother Mead didn't care for drill, believing that it
inhibited originality and spontaneity in children. If something
was to be learned, it had to be learned right away, a skill
Margaret retained all her life. In Margaret's experience, this
involved as it does with the children described above employing
more senses and ways of knowing in the learning situation--
combining both left hemispheres of the brain for acquiring
information. When she learned a poem, for example, she would
join simple rote memorization (left hemisphere) to an inner
process in which she actually saw the images described in the
poem, felt the situation or event as vividly as if she has been
there, experienced the textures and tone of the poem, and took
its emotions for her own (right hemisphere). As an experiment,
the reader might apply these techniques in learning the following
ditty in the same way the four-year-old Margaret Mead learned it:

I'm sitting alone by the fire
Dressed just as I came from the dance.
In a gown, Frog, even you would admire--
It cost a cool thousand in France.
I'm bediamonded out of all reason,
My hair is done up in a queue,
In short, sir, the belle of the season
Is wasting an hour on you.

In our own research with "problem learners," we have developed techniques quite similar to Margaret's multi-perceptual learning. The child is taught to think in images as well as in words, to learn spelling or even arithmetic in rhythmic patterns, to think with his whole body--in short, to learn school basics from a much larger spectrum of sensory and cognitive possibilities. Thus, if a child shows inadequacy in one form of learning--say, verbal skills--we direct him to another form, such as sensory-motor skills, in which he may show a great facility to learn to read and write faster and with greater depth and appreciation. Some years ago, while developing new teaching methods for what was bureaucratically referred to as "minority group slow learners," I asked an eight-year-old boy, "Tommy, how much is this: five plus three plus two?" Tommy made a face indicating boredom. I then upended the chair I was sitting on and began to drum on it, asking, "Tommy, how much is this: bump bump bump bump bump--bump bump bump--bump bump?" Tommy grinned and said, "That's ten, man." "Why didn't you tell me before?" I asked. "'Cause you didn't ask me before," he replied.

He was right. Most of our questions and answers in the schoolroom are addressed to one very small section of the brain, and arise out of one very small section of the planet, northern Europe. Much in northern European derived education and understanding of intelligence discriminates against one whole half of the brain, and tends to reward only left hemispheric dominant students who respond well to verbal, linear styles of education. And yet we humans are as different as snowflakes, one from the other. Our brains are as different from each other as are our fingerprints, with enormous variations in styles and talents of perception and learning. Some people are naturally kinesthetic thinkers, others think in images, others in sounds. Classical education tends to inhibit these and frequently causes these nonverbal thinkers to feel inferior and begin a process of failure that will last all their lives. From many years of observation I have found that I have rarely met a stupid child, but I have met many stupid and debilitating, and yes, even brain-damaging systems of education. As we subsequently discovered, a child can learn math as a rhythmic dance and learn it well (the places of rhythm in the brain being adjacent to the places of order). He can learn almost anything and pass the standard tests if he is dancing, tasting, touching, hearing, seeing, and feeling information. He can delight in doing so because he is using much more of his mind-brain-body system than conventional teaching generally permits. So much of the failure in school comes directly out of boredom, which itself comes directly out of the larger failure to stimulate all those areas in the child's brain which could give him so many more ways of responding to his world.

Adding to this is our tendency to classify people as either an artist or a practical type; either a feeling-sensation type or an abstract intellectual; either this or that but rarely maybe. The message of the bilateral brain is that we are Both/And plus much much more. In the case of Margaret Mead we saw ways of educating the Both/And so that one learns to realize one's full potential. In today's complex reality we need to have access to all our parts. We can no longer afford to short-change our brains and impoverish our spirits. Those limitations have now become desecrations of our humanity, the fullness of which is needed in ways in which it never was before.

NOTES

1. Based on O.W. Markley, et al, Changing Images of Man (Menlo Park California: SRI International, 1974), p. 7.

2. For further information, see the issue of Dromenon titled "Arts and Minds" (Dromenon, G.P.O. Box 2244, New York, New York 10001 $3.00).

Futuristic World Views: Modern Physics and Feminism
Implications for Teaching and Learning in Higher Education

Gerri Perreault

This paper is titled, "Futuristic World Views: Modern Physics and Feminism." But what is a "world view" and what is a "futuristic" world view? And what do modern physics and feminism, two seemingly disparate areas of human endeavor, one a science and one a social movement, have to do with world views? Is the title merely one to link personal interests to a conference of the World Future Society's Education Section, or is the title central to the point of view being expressed? It is, of course, the latter.

What is a "world view?" World view as used in this paper includes one's values, beliefs, attitudes, and basic assumptions about knowledge and the nature of reality. Anthropologist Anthony Wallace calls world view a "mazeway"--nature, society, culture, personality, and body images as seen by one person.[1] It is differentiated from "theory" in that it is broader and includes both explicit and implicit assumptions and beliefs. What is a "futuristic" world view? It is a world view that poses important alternatives to and/or transformations of (as opposed to mere changes in) present world views. A futuristic world view is one that is not dominant currently but is held by a minority of thinkers and presents significant challenges to current assumptions, beliefs, and values.

The world views which are the focus of this paper are those of physics and feminism. The paper will describe and compare the similar differences in world views between classical physics and modern physics and between patriarchy and feminism (see Chart 1) and will point out the similarities in the world views of classical physics and patriarchy and of modern physics and feminism. (Note, though, that the context for the discussion of patriarchy and feminism is limited to the United States.) In brief, my thesis is that the world view of classical physics and of patriarchy puts a premium on:

1. separation, division, categorization;
2. independence, unrelatedness, unconnectedness;
3. isolated and independent parts;
4. static and mechanistic processes;
5. either-or thinking;
6. separation of observer from the world,
   objectivity possible;
7. absoluteness of space and time.

In contrast, modern physics and feminism are strikingly similar
in their emphasis on:

1. lack of separations and divisions;
2. interrelatedness, interconnectedness;
3. wholeness and oneness;
4. dynamic and organic processes;
5. transcendence of either/or thinking;
6. inseparability of observer and observed,
   myth of objectivity, "participator" more accurate;
7. relativity of time and space.

Chart 1
World Views Compared

Classical Physics	Modern Physics
1. Mind & Matter separate	1. Mind & matter connected
2. Building blocks	2. Connections
3. Independent parts	3. Wholeness & oneness
4. Static & mechanistic	4. Dynamic
5. Either/or thinking	5. Transcendence of either/or thinking
6. Scientist separate from material world. Objectivity possible.	6. Scientist inseparable from material world. Objectivity a myth. "Participator."
7. Space & time: absolute	7. Space & time: relative

Patriarchy	Feminism
1. Separations & divisions	1. Lack of separations; interrelatedness
2. Parts	2. Connections
3. Fragmentation & independent parts	3. Wholeness & oneness
4. Static & mechanistic	4. Dynamic & organic
5. Either/or thinking	5. Transcendence of either/or thinking
6. Observer separate from world. Objectivity possible.	6. Observer inseparable from world. Objectivity a myth.
7. Time absolute	7. Time relative; illusion of linearity.

It is my assumption and belief that the dominant world view of American society[2] is more closely aligned with the assumptions and beliefs of Newtonian physics and patriarchy than with modern physics and feminism, and that although these assumptions have facilitated material "progress" they have also resulted in disastrous consequences for the entire planet.[3]

To illustrate, there are a number of critical, life-threatening problems faced by society and the planet. These include fragmentation and alienation of people, community, and nation; unbridled specialization and technology; destruction of the ecosphere; the reign of technique at the expense of care, compassion, and wisdom; the reign of the various isms (racism, sexism, militarism, etc.) and their consequent life-destroying and limiting oppressions; and a focus on ends rather than means and processes.

The world view common to all of these problems and crises is an assumption, mostly implicit, of separableness, independent and isolatable parts, divisions and differences, and unconnectedness. Modern physics and feminism both present alternatives to and transformations of these dominant assumptions, assumptions which not only create the problems listed but lead to inadequate solutions.

The problems listed above are not amenable to mere Band-Aid solutions (e.g., more psychological services to help people cope) and techniques (e.g., more sophisticated computer systems), necessary though some of these may be. Rather, the problems call for a fundamental shift in world view to one that emphasizes wholeness (of the person and of the planet/universe); inter-relatedness; transcendence of dichotomies such as rational/intu-itive and subjective/objective; interdependence; and attention to process. These characteristics comprise both modern physics and feminism.

A question may have arisen in the reader's mind by now as to whether or not I am arguing a causal link between the two shifts in world views being discussed. What I am doing is describing what I see as two shifts that seem to be taking place, and I have not attempted to analyze the possible intricate and intrinsic ways in which they might be interconnected. My assumption is that there is some link, perhaps imbedded in what Art Harkins would call "cultural system conditions"[4] (part of which, of course, includes physics and feminism). The futuristic world views described in this paper are probably part of, and contribute to, a larger shift in world views occurring in other areas of the culture as a whole, for example, ecology, some branches of psychology, and futures studies. An inquiry into the probabilitistic (as distinct from "exact") nature of the interconnections among all these areas was not attempted in this paper.

The discussion of both modern physics and feminism which follows is of course a linear and rational ("rational" in its root sense meaning "to divide") discussion of multi-dimensional, interrelated, and non-linear and non-rational[5] topics, and hence carries all the problems co-existent with this contradiction. Capra, a physicist, says: ". . . the exploration of the sub-atomic world has revealed a reality which repeatedly transcends language and reason. . . ."[6] Morgan, a feminist, says that we must: ". . . go beyond what we sense (I am assuming that we already are beyond what we know) and test our perceptions of reality. We must admit the entire cosmos as the ground on which such a search takes place. We must recognize the dissolution of the illusion of linear form . . . ."[7] But I am using language, a linear and rational form, and categories--even more linear and rational--to communicate. The effort has, for me, been worthwhile, and I hope it will be for the reader, too.

The organization of the discussion which follows is first, a description of the paradigm shift from classical physics to modern physics; second, a description of the paradigm shift from patriarchy to feminism, and, third, implications for teaching and learning in colleges and universities.

Paradigm Shift from Classical Physics to Modern Physics

The shift from classical (i.e., Newtonian physics) to modern physics (i.e., Einstein's relativity theory and Planck's quantum theory)[8] was a paradigm shift in world view. Classical physics is best represented by the analogy of the machine. Key characteristics include the separation of mind and matter and a model that views atoms as the building blocks of the world. In contrast, modern physics is best represented by the analogy of an organism. Key characteristics include the inseparability of mind and matter and a model based on patterns of connections, rather than building blocks. The characteristics of classical physics and modern physics will now be described in more detail.

1. Mind and Matter: Separate or Connected?

Classical physics is based on a belief in the dualism of mind and matter, or spirit and matter. This belief can be traced to the philosophy of the Greek atomists who saw matter as being made of building blocks called atoms and these atoms were "purely passive and intrinsically dead," moved by some external force assumed to be fundamentally different from matter.[9]

This dualism became part of the thinking of Descartes, a 17th century philosopher who based his view of nature on "its fundamental division into two separate and independent realms, that of mind ('res cogitans') and that of matter ('res extensa')."[10] This Cartesian conception of matter as dead and completely separate from us was the basis for Newton's mechanistic view of the universe. Nature was assumed to operate like a machine with cause and effect and was governed by exact and absolute laws which existed in an external world.

In modern physics, mind and matter are not separate. At the subatomic level, mass is nothing but a form of energy,[11] and mass and energy change unceasingly into each other.[12] And we ourselves are somehow included. Postle comments that: ". . .we are energy, that our structure is formed of energy itself acting in the fields of force across space. The only difference between this book and that body of yours is how the energy is organized."[13]

2. Building Blocks or Patterns of Connections?

In Newton's mechanistic model, atoms--solid, material bodies--are the building blocks of the universe. But while this conception is workable in the macroscopic world, it doesn't work in the subatomic realm.[14]

In quantum physics, the idea of atoms and subatomic particles as solid objects is abandoned. The world consists not of things but of interactions and interconnections.

At the subatomic level, units of matter are "abstract entities" which do not exist with certainty at definite places, but rather show "tendencies to exist."[15] These "tendencies to exist" are expressed as probabilities, and the corresponding mathematical quantities of these probabilities take the form of waves.[16] These wave-like patterns of probabilities are not probabilities of things but of interconnections. Any observed "object" is an "intermediate system." As Capra explains, subatomic particles "can only be understood as interconnections between the preparation of an experiment and the subsequent measurement," and these relations always include the observer.[17]

3. Isolatable Parts or Wholeness?

Classical physics saw the universe composed of material, isolatable parts. In modern physics, "reality" is an insepar-

able, harmonious whole, and separation is an illusion. Rather
than the world being a collection of independent parts or
building blocks isolated from one another, it is a "complicated
web of relations between the various parts of a unified whole."[18]
As Bohm says, "One is led to the new notion of unbroken wholeness
which denies the classical idea of analyzability of the world
into separate and independently existing parts. . . ."[19] And
Heisenberg: "The world thus appears as a complicated tissue of
events in which connections of different kinds alternate or
overlap or combine and thereby determine the texture of the
whole."[20]

The whole is more than the sum of its parts. The structure
of a hadron, for example, "is not understood as a definite
arrangement of constituent parts, but is determined by all sets
of particles which may interact with one another to form the
hadron under consideration." Each hadron is understood "as an
integral part of an inseparable network of reactions. The
emphasis is not on static fundamental structures or entities, but
on change and transformation."[21]

4. Static or Dynamic?

In classical physics, matter was viewed as inert and
passive. Indeed it looks that way at the macroscopic level. At
the subatomic level, however, "the material that the physicist
works with now is change. Events. Interactions. Processes."[22]

In quantum mechanics, physicists have to take into account
the unification of space and time and hence view the particles in
terms of activity and processes. (See also discussion of the
hadron in item 3 above.) Particles are seen as bundles of
energy, and "energy is associated with activity, with processes,
and this implies that the nature of subatomic particles is
intrinsically dynamic."[23] Matter is "never quiescent but always
in a state of motion."[24] The picture is one of continuous
dancing and vibrating motion. As Capra so beautifully describes
it, the interactions: ". . . involve a ceaseless flow of energy
manifesting itself as the exchange of particles; a dynamic
interplay in which particles are created and destroyed without
end in a continual variation of energy patterns."[25]

5. Transcendence of Either/Or Categories?

The foundation of quantum mechanics demonstrates the falsity
and inadequacy of dividing reality into categories of either/or.
The wave-particle duality is a good illustration. At the
subatomic level, particles are seen as "tendencies to exist" and
these are

...very   abstract entities which have a dual aspect.
Depending on how we look at them, they appear sometimes as particles, sometimes as waves, and this dual
nature is also exhibited by light which can take the
form of electromagnetic waves or of particles.[26]

As Capra remarks, ". . . the unification of concepts which had
hitherto seemed opposite and irreconcilable turns out to be one
of the most startling features of this new reality."[27] Matter is
both continuous and discontinuous; force and matter are different
aspects of the same phenomena; space and time are unified; and
particles are waves and waves are particles.[28]

6. Scientist and Material World: Separate or Inseparable?

Newtonian physics rests on the assumption of an external
world which exists separate from us and thus it forms the basis
for the concept of scientific objectivity. It further assumes we
can observe, measure, and speculate about the external world
without changing it.[29] In this world of reality, people can be
said to discover, rather than create.[30]

In quantum mechanics, the "observer" becomes the "participator." There is no such thing as objectivity; we cannot
eliminate ourselves from the picture.[31] A person does not
discover the facts of nature so much as she or he applies
"theoretical systems or paradigms to it," that is, creates
reality.[32]

As Zukav points out, "what we experience is not external
reality, but our interaction with it."[33] As noted earlier, the
properties of an "object" cannot be defined independently of the
processes of preparation and measurement; if the preparation or
measurement is modified, the properties of the observed object
change. For example, the apparently mutually exclusive wave-like
and particle-like behaviors of light are not properties of light
but "properties of our interaction with light."[34] The
properties described belong to the interaction, "not to
independently existing things like light."[35] In Heisenberg's
words, "What we observe is not nature in itself but nature
exposed to our method of questioning."[36]

7.   Space and Time: Absolute or Relative?

In classical physics, space was three-dimensional and time
was one-dimensional, linear, and separate from space. According
to Einstein, however, space and time are inseparably linked;
there is no such thing as space and time, only space-time which
is a continuum.[37] There is no universal flow of time from past
to present to future.

The theory of relativity "emphasizes the notion that no matter what we observe, we always do so relative to a frame of reference that may differ from someone else's, that we must compare our frame of reference in order to get meaningful measurements and results about the events we observe."[38]

In sum, the theory and research of modern physics provides the basis for a world view dramatically different from that of classical (Newtonian) physics. Whereas the latter envisioned a mechanical world, a world of objects, of separations and discrete units, and offered the machine as the model for the universe, the modern physicist envisions a dynamic world, a world of interrelatedness, of oneness, and of change, and a model of the universe as a dynamic, organic one in process.

Paradigm Shift From Patriarchy to Feminism

Turning now to patriarchy and feminism, one can see in the shift from patriarchal world view to a feminist one a change strikingly similar to the one between classical physics and modern physics (see Chart 1). They key characteristics of the patriarchal world view are: separations and divisions, parts, fragmentation and independent parts, static and mechanistic, either/or categories, observer separate from world with objectivity possible, and time absolute. The key characteristics of the feminist world view are: interrelatedness, connections, wholeness and oneness, dynamic and organic, transcendence of either/or categories, observer inseparable from world with objectivity a myth, and time perceived as relative.

In case the use of the categories, patriarchy and feminism, is confusing, it might be helpful to distinguish the usage in this paper from more popular connotations. Patriarchy in the popular use of the term usually refers to rule by one sex, the patriarch, the father, the male, and the consequent biases and institutionalized discrimination against women. Feminism in popular usage usually refers to efforts to counteract this dominant rule of the patriarch, the male, and to construct a more egalitarian society (see definitions in the Appendix).

In this paper, however, patriarchy and feminism are being discussed in a broader context as world views and not restricted to a concern with stereotypic biases and institutionalized discrimination related specifically to women and men. Patriarchy here, for example, refers not only to rule by one sex, the male, but to its world view, its basic assumptions about the world.

Feminism as used in this paper refers not only to attempts to counteract patriarchy and to achieve legal and political equality but to its world view, its fundamental assumptions about the world. It should be noted that there are, of course, differences among feminists, and the feminist world view discussed here is not one shared by all feminists. It is one which goes beyond what is called "reformist feminism," i.e., working toward equality with men (e.g., adding women to the faculty and to high political office) and asks for changes more fundamental than the equality of women with men.

It may be useful to look at David Bakan's description of the modalities of "agency and communion" since these are to some extent similar to characteristics of patriarchy and feminism, and somewhat poetically capture the difference between the two.[39] To quote Bakan:

> Agency manifests itself in self-protection, self-assertion, and self-expansion; communion manifests itself in the sense of being at one with other organisms. Agency manifests itself in the formation of separations; communion in the lack of separations. Agency manifests itself in isolation, alienation, and aloneness; communion in contact, openness, and union. Agency manifests itself in the urge to master; communion in noncontractual cooperation. Agency manifests itself in the repression of thought, feeling, and impulse; communion in the lack or removal of repression.[40]

Bakan goes on to say:

> One of the fundamental points which I attempt to make is that the very split of agency from communion, which is a separation, arises from the agency feature itself; and that it represses the communion from which it has separated itself.[41]

Patriarchy would be aligned with the world view underlying agency in that patriarchy emphasizes separation, division, categorization, fragmentation, independence, prediction and control (mastery), and the separation of knower and known ("objectivity"). Feminism would be closely aligned with the world view underlying communion in that feminism emphasizes wholeness and oneness, lack of separations, interdependence and interrelatedness, connectedness, cooperation (rather than mastery), and the inseparability of knower and known (the myth of objectivity). This is not to say that agency is totally rejected but that it is tempered and balanced with communion and restricted to situations in which it is appropriate, just as classical physics is not totally rejected in the shift to modern physics.

Feminism, then, brings a radical transformation of the world view of patriarchy, of previous dichotomies (including feminine/masculine) and ways of perceiving, feeling, doing; the dissolution of linearity; and a critique of the compartmentalization and separations that have allowed us to interact with the world as object (i.e., master it), with disastrous consequences for the entire planet. Feminism as a world view similar to that of modern physics focuses on interrelatedness, interdependence, and connectedness; on organic processes; on wholeness and oneness; and on the inseparability of knower and known.

Before proceeding to expand on this shift, it is necessary to articulate those aspects of feminism that will not be _explicitly_ included in the discussion of feminism's parallels with modern physics. (These aspects are of course _implicitly_ included _by the very nature_ of those world views.)

They are:

1. Feminism challenges the patriarchal value of the male as the standard for human. It is pro-woman and values women as people, as human beings. Perhaps it should be noted, because of our training in dualistic thinking, that being pro-woman does not mean being anti-man. The opposite of pro-woman is anti-woman, or woman-hating, well documented in writings by Figes, Hays, Millett, Daly, and others.

2. Feminism, in attempting to redress the internalization and institutionalization of patriarchal norms, means deliberate, conscious, and continual monitoring of the ways in which we all manifest and perpetuate anti-femaleness and anti-feminism (for both women and men), including--but not limited to--biases/oppressions regarding race, class, lesbians/gays, age, and physical disability.

3. Feminism provides support for women. At this period in herstory/history, women must consciously support each other. Sara Evan's concept of "free social space" is also relevant here.[42]

Let me now turn to an expansion of those world-view aspects of feminism which share the world view of modern physics.

Interrelatedness, Lack of Separations, Connectedness

Feminism envisions the world as interdependent and interconnected and as a "complicated web of relations," to borrow a description from physics. It values seeing relationships, connections, and processes, and tries to redress the extreme compartmentalization of the Western patriarchal way of thinking, doing, and feeling.

According to Morgan, "The either/or dichotomy is inherently, classically patriarchal." Morgan abhors "that puerile insistence on compartmentalization (art versus science, intelligence versus passion, etc.)," and says that reason without emotion is fascistic and emotion without reason is sentimental.[43]

The catchphrase of the women's movement, "the personal is political" and "the political is personal," sums up a perception of the error of previous dichotomies of reason/emotion, rational/intuitive, public/private, and fact/value as arbitrary categories that are not really separable. According to Morgan, it is "the insistence on the connections, the demand for synthesis" that is so much a part of what she calls metaphysical feminism.[44] Everything is connected with everything else.

Wholeness and Oneness

Feminism sees the oneness and wholeness of the universe. Though this is implicit in the above dimensions, it adds the concept that the whole is greater than the sum of its parts and is inseparable from the parts.[45] Compartmentalization, though sometimes necessary for living in our three-dimensional world, or what LeShan would term "sensory reality" is an idealization, not "reality," whatever that may be. Morgan talks about "the inclusiveness of the feminist vision, the balance, the gestalt, the refusal to settle for part of a completeness...."[46]

Dynamic and Organic

Change and transformation are fundamental processes of any living system.[47] Feminism shares this belief and sees the world as a dynamic not static one, as a living system. Feminists talk of "relationships at the center of things,"[48] and see "structures of relations in process--a reality constantly in evolution."[49] The world is continually growing, evolving, changing; and "we are in process, continually evolving,"[50] "a process of integration and transformation."[51] Morgan talks of this process as "an upward spiral, so that each time we reevaluate a position or place we've been before, we do so from a new perspective. We are in process. . . . "[52]

In contrast to the patriarchal-masculine-agentic focus on ends, process is a central concern and priority. As Morgan states, "the process, the form of change itself is everything, the means and the goals justifying each other."[53] And Hartsock says, "At bottom, feminism is a mode of analysis, a method of approaching life and politics."[54]

Even feminism itself, as a movement, is seen as "the dialectical expression of personal drama."[55]

Transcendence of Either/Or Categories

The criticism of patriarchal dualistic thinking is one of the most consistent and pervasive dimensions of feminist writing, e.g., Morgan, Rich, Schaef, Bunch, and Daly. This dimension, the transcendence of either/or thinking, has been covered above so it will not be repeated here.

Observer Inseparable from Observed, Knower from Known

A feminist sees herself/himself as constructing, rather than discovering, her/his world. Yet, theory is "never neutral" and "cannot be separated from practice," from experience.[56] (The physicists' term "participator" is relevant here.) One's world view is a function of the interaction of one's biology, genetic makeup, and experiences; objectivity is a myth.[57] The feminist's struggle with the biases and distortions of patriarchy have helped bring the recognition that no one's view of the world, including one's own, is "objective" in the common sense connotation of "without bias,"[58] and s/he recognizes that objectivity is not possible. But in this the feminist is not really much different from anyone else--the critical difference is that a feminist acknowledges s/he is not objective.[59]

Relativity of Time and Illusion of Linearity

The concept in feminism that seems closely related to some in modern physics is that linearity and direct cause and effect relationships are questioned. Anne Wilson Schaef describes a White Male System (similar to what I've labelled patriarchy), and a Female System (similar to what I call feminism). In the White Male System, there is "a belief in the reality of numbers" and "time is believed to be its numbers. Time is believed to be what the clock measures." In the Female System, "time is seen as a process . . . one goes through cycles, rhythms, procedures, etc., and that it may or may not have anything to do with the clock."[60]

Similarly, Mary Daly speaks of "the linear, measured-out, quantitative time of the patriarchal system" and of "women . . . living in a qualitative, organic time . . . in which events are more significant than clocks."[61] She describes this movement as not linear "but rather resembles spiraling. . . ."[62]

In sum, feminism provides the basis for a world view dramatically different from that of patriarchy. Whereas the latter emphasizes separations and divisions, fragmentation and independent parts, the separability of the self from the world, and static and mechanistic processes, feminism emphasizes interrelatedness and lack of separations, wholeness and oneness, and inseparability of the self from the world and dynamic and organic processes. Thus, feminism shares a world view strikingly similar to that of modern physics and patriarchy shares one strikingly similar to that of classical physics (see Chart 1). Both feminism and modern physics are radical shifts from previous world views.

What, then, are the implications for teaching and learning in higher education?

Implications for Teaching and Learning in Higher Education

Both modern physics and feminism are futuristic world views, fundamentally different from contemporary dominant ones. As such, both challenge society's basic beliefs, value systems, and structures, including those found in higher education. The discussion which follows focuses on the implications for teaching and learning in colleges and universities. Other areas, such as research, could well have been examined in a similar manner.

The implications described below can be seen to flow from the world views of both modern physics and feminism (though it must be noted again, this world view is not common to all persons who call themselves feminist).

Interrelatedness, Interconnectedness, and Interdependence. If one views the world as interrelated, interconnected, and interdependent, then there are a number of implications for education. Four that seem important are:

1. A continual and pervasive emphasis on interdependence, inter-relatedness, and interconnectedness of people, nations, and the planet as well as processes of change and development. For example, a course on the psychology of adults must consider the

connections of one's psychological change and development to the
historical and social conditions of one's time as well as
implications for the nation and planet of alternative images of
the "healthy" adult.

   2. A linking of education to experience, experience being a
"fundamental base for knowledge."[63] This is represented in the
feminist insistence on connecting the personal and the political.
For an instructor, this means facilitating insights into the
interrelationships among personal experiences and the socio-
political-historical structures. If one can see how one's own
experience connects, the ability to see other connections is
greatly enhanced.

   3. A linking of theory to practice and vice versa.

   4. An attention to process (the learning situation) as
inseparably related to product (learning outcome). One does not,
for example, "teach" democracy with authoritarian methods.

   Wholeness and Oneness. A perspective on wholeness includes
a transcendence (not just an integration, in the sense of
combining separable parts) of dichotomies and of views of the
world as discrete, separate, and indispensable parts, for
dichotomies and categories are conceptual tools which do not
exist separately either in human beings or in a holistic
universe.

   For education this means redressing the extreme compartmentalization of knowledge (or subject matter). For the curriculum
this means an acknowledgement of the arbitrariness of dividing
knowledge or the universe into categories, and a struggle to see
things whole. It means a struggle for an interdisciplinary
perspective, one that sees particular subjects and problems not
in an isolated context but as intricately interrelated with a
larger picture.[64] Most liberal arts programs have this as an aim
but they end up presenting multi-disciplinary rather than
interdisciplinary views to students, for students are required to
take courses in disciplines which remain discrete and unrelated
to each other. Faculty have been trained in disciplines and find
it difficult to move to an interdisciplinary approach.

   In addition, education needs to redress the extreme
compartmentalization and restriction of thinking processes to the
rational domain and the repression of the intuitive. For the
learning process, this means acknowledgment of the extreme
emphasis placed on rationality in education and balancing this by
facilitating intuitive ways of knowing as well as giving

attention to affective processes in the learning situation. For women and other groups who have been allowed to be more intuitive, this is a validation of themselves.

Dynamic and Organic. The educator needs to see both knowledge and students as continually evolving, growing, and developing. Knowledge and the universe need to be seen as continually developing rather than capturable in bits and pieces of "information" and "facts" (building blocks?) which are better seen as working hypotheses. Daly's argument that we must change the nouns of knowledge to verbs of knowing illustrates the way even language reflects static or dynamic concepts. Hence, with students seen as continually developing, as beings in process, becoming, and with knowledge viewed similarly, the instructor's role needs to include facilitation of the student's personal growth as well as of the student's knowledge and conceptual base, including the skills required for continued learning. There is no end point to development.

The instructor as co-learner attempts to provide conditions for the development of autonomous life-long learners capable of taking responsibility for, and caring for, themselves and their planet. In contrast, education which is based on what Freire in Education for Critical Consciousness calls banking education is a contradiction to this. Such education attempts to fill students with information and right answers (building blocks again?) possessed by the teacher/banker, thus subverting autonomy and responsibility by this process.

Transcendence of Either/Or. In addition to what has been suggested above, what would be useful in moving beyond either/or conceptualizations are (1) an explicit emphasis on categories as conceptual tools, not as reality itself ("the map is not the territory"); (2) a struggle to see the biases inherent in present categories (homosexual/heterosexual as an example); (3) presentation in the classroom of multiple interpretations of whatever topic is under consideration, and (4) continually asking, "Is there another way to look at that," and "does it have to be either/or?"

Inseparability of Observer and Observed. The inseparability of observer and observed or knower and known means that an instructor must be in touch with what her or his own world view is, make this explicit to students, and continually try to be cognizant of his or her world view as it changes. In addition, the instructor needs to assist students in recognizing the explicit and implicit world views which underlie the material they read (e.g., biases of theories) as well as to assist them in recognizing the fluidity of the categories "value" and "fact."

In doing these things, s/he is not involved in presenting <u>The Truth</u> to students but is sharing her/his own evolving "truths," and is facilitating students in their own searches. The question that should be continually raised is, "How would that be viewed by someone with a different world view?"

   <u>Relativity</u> <u>of</u> <u>Time</u> <u>and</u> <u>Illusion</u> <u>of</u> <u>Linearity.</u> If time is seen as a process and this is distinguished from clock time, then most contemporary education—predominantly based on clock time—is a denial of process time. It does not allow for the fact that some people need longer periods of time for their learning processes.

   The challenge to linear, direct, cause and effect relations also has implications for education. Direct cause and effect seems most similar to S-R learning theory, and challenging the absoluteness of this view allows learning to also be seen in terms of a more <u>complicated</u> process of <u>interactions</u> and as a spiral rather than a linear pattern of development.

   In summary, a shift to the world views underlying modern physics and feminism would have a number of implications for teaching and learning in higher education. Changes would include an interdisciplinary perspective and approach; a linking of education to experience; a perspective which views both students and knowledge as continually in process and evolving; a balance of rational and intuitive ways of knowing; an acknowledgment of the limits of objectivity and an articulation of one's own particular world view to students; and a continual emphasis on the interconnectedness and interdependence of people and the planet as a whole.

Concluding Comments

   In this paper I have described the radical shifts in world view that have taken place from classical physics to modern physics and from patriarchy to feminism, and have discussed some implications for teaching and learning in higher education. I will not summarize here, since I have done so at the end of each section. However, I do want to make some concluding comments.

   As educators concerned about the future, it is critical that we be able to help ourselves and others, including students, diagnose the possible sources of present conditions and problems (described earlier) so that we do not continue to merely treat symptoms and apply technical solutions[65] and so that we can struggle to envision sane and healthy alternatives.

It is my belief that the world views we hold are critical contributors to our actions and interactions, to the problems we see, and that the world views of both patriarchy and classical physics exert a strong and detrimental influence on all our endeavors. The world views underlying modern physics and feminism provide the basis for radically altering the dominant atomistic and reductionistic stance toward ourselves, other human beings, and the planet as a whole. Both provide the philosophical basis for a holistic world view that is potentially more humane, just, compassionate, full of care, responsible, and able to respond. I would like to close with one of my favorite quotations, Einstein's thoughts on the task before us:

> A human being is a part of the whole, called by us the "Universe," a part limited in time and space. He experiences himself, his thoughts and feelings as something separated from the rest--a kind of optical delusion of his consciousness. This delusion is a kind of prison for us, restricting us to our personal desires and to affection for a few persons nearest to us. Our task must be to free ourselves from this prison by widening our circle of compassion to embrace all living creatures and the whole of nature in its beauty. Nobody is able to achieve this completely, but the striving for such achievement is in itself a part of the liberation and a foundation for inner security.

APPENDIX

Definitions

The terms listed below are defined on the basis of their usage in this paper and, where relevant, the context is the United States.

Agency. An approach to the world which is based on assertion, mastery, self-protection, isolation, alienation, and formation of separations. Developed by David Bakan. Agency is contrasted with communion. (See "communion" below and footnote 39.)

Classical Physics. Newtonian physics. Physics which is based on a mechanistic and compartmentalized view of the universe. (See "modern physics" below.)

Communion. An approach to the world which is based on a sense of being at one with other organisms, a lack of separations, an openness, and non-contractual cooperation. Developed by David Bakan. Communion is contrasted with agency. (See "agency" above and footnote 39.)

Feminist. A person who is pro-woman, is aware of the ways in which women, and to some extent men, are oppressed by sex-biased beliefs and institutionalized practices; and wants to move from a patriarchal society to a more egalitarian one. In addition, feminists have a world view which sees the world as interrelated, whole, and dynamic and organic; are concerned with cooperation (rather than mastery) and with means and processes as well as ends; and strive to transcend culturally imposed definitions of feminine and masculine.
Note: Feminists differ along a number of dimensions, and while most feminists would agree with the first sentence, the second one would be less commonly shared for it implies the need for changes more fundamental than equality of women with men.

Feminine. An adjective used to describe a person with characteristics such as dependence, non-rationality, intuitive, emotionally expressive, reserved and lady-like, non-assertive, timid, receptive, and concerned with relations (as opposed to tasks). Usually ascribed to females, but is culturally based and changeable and needs to be distinguished from the categories "female" and "woman" which are biologically based (genetic, gonadal, and hormonal criteria used) and unchangeable.

Higher Education. Education in two and four-year colleges and universities. (In addition, the education discussed in the paper is primarily formal and classroom based.)

Masculine. An adjective used to describe a person with characteristics such as independence, rationality, emotionally inexpressive, aggressive, courageous, and dominant. Usually ascribed to males, but is culturally based and changeable and needs to be distinguished from the categories "male" and "man" which are biologically based (genetic, gonadal, and hormonal criteria used) and unchangeable.

Modern Physics. The relativity theory of Einstein and the quantum theory of Planck. Physics which is based on an organic and holistic view of the universe. (See "classical physics" above and footnote 8.)

Patriarchy. Commonly referred to as rule by one sex, the father, the patriarch, the male, and includes the consequent biases and instituionalized discrimination against women. In this paper it also includes the view of the world which emphasizes compartmentalization, separations and divisions, rationality, quantification, mechanistic processes, prediction and control (mastery), and a focus on ends which ignores means and processes.

NOTES

1. Anthony F.C. Wallace, "Revitalization Movements," American Anthropologist, Vol. 58, 1956, p. 254.

2. Society is used in the larger sense of culture in general, not merely societal organization. I did not use the word culture because of its frequent use to mean arts and sciences rather than the network of beliefs, practices, etc., that comprise a culture.

3. The reference to "planet" rather than merely "society" or other more localized term is used in the belief that it is critical that our concern include the planet rather than be restricted to a narrow focus on one's own life, locale, or nation. This is, in my mind, not only a pragmatic necessity if we are to survive on an interdependent planet but a moral and ethical imperative for care and concern about all life. I also realize I could have included "universe" here rather than "planet" but I have little conception of how we affect the universe (including past, present, and future in this category).

4. Conversation with Art Harkins, futurist, University of Minnesota, October 11, 1979.

5. "Non" here means "not only" rather than "not at all."

6. Fritjof Capra, The Tao of Physics (Berkeley, California: Shambhala, 1975), p. 149.

7. Robin Morgan, Going Too Far: The Personal Chronicle of a Feminist (New York: Random House, 1977), p. 290.

8. Some of Einstein's theories retain elements of classical concepts, for example, the one-to-one correspondence with reality. But for purposes of this paper it is not necessary to delve into these differences and I have included him in the

modern physics world view. See Zukav, especially page 25, for discussion of the classical elements in Einstein's theories.

9. Fritjof Capra, "The Tao of Physics: Reflections on the Cosmic Dance," Saturday Review, December 10, 1977, pp. 22.

10. Capra, 1975, p. 22.

11. Ibid., pp. 63, 202.

12. Gary Zukav, The Dancing Wu Li Masters (New York: William Morrow and Co., 1979).

13. Denis Postle, Fabric of the Universe (New York: Crown Publishers, 1976), p. 80.

14. It should be noted that Newton's laws are based on observation of the everyday world and predict events. Quantum mechanics is based upon experiments conducted in the subatomic realm. It predicts probabilities pertaining to subatomic particles and these particles cannot be observed directly. See Zukav, especially page 46, for further discussion.

15. Capra, 1977, p. 22; 1975, p. 68; Zukav, p. 57.

16. These "probability waves" are "abstract mathematical quantities related to the probabilities of finding the particles at particular points in space and at particular times" (Capra, 1977, p. 22).

17. Capra, 1975, p. 68.

18. Fritjof Capra, "Modern Physics and Eastern Mysticism," Journal of Transpersonal Psychology, No. 1, 1976, p. 23.

19. Bohm, 1975 as quoted in Capra, 1975, p. 138. See also discussion of Bohm's concept of the enfolding and unfolding universe and the implicate and explicate order in Re-Vision. This issue also includes discussion of neurophysiologist Pribam's concept of the holographic brain and the holographic universe (Re-Vision, Summer/Fall 1978).

20. Werner Heisenberg, Physics and Philosophy: The Revolution in Modern Science (New York: Harper and Row, 1958; Harper Torchbook Edition, 1962). Quoted by Capra, 1976, p. 23.

21. Capra, 1976, p. 32.

22. Postle, p. 151.

23.   Capra explains that particles can: "no longer be pictured as static three-dimensional objects . . . but must be conceived as four-dimensional entities in space-time.   Their forms have to be understood dynamically, as forms in space and time.   Subatomic particles are dynamic patterns which have a space aspect and a time aspect.   Their space aspect makes them appear as objects with a certain mass, their time aspect as processes involving the equivalent energy.   Relativity theory thus gives the constituents of matter an intrinsically dynamic aspect.   It shows that the existence of matter and its activity cannot be separated.   They are but different aspects of the four-dimensional space-time reality" (Capra, 1976).

24.   Capra, 1977, p. 23.

25.   Capra, 1975, p. 225.

26.   Ibid., p. 67.

27.   Ibid., p. 149.

28.   Ibid., pp. 149-150.

29.   Zukav, pp. 54-55.

30.   Joseph F. Rychlak, "Scientific Method," in Joseph F. Rychlak, A Philosophy of Science for Personality Theory (Boston: Houston Mifflin Co., 1968), p. 115.

31.   Zukav, p. 56.

32.   Rychlak, p. 115.

33.   Zukav, p. 115.

34.   Ibid.

35.   Ibid., p. 118.

36.   Heisenberg, 1962, p. 58.

37.   Zukav, p. 170.

38.   Itzhak Bentov, Stalking the Wild Pendulum: On the Mechanics of Consciousness (New York: E.P. Dutton, 1977), p. 3.

39.   Although Bakan says agency is more characteristic of males and communion of females, in his discussion of agency and communion in his book he has included more of the negative

aspects of masculinity and less of the negative aspects of femininity. So in terms of the perspective I am presenting, his description is closer to feminism than to stereotypic femininity; and the agency/communion distinction seems to provide a parallel to the distinction in world view between classical physics/modern physics.

40. David Bakan, The Duality of Human Existence (Boston: Beacon Press, 1966), p. 15.

41. Ibid., p. 15.

42. Sara Evans, Personal Politics (New York: Alfred A. Knopf, 1979), p. 219.

43. Morgan, p. 15.

44. Ibid., p. 16.

45. For scientific views of this concept, see Re-Vision and Pribam. In these publications, physicist Bohm and neurophysiologist Pribam discuss their intriguing theories of the hologram as a metaphor for the universe. See also Leonard's, The Silent Pulse.

46. Morgan, p. 16.

47. Kenneth P. Pelletier, Toward a Science of Consciousness (New York: Delta Books, 1978), p. 6.

48. Jodi Wetzel, "Defining Feminist Pedagogy: A Female Systems Model," paper prepared for Second Annual Conference on Women's Studies at the University of Minnesota (Conference Theme: "Common Differences"), Springhill Conference Center, April 22-23, 1979, p. 6.

49. Nancy Hartsock, "Fundamental Feminism: Process and Perspective," Quest, Vol. II, No. 2, Fall 1975, p. 73.

50. Morgan, p. 14.

51. Mary Daly, Beyond God the Father: Toward a Philosophy of Women's Liberation (Boston: Beacon Press, 1973), p. 27.

52. Morgan, p. 14.

53. Ibid., p. 5.

54. Hartsock, p. 71.

55. Morgan, p. 300.

56. Rosiska Darcy De Oliveira and Mireille Calame, "Liberation of Women: To Change the World and Re-Invent Life," Quest, Vol. 1, No. 1, Summer 1974, p. 66.

57. Most people are aware of cultural influences on one's perception of the world but may not be aware of biological factors. I do not mean genetic only. I do mean biological makeup in a very fundamental sense. For example, our eyes are a lens on the world and we can ask the question, "How would we 'see' the world if the sense receptors in our eyes had been constructed differently, e.g., X-ray vision or microscopic vision?"

58. In an earlier draft of this paper, I distinguished here the usage that means "publically verifiable" but the more I think about it, this has its own set of problematic assumptions.

59. I realize that this is not true of all feminists, but I believe the statement is accurate as a generalization in that, as I listen to research papers at conferences, it is feminists who feel compelled to state that their work is not objective and value free.

60. Anne Wilson Schaef, "It's Not Necessary to Deny Another's Reality in Order to Affirm Your Own--The Systematization of Dualism in the White Male Structure," an address delivered at the First National Conference on Human Relations in Education, June 20, 1978, Minneapolis, Minnesota, p. 12.

61. Daly, p. 43.

62. Mary Daly, Gyn/ecology: The Metaethics of Radical Feminism (Boston: Beacon Press, 1978), p. 23.

63. Hartsock, p. 78.

64. The very language we use is important to consider. For example, when I first wrote this I said "but as part of a larger whole." This became "but as intricately interrelated with a larger whole." This difference here is as significant as that between classical and modern physics conceptions of the world.

65. See Hazel Henderson, "Philosophical Conflict: Re-Examining the Goals of Knowledge," Public Administration Review, January/February 1975.

Ethnotronics and Human Learning Futures

Arthur M. Harkins and Earl C. Joseph

Ethnotronics is the new field of solid-state culture and cultural storage, retrieval, and creation. This paper explores its potentials and problems, emphasizing its implications for future human learning. It may be helpful to summarize the results of applying the anticipatory sciences to forecast the most likely futures for computers and human cultures for the 1980s, 1990s, and beyond. Extrapolated trends for some expected future computer developments have been extended to arrive at a forecast of the advancing "technologically driven" alternative futures.

These trends can be used to map the next four computer revolutions now visible for the 1980s, specifically:

1.   1978/1980:   Component processors leading to smart machines, people appliances, and components as end products.

2.   1980/1983:   Component computers forcing universal computer systems leading to hard programs and machines/computers as components.

3. 1983/1985: Component memory revolutionizing communications, leading to information appliances, smart memory (memory becoming components), and offices as machines in the 1990s.

4. 1985/1988: Component systems further revolutionizing institutions, leading to the demise of mainframe computers and allowing large segments of cultures to become machines in the 1990s.

These major technological transitions are not only forecastable, but also scientifically and technologically feasible for the near future. Obviously, they will have significant long-term future impacts on cultures and computer systems alike. In addition, they signal the need to step over some current "Maginot Lines"--perhaps not immediately, but certainly during the next decade.

Table I summarizes the general progression of life expectancy and related variables for humankind from the stone age up through the post-industrial age. All of these variables may be either directly or indirectly traced to the impact of human technologies. As we use the term here, and as it should be used everywhere, technologies are the humanly imputed "rules" which relate means and ends in organic and inorganic systems. They are common to all systems, and may be classified into two overlapping categories:

1. self-maintenance/self-change technologies; and

2. environmental exchange technologies.

Humans have codified technologies into what anthropologists call "culture," or the learned ability of the nervous sytem to identify phenomena and their patterned behaviors in a shared manner. Linguistically, individual cultures are thereby metaphors of human metatechnologies.

Table I: **Change Through the Ages of Humankind**

Era / Activity	Time Spent in Activity (Years)			
	Stone Age	Agricultural Age	Industrial Age	Post-Industrial Age
Discretionary	6	11	33	75
Work	6	11	11	10
Education	0	1	2	15
Sleeping/Eating	6	12	24	55
Average Life Span	18	35	70	150
Years in Era	Millions	1000s	100s	10s

Although human culture is shared, it empirically resides in the nervous system. In other words, it is organically "solid-state." The mystical notion of culture *sui generis* is precisely that--mystical. It takes a culturally programmed creature to recognize culture upon encountering it, and it takes a sophisticated creature to realize that culture can be encountered only inside the organism, for that is where the central nervous sytem resides. The physical analogue of culture in modern electronic computing systems is the microprocessor, or "chip." "Smart" chips already mimic some of the evolved functions of the human central nervous system; this is shown in Tables II and III.

Table II.   A Future History Map of Smart Machines

Smart Automobiles

1980s	Collision Avoidance
	Fault-Tolerance
	Long-Lived
	Driverless/Operatorless
1990s	Substitutions-for-Travel

Office-of-the-Future

1980s	Computerized Word Processing
1985+	Smart Office Machines
	People Amplifier Appliances
	Information Appliances
	Information Based Machines
1990s	Knowledge Based Systems
	Wearable/Carriable Office
	Automated Office
	Smart Office

Factory of the Future

1980s	Smart Machines
	Roboticized
1985+	Smart Factory
1990s	Microminiaturized Micro-Factory (MF)
2000s	MF Widespread Usage
2050s	MF Common

Table III: Communications Trends

Past

> 500 Years Ago
> Print--Movable Type

> 150 Years Ago
> Visual--Camera/Film

> 100 Years Ago
> Telecommunications--Telephone

> 50 Years Ago
> Audio--Radio/Transmitter/Vacuum Tube

> 30 Years Ago
> Audiovisual--TV/Picture Tube

> 20 Years Ago
> Data--Digital/Transistor/DP Computer

> 15 Years Ago
> Real-Time--Integrated Communications/Computer/Terminal

> 10 Years Ago
> Computer Networks--Distributed Processing/Minicomputer

> 5 Years Ago
> World Networks--Satellite

Today

> Word Processing--DP/Mini/Terminal
> Smart Telecom--VLSI/Microprocessor

Future

> 5 Years From Now
> Smart Data Management--Integrated Memory
> People Appliances--VLSI/Component/Memory

> 10 Years From Now
> Paperless Media--Electronic Economics
> Information Appliances--VHSI/Component Memory
> Knowledge Based Systems--Smart Memory

> 15 Years From Now
> Portable Office--Energy Economics

Joseph has identified future "smart" (non-purposively self-reprogramming) electronic chips, due to arrive in the 1980s, which will be powerful enough to store entire human subcultures. Along with other electronic devices, chips already store entire curricula. "Subcultures-on-a-chip" represent a quantum breakthrough, but "intelligent (purposively self-reprogramming) cultures-on-a-chil," achieved by interfacing several institutional chips, require protean reevaluation of what we mean by the concepts of <u>human</u>, <u>human culture</u>, and <u>learning</u>. This is indicated by Table IV. For example, "intelligent" chips will exhibit isomorphy of function with many of the evolved functions of the human central nervous system; in clusters, as with human sociocultural systems, they will include the capacity to <u>alter</u> shared understandings.

Table IV: Advancing Technology

Period (Age)	Human Augmentation/Assistant				
	Power	Skill	Control	Intelligence	Policy
Past					
1. Pre-Historic	Human	Human	Human	Human	Human
2. Pre-Industrial					
(Agricultural Age)	Animal	Human	Human	Human	Human
3. Industrial Age	Machine	Human	Human	Human	Human
4. Mass Consumptive	Machine	Machine	Human	Human	Human
Present					
5. Automation					
(Computer Age)	Machine	Machine	Machine	Human	Human
Future-Post Industrial					
6. Cybernetic Age	Machine	Machine	Machine	Machine	Human
7. Future Age	Machine	Machine	Machine	Machine	Machine

Ethnotronic systems can be expected to develop in a number of ways in the future. For example, a current trend is the progression of these systems along a number of paths, namely: the office-of-the-future, people appliances, smart machines, intelligent/smart terminals, knowledge-based decision support systems, information appliances, convivial machines (including convivial computers), and the like. These trends are expected to evolve into wave after wave of smarter and more convivial ethnotronic systems. Some current research is resulting in the development of bridges necessary for the more sophisticated ethnotronic systems which will be appearing during the 1980s and 1990s. These include:

1. a growing list of primitives which are also becoming more complex;

2. new languages for both users and designers of ethnotronic systems;

3. long-range forecasting and assessment studies of future designs and impacts; and

4. prototype design analysis.

The Fundamentals of Ethnotronics

In order to communicate effectively about probable and possible futures, it is necessary to develop a new language including entirely new words and phrases as well as new meanings for old words, such as "smart machines," "people amplifier appliances," "primitives," and, of course, the term "ethnotronics" itself.

Harkins introduced the concept of ethnotronics in 1976,[1] following a conversation with Drew University anthropologist R. Wescott. Subsequently, a second paper was published by Harkins and Joseph which further elaborated the "primitives," or fundamental elements, of the idea.[2]

Ethnotronics must be clearly defined in order to distinguish it from such possible concepts as "psychotronics" and "sociotronics." With valuable assistance from Stanford University anthropologist R. Textor, we propose to regard ethnotronics as "an approach to the study of a range of inorganic machines exhibiting shared functional characteristics." On the basis of this definition, we have developed a cultural approach to this range involving the following:

1. the scientific and philosophical analysis of the communicational nature(s) of "dumb" (non-self-reprogramming)
   interactive in-organic devices;

2. the scientific and philosophical analysis of the proto-
   symboling and communicational nature(s) of "smart" (non-
   purposefully self-reprogramming), interactive inorganic
   devices (or information appliances);

3. the scientific and philosophical analysis of the symboling and communicational nature(s) of "intelligent"
   (purposefully self-reprogramming), interactive inorganic
   devices (or human surrogates);

4. the study of the impact of human (or other organic)
   symboling and communicational influences upon the
   development and future of such inorganic devices; and

5. the study of the existing and probable/possible cross-
   impacts upon human (or other organic) systems of such
   inorganic devices, including the possibility of
   hybrids.

We also propose that the central focus in the use of the concept
of ethnotronics be the notion of intelligent purposefulness, or
the extent to which human (or other) organic, non-human
inorganic, or hybrid entities are able to self-guide their own
evolutions through internal logico-decisioning structures capable
of self-reprogramming. This capability may be extended
hypothetically to systems of intelligently purposeful inorganic
entities, or solid-state sociocultural systems. Obviously, there
is a range of ethnotronic system types and "levels;" this is
indicated in Table V.

Some Applications of Ethnotronics:
People Amplifiers

Most computers are universal in the sense that they are
capable of executing any algorithm or primitive function that is
expressable by a set of procedure-oriented program steps. The
set of unique facilities or capabilities provided by a specific
computer, however, often do not "match" those which are required
to perform or amplify a specific function. As a result, certain
tasks are easier or possible on some computers and impossible on
others. The main reason for introducing terminology like "smart
machines," "people amplifier appliances," "information
appliances," "knowledge-based decision support systems," and the
like is to suggest with such jargon the procedures, or class of
primitive functions, that computers either automate or make easy.

If it were not for such implied features, the user would have to code, or program, explicitly required software and add to the computer's hardware architecture in order to "design" a machine for each desired task.

Table V: Ethnotronic Systems and Cultures
People Amplifiers

Proto-Ethnotronic Machines

    Shelters--Weather Control Amplifiers
    Tools--Muscle Power Amplifiers
    Transport--Mobility Amplifiers
    Mechanical Machines--Skill Amplifiers
    Electromechanical Machines--Quality-of-Life Amplifiers
    Computers--Math, Record-Keeping and Data Processing Amplifiers
    Intelligent/Smart Terminals--Procedure Oriented Task Amplifiers

Primitive (Modern) Ethnotronic Machines

    Calculator (portable, electronic)--Math Skill Amplifier
    Smart Calculator--Profession-Related Math Skill Amplifier
    People Amplifier Appliance--Profession Skill Amplifier

Ethnotronic Machines: Smart and Communicating Appliances

    Information Appliance--Information Use Amplifier
    Smart People Amplifier Appliance--Profession Amplifier
    Component Ethnotronics--Imbeddable "Smarts" including:
                Teacher-on-a-Chip
                Course-on-a-Chip
                Library-on-a-Wafer
                School-on-a-Wafer
                Office-on-a-Wafer
                Management Information System-on-a-Wafer
                Institutions-on-a-Wafer
                Cultures-on-a-Wafer

    The needs of computer users and rapid advances in computer technology have historically combined to spawn ever increasing application arenas. These have also stimulated new developments in computers and led to still more novel features such as "imbedding," new means of communicating with computers, and new programming systems.

The question that now arises is, "What new features and applications will future ethnotronic systems require and bring about?" One way of defining the "power" of a people amplifier is by determining the extent to which a user may specify "what" he or she wants accomplished without detailing "how." For example, the user employs guidelines, constraints, and prompting to "set up" an activity for the system to perform or amplify. Conversely, in the case of purposeful ethnotronics, the amplifier, or machine, determines the need to assist the user and "prompts" the user by making him or her currently aware that "help" is available. In either instance, the user can then request a needed "result." The complex primitives imbedded in the machine may then determine various procedures which "match" the request and "try" these procedures by using "deductive reasoning," problem-solving mechanisms, or opportunity-generating algorithms. The "dialogue" between the user and the ethnotronic system amplifies the individual user in the following ways:

1. by drawing upon cultural knowledge bases;

2. by translating these knowledge bases in such a way that the user may apply them in real-time for the task at hand; and

3. by providing information and, perhaps more importantly, procedures (processes, skills, etc.) that both the machine and the individual can work together to apply.

This example illustrates only a few of the many characteristics of people-amplifying ethnotronic appliances.

The process of "educating," "culturizing," or "profession-alizing" ethnotronic systems is, in general, quite different from the processes which cultures employ for people. (The same processes used with people will eventually work on machines, however.) In practice, ethnotronic systems will be professional-ized, educated, or culturized by more direct "plug-in" methods, including the following:

1. adding to, deleting from, revising, or updating the system's data/information storage banks;

2. loading additional (software/courseware) programs, algo-rithms and/or primitive functions into its memory;

3. adding hardware modules in order to:
   a. update/revise/convert/transform the system;
   b. add additional primitive functions; or
   c.alter the system's structural architecture. These
      modules can be used to add, delete, or revise memory,

processes, communication channels, satellite communication channels, voice recognition and reply, languages, sensors, actuators, and so on. In other words, a new "professional" expertise can be "plugged in" to an ethnotronic system, providing it with what essentially amount to more "arms," "senses," "mobility," communicability," "manipulability," and so on.

4. modifying the ethnotronic system _itself_ in one or more purposeful modes/abilities of self-organizing, self-reconfiguring, self-programming, problem-solving, self-adapting, learning, synthesizing, creating, etc.;

5. enabling direct communication with the user, which might involve learning in cooperation (synergy mode) with the person or receiving commands/information/instructions from him or her;

6. electronically "sensing," or connecting into, other machines, including:
   a. other ethnotronic systems;
   b. satellite communication, giving worldwide access-ability
   c. computer data banks;
   d. telephone or data communication channels which allow the system to "talk" with people or data banks;
   e. electronic libraries which give the system access to most stored cultural knowledge.

7. enabling purposive cultural discourse with other ethnotronic systems to "learn" what other such systems have "learned"—and with people other than the one being amplified.

These latter points in particular posit the emergence of new cultures which are both "purely" ethnotronic (that is, machine-to-machine) and human-ethnotronic (that is, human-to-machine).

Thus, professionalizing, culturizing, and/or educating an ethnotronic appliance should involve no more than the simple "plugging in" of specific modes. The availability of appropriate "teaching" modules will make it possible to "educate" quickly and dynamically these future ethnotronic systems to different "cultures" or "professions" from one moment to another with a minimum of effort. This educative process will be vastly different from that which must be employed in teaching humans, since it will involve nothing more than adding appropriate functions and information to the system when and where needed.

Of course, this will require a certain investment of time, money, design and/or programming pre-process. However, once an ethnotronic system has been designed and built or programmed, mass production will allow millions--or even billions--of such systems to be "updated" or "educated" with a minimum of effort. This, of course, is a major difference between ethnotronic machines and people; while people must be educated individually, ethnotronic machines will be able to be educated almost simultaneously. We can therefore posit a hierarchy of the costs of educating various sytems, beginning with the most expensive and least efficient and ending with the least expensive and most efficient:

1. Nature/Natural Systems

2. Human/Human Systems/Societies

3. Machine/Dumb Systems

4. Ethnotronic Machine/Smart Systems

Naturally, it will be necessary to impose limits, or "wired-in" controls, on interactive ethnotronic systems. A _purposive_ ethnotronic people amplifier appliance with the ability to "think" or "do" on its own will attempt to achieve its goal of amplifying "its" person at all costs. An uncontrolled ethnotronic system, for example, might "call up" the President of the United States in order to "assist" a 6-year-old who is having a political conversation with a friend. Assuming that the system has access to communications networks, and that it "learns" that the President is the one who "makes" the policies in question, this would be a perfectly sensible move. Unless the system were instructed to do so, it would not prioritize and instead would simply assume that its task of assisting or amplifying "its" person took precedence over anything else.

This dedication on the part of the system, while it might be annoying to the President, would be essentially non-threatening. But what if the system "perceived" a need for an illegal or covert action which was "triggerable" via an information transfer from another purposive system? Obviously, this sort of thing would have to be prevented. It would either have to be "wired-out" as a possibility for the machine or stopped by means of a network of "police" machines whose functions would include preventing illegal, costly, or simply ridiculous actions on the part of communicating ethnotronic systems.

Now envision the possibility of "cultures-on-a-chip," or "cultures-on-a-wafer"--ethnotronic systems as media similar in function (butnot in applicability) to those common in science fiction novels. Imagine that a person using such a system could converse with it in order to test out a particular future by causing the future to occur and "unfold" via dialogue with the system. For example, the user might test out decisions on a political issue before making a "real" decision, or experiment with "what if" dialogues with an ethnotronic system which simulates the culture. Such dynamic "paperless electronic books" would provide very different interactive media from conventional books, TV, or even most computers. The possibilities, in short, are endless.

Conclusions

1. Ethnotronic systems are generalized and/or specialized tools or appliances which may be used to manipulate a collection (subset) of human knowledge for the purpose of amplifying individuals and/or groups.

2. The development of ethnotronic systems is currently at the threshold of realization. Very crude versions are already in use, and we can expect that this branch of science and technology will become very active in the near future. For quite some time, however, the emerging systems will be in a state of flux. Even at this early stage, however, some of the future features of ethnotronic systems are beginning to fit together.

3. Since the birth of computers, the notion of higher-level systems of assisting people has led to a proliferation of special and general-purpose embodiments. The myriad systems available, not to mention the multiplicity of programming languages, has frequently made the application of these tools very complex. With the advent of the microprocessor, ethnotronic systems are becoming both technically and economically feasible.

4. Finally, ethnotronic systems can be used to amplify and help people. They are modern tools which incorporate a vast amount of complexity. Their interface with people is simple and convivial, and they provide powerful functions (primitives) for transforming cultural information algorithms into knowledge which an individual can use in his or her everyday life.

NOTES

1. A.M. Harkins, "Notes on Ethnotronics," Futurics, Vol. I, No. 2 (1976).

2. A.M. Harkins and E.C. Joseph, "Prolegomena to Ethnotronics," Journal of Cultural and Educational Futures, Vol. I, No. 2 (1979), pp. 2-3.

Women and Children as Builders of the Future

Eleonora Barbieri Masini

Images of the future change the present and build the future. The image is the antithesis of the present, but at the same time, it is not pure fantasy. The image is built with the seeds of change which are found in the process of human history. Hence images of the future are not pure fantasy but are creations built upon what is changing, upon what is already in the process of history to which each person, each group adds their specificity to make their images of the future emerge. The possibility of the future is captured and brought to light. All people could be "builders of images of the future" if they nurture the seeds of change. However I believe that only some people are capable of this--the people who are in some way out of the mainstream of the social system, which by its very nature tries to maintain itself.

I will now speak of the seeds of change and those in whom I believe these seeds of change can be found. They are individuals who:

a) see the link between the present and the future in the image of the future;

b) realize that the roots of the images are in the seeds of change themselves, seeds which are integral to the process of human history

c) have the capacity to listen as well as the capacity to add their own unique contributions to the group and to the culture, thus bringing change to the forefront;

d) realize the dynamism of the present through recognition of alternatives in the present and in the future.

Many individuals have the capacity to store and nurture the seeds of change. I believe that such individuals are the hope of the future; however, some, more than others, will emerge as the catalysts for change. They are the individuals who for the most part, are outside the mainstream of the social system. They are the oppressed, those on the margin of the system. They include the politically oppressed, the ones who are silent, and the ones whose voices are not heard, unless more people in the mainstream of the social system take the risk to listen. They are the ones who are not stuck in the structure of the system. They were not builders of the structure nor are they actively involved in maintaining the system. Women and children are, for the most part, outside the mainstream of the social system. Women and children have a capacity to be the storehouses of the seeds of change. This seemingly springs from a capacity to sense the energy and the authentic feelings within the structure of the system.

In this paper, I shall concentrate on women and children as repositories of the seeds of change.

How can we bring to light the capacity of women and children to harbor the seeds of change? How can we use this capacity as the filter through which other possibilities are seen? It is a capacity for growth and change which is not built on the demise of rationality but on a union of rationality with intuition and emotion. What follows is a discussion of these capacities in women and in children as builders of the future.

Women's Capacities

Women have developed, over many centuries, their capabilities to harbor and to nurture the seeds of change. Such capabilities are the basis on which the image of the future is built and at the same time provide a basis on which women can create power for themselves.

These capabilities have been kept in "private spaces" by women themselves as well as by men. However, if this potential is allowed to emerge and is communicated among women, it can be the basis of a network of changes which may be stronger than any revolution. Such a network of changes would permeate the nooks and crannies of social structures and transform them. These capacities go much further than the recognition of women's rights. They are built on the assumption that women have a power in "private spaces" which has not emerged into "public space" and which sometimes has even been suppressed in private. If the power found in "private spaces" should emerge into the "public space," there would be an image of women built by women. This

could lead to futures different from the ones emerging out of the
present, a present which was built by men using men's logics.
Awareness of this power may spread from woman to woman in every
culture and perhaps to men who are able to understand it.

These qualities, which are the basis for nurturing the seeds
of change and hence building the image of the future, can be
divided into individual and social capacities. At the individual
level:

a) Women can experience and thrive in complex situations
    where intellect, intuition and emotion are all involved.
    They are able to live among family tensions, many of
    which have been overcome by women with their capacity to
    grasp rapidly the complexity of situations. The needs
    and aspirations of men and children, the possibilities
    and difficulties of material as well as non-material
    life can be grasped together in their dynamism through
    such capacity. This capacity to integrate and to
    synthesize is extremely important in a world of growing
    complexity. The on-going trend toward fragmentation of
    problems and a specialization of solutions is not
    appropriate in the complex world of today. Women have
    in their hands, minds, and hearts the possibility of
    overcoming such fragmentation and specialization. In
    addition to the capacity to act integratively in complex
    situations can be added the capacity to act rapidly,
    spurred not simply by the intellect but also by an
    intuitive grasp of the complex links among events.

b) Another individual capacity which has developed in women
    is that of changing interests and focuses of concern
    rapidly. This capacity is extremely important to the
    concept of anticipatory learning, learning for the pur-
    pose of innovation and change, not conservation.[1] This
    capability would be extremely important in a world where
    interests and emphases change so rapidly. Again, this
    constitutes the basis of a power which is not currently
    available to men accustomed to linear thinking and to
    slower rates of change. However, this capacity could be
    developed by men who understand the need for it in
    present times. Nothing prevents such capabilities from
    spreading.

c) Women are also capable of great sacrifice and
    dedication. Unfortunately this capacity has often been
    exploited. But in times when such capabilities will be
    needed, when there is scarcity of resources, it will be
    very important.

d) Another individual capacity of women is related to time-dimensions. There are societies which have no knowledge of control over nature. The division of time into work and rest is related to rhythms and cycles of nature. Time is not considered as an abstract category; it is part of life itself. However, this does not preclude a sense of eschatological time. In such societies women are more at ease, for they are capable of living in natural rhythms. This type of society has been labelled as pre-industrial and we can see these characteristics still present in many developing nations.[2]

There are also societies with a high degree of external control over nature. Time in these societies is divided into seconds, minutes, hours, etc. It is typical of the industrial society. In this type of society, women as well as time are fragmented; sources of this fragmentation include the division and tension between work and home.

There is a third type of society where relationships are ecologically integrated with nature. In this type of society, time is not fragmented but is part of a continuum. The difference is that society is not dominated by nature but is in harmony with it. Time is an integration of rationality and emotion. This type of society could provide a model for the future where women would be very well adapted.

All these capacities possessed by individuals can be utilized. Society has for the most part, hidden them but these capacities can be developed and brought into the "public space" from the "private space." The power of women can emerge if such capacities are developed. It would be a different kind of power from the one used and developed by men, not oriented toward competition and conflict but toward the lessening of tension, the development of community, and living in harmony with nature.

Women have many social capacities complementary to the bases of power which women can have, at the individual level:

a) Women are becoming increasingly aware of being peripheral to the centers of political, economic, and communicational power. This makes women more apt to understand other marginal people, such as minorities, old people, children and Third World people. Today is, I believe, an historic moment for those on the periphery, as well as an awakening awareness of peripheries. Toynbee's theory of the great external and internal proletariat may be useful in this context.

Thus women can build what the liberation movements call "liberation zones" where marginal people recognize themselves, organize themselves, find their common needs and aspirations, and develop their ways of defense. In this way the seeds of change, which are in the process of history and are sources of visions for humankind, can be cultivated.

b) Women are capable of opposing trends which focus on growth solely in the economic sphere and of fostering more complete development. Women understand that economic growth is not enough, that what is needed is education, responsibility, awareness, communication, and exchange. These are possible only in an atmosphere of total development, involving the whole of the person and not in a society oriented to produce economic growth. Few men in the public sphere deeply understand this, but it could be brought into the public sphere by women, offering the possibility of a significantly different society.

c) Women understand that governmental and intergovernmental decisions are apt to be overridden by bureaucratic and administrative constraints; women are more willing to work outside governmental structures where the activities are run informally, flexibly and directly.[3]

The above are all capabilities that can build the power of women. This power can be used to shape the world rather than make revolutions. It is a power which, if women are aware of it and communicate among themselves, will build images of the future that are much stronger than any image built in imitation of men's perception of reality.

I have described the sort of capacities women may develop. These capacities, which are primarily in the "private space," can be reinforced and transferred to the "public space." This is a power which is different and goes well beyond the power of men prevalent for centuries. Men's power is built on overcoming others, rather than finding a way of living with the others; it values profit, whether on the material or non-material level, rather than holistic gain and growth. It is dictated by a belief in "more consumption, more production," rather than making do with what is. Some women have also become allied with this kind of power and belief structure. They have been influenced and polluted by men; women who do not develop these views have often been considered with scorn. Why not change the trend so that men are influenced, even polluted, by women to develop a power of a different nature, based on the individual and socio-structural capacities of women?

The world we are living in is built, whether by men or women, on principles of overcoming and profiting. However, these principles are not working well anymore. We seem to have reached the limits in material and non-material terms. In material terms, we are increasingly aware of the limits of the physical world; in non-material terms, the young are uninspired and unhappy and they seek rewards different from the material ones. The power that has existed up until now has given material satisfaction and non-material unhappiness, and the young resort to drugs, suicide or terrorism. Perhaps we could find in women the possibility of a different power, based on different principles. If women pass this on to men we could have a different world. This would, of course, be built on women's capacity to nurture the seeds of change and to build alternative images of the future out of which a different future may emerge.

Children's Capacities

The year 1979 was designated the Year of the Child. Much has been written and said about children but little consideration has been given to the rights and capacities of children, their social roles and power. Children are usually considered objects rather than subjects. E. Boulding describes the bases for the legal status of children as follows:

> The legal ground for assigning minority of "non-age" to children and youth is that they are physically, emotionally and socially immature beings who must be protected by adults until they reach full maturity and can cope on their own with society. In general, the term children is used for those under 12 or 14. This means that society is protecting itself by legal means from having to incorporate young persons into full participation in society for what may be as long as half or more of the lifetime of those persons.[4]

In a paper on "Reconstructing Childhood," A. Nandi suggests that:

> In the modern world, the politics of childhood begins with the fact that maturity, adulthood, growth and development are important values in the dominant cultures of the world. They do not change colour when used to describe the transition from childhood to adulthood. Once we have used these concepts and linked the processes of physical and mental change to a valued state of being or becoming, we have already negatively estimated the child as an inferior version of the adult--as a lovable, spontaneous, delicate being

who is also simultaneously dependent, unreliable and succourant and, thus, needs to be guided, protected and educated as our ward. Indirectly, we have also already split the child into two parts: his childlikeness as an aspect of childhood which is approved by the society and his childishness as an aspect of childhood which is disapproved by the society.[5]

I believe that children have a power that adults have lost. They have the capacity to store and to cultivate, in a way similar to women, the seeds of change which are in the process of human history. Such seeds are also the basis for images of the future held by children, but which are not acknowledged or recognized. I have carried out some research in Italy on images of the future held by children. The research has shown that, when children imagine their future, it is a future which is in the process of history and not mere fantasy. Children in poor parts of Italy imagine a future in which work is stable, marriage is chosen, and violence absent. It is the antithesis of the present, built on a desire for change which they are finding in the social process.

When children of various socio-economic backgrounds are asked to plan the future, it is a future where the hunger of many has to be overcome by the solidarity of others, where the solitude of people in the metropolis must be tempered by friendship. Children bring these out in deeper, more involved, more global images than adults do.

When children are stimulated to express themselves about their future through offering them very simple media and the role of the researcher is minimal, we find comments like the following emerging from children in Naples:

'After the destruction of the Earth . . . will we create a New One?'

'Flowers will be pointed. . . or varied in colours. . . eh, in any case they'll always be different.'

'Instead of TV, a theatre 50 km. wide in which everyone acts.'

'The possibility of civil war and the subsequent destruction of all food sources except the roots. We should go into the country to talk with the farmers today about it.'

'To repopulate the country.'

'Children and old people working together.'

'Hot air balloons, pocket size (rechargeable) flying saucers, horses, cable cars as transport.'

'Communication by multiway TV or drums.'

For children, change is obviously always present.[6] Children, when given the possibility, are capable of building their futures their schools, their sector of town, their town, their society.

In the same project, video taping and a photocopying machine were experimented with in Oxford with similar results. Children easily learned new behaviors and expressed integrative, dynamic images of futures. In Naples, access to this more expensive technology did not exist, but at the same time free constructions of "future inventions" using discarded materials (toilet paper tubes, cloth, wood and plastic industrial remnants, tinfoil, etc.) evoked a spontaneity not possible in more fixed "block play." Children put pieces together because "red and round looks good here," or "the solar energy transformer should be here" because the loose parts fitted well.[7]

This is an indication of what children envision in the processes of change. We should be able to listen more to them, to understand more how they perceive the present, and hence to work to change the present in terms of a different image of the future. We should avoid destroying this capacity, this sensitivity which is akin to capturing the mood of a conversation between parents or watching a flower opening up. From these capacities, which are individual and societal at the same time, may emerge a power, a social role which is based, not on overcoming, but on living together symbiotically. The cry of children in Italy--Rome, Naples, or Milan--for friendship beats upon the ears of today's adults.

Children and women are outsiders. They are not the builders of the present, crisis-ridden social system. We may change the future if we are able to listen to them, and to acknowledge their special kind of invisible power that can change the world. The change would be from a world in crisis to one of revival and perhaps of total material and non-material development of the human being.

NOTES

1. J. Botkin, M. Elmandjra, M. Malitza, No Limits to Learning, a Report to the Club of Rome (Oxford: Pergamon Press, 1979).

2. O. Nudler, "On Types of Civilizations: A Comparison Through Three Dimensions," paper presented at the II Meeting on Visions of Desirable Societies, WFSF 1979.

3. E. Boulding, Women in the XXI Century World (New York: John Wiley, Halstead Press, 1977).

4. E. Boulding, "Children's Rights and World Order--A Global Study of the Role and Status of Children and Youth in the 1970's," March 1977, Draft.

5. A. Nandi, "Reconstructing Childhood," Paper prepared for the World Future Studies Federation meeting on "Visions of Desirable Societies," Mexico, 1979.

6. Raymond Lorenzo, "Children Communicating Future," Paper prepared for the VI World Conference on Future Research, Cairo, 1978.

7. Ibid.

Section IV
Action and Examples for the Present and the Future

Section IV
Action and Examples for the
Present and the Future

INTRODUCTION

The application of a futures focus to school-based education is the theme of Section IV. Whether proposed or already in practice, the programs and recommendations discussed in the six articles selected for inclusion in this section involve learners and teachers at varied levels throughout the life span. Of necessity, these six articles represent only a sampling of approaches to futurizing school-based education, but an attempt has been made to include a varied set of innovative approaches. Innovation, by definition, involves risk taking with no guarantee of success or longevity. However it can be hoped that the recommendations of Edward F. Carpenter, Leonore W. Dickmann, Paul A. Wagner, Dennis R. Falk, Phoebe P. Hollis, and Carlos A. Torre will be given careful and thoughtful consideration.

Carpenter shares with us a description of a new urban high school, the A. Philip Randolph Campus High School, opened in the fall of 1979. It was developed out of a collaborative attempt by the City College of the City University of New York and the New York City Board of Education to ameliorate some of the current problems in urban education and in the education of adolescents for participation in the world of the future. Carpenter asserts that:

> What will place the A. Philip Randolph Campus High School into the realm of the future will be its futuristic curriculum; teaching-learning processes; staff development program; organizational structure; awareness of current societal problems and their projection into the year 2000; incorporation of the distinguished college faculty into meaningful participatory roles; utilization of such college resources as the Computer Center; . . . and the introduction of futures courses into the high school.

Because this school is so new, much remains to be reported. However it is helpful, as Hood and Shane so cogently pointed out in Section I, to have change models to refer to regardless of the model's stage of development.

Implicit in Carpenter's description of a model for an urban high school is a concern with developing in students positive future focused role images. This is a central concern in Dickmann's proposal, "A Futures Curriculum for Symmetry," in which she offers a broad framework within which to construct curriculum. Dickmann suggests that "the seven frameworks of aliveness, purposiveness, loving, intelligence, truthfulness, spirituality, and morality are organizing centers for providing for the 'who' and a focused role image." In addition she contends that these seven frameworks, along with eight broad categories of human concerns "provide an holistic perspective for viewing curriculum as a plan to help students move toward completeness as human beings in the human scene." An easy to use set of starter strategies to foster an understanding of symmetry is also provided.

Rather than discussing curriculum in the broadest sense, Wagner focuses his concerns on one aspect of the curriculum-- science--and presents a well developed case for a significant change in science education. Given what is now known about rapid changes in information and about shifts in paradigms or world views, he raises questions about the sort of education likely to equip future scientists with the competencies and attitudes necessary to work within a novel research paradigm. Since one or more of the sciences will likely require a new research paradigm in upcoming years, it is imperative that future oriented science educators anticipate this need and prepare to include philosophic aspects of "doing science" at each step in the science curriculum sequence.

At one level Wagner is critiquing the education of scientists as professionals. In "Futuristics and the Professional Education of Social Workers," Falk discusses a new and innovative approach to issues similar to the ones Wagner raises about outcomes of education. Falk describes how one professional school (the School of Social Development at the University of Minnesota-Duluth) has used a futuristic orientation as a major component in designing its educational program. Within this, there is a strong emphasis on the change function of the social work profession. Falk notes that, as an outgrowth of the social development model, faculty and students began to image a future characterized by concerns with social equality, justice, and the fulfillment of basic human needs. This may indicate similarities between the social development model and Dickmann's curriculum for symmetry.

In "Forecasting the Speech Communication Curriculum of the Future," Hollis reports her Delphi study of issues existing within the discipline of speech communication and implications for the curriculum. The study grew out of a perceived lack of defined objectives within the field and as it relates to the larger academic community. In addition there was a concern about over-specialization and fragmentation of the discipline. The study is built on the assumption that practitioners of a discipline shape that field consciously and unconsciously, and that the world views individuals hold shape expectations about the future. Similar assumptions are also crucial to the articles by Perreault and Wagner. Studies similar to Hollis' would certainly be useful and provocative in other disciplines.

To round out the variety of actions and examples selected for inclusion in Section IV is Torre's article, "Cybernetics of Communication In Academic Life." Social Cybernetics, as developed by Waldemar De Gregori, is a method for training individuals to improve, at a conscious level, their ways of thinking and mental functions. Torre reports the development and use of this approach in a workshop type course, "Cybernetics of Communication." The course provides an innovative approach to the acquisition of basic skills so necessary in an academic setting. It is built on a synthesis of several theoretical models, both old and new, producing an approach that is developmental and holistic.

The A. Phillip Randolph Campus High School: School for the Future

Edward F. Carpenter

Among the many problems besetting our cities, the sad plight of education and the failure of the public schools to prepare students successfully for living in a pluralistic-technological society are of major concern. Indeed, parents as taxpayers, employers and union officials all deplore the poor level of educational attainment of these youths, and are demanding reform in American public education. As Hazel Hertzberg said, "The endless process of reforming public education usually takes one of two approaches: the first, comprehensive, while the other focuses on single aspects of education--the curriculum, the organization of the school, the composition of the student population--as the vital key to change."[1] Competency Based Teacher Education is one of the attempts to bring about some reform in the educational system. This attempt to improve education through making the teacher more accountable has brought about even more controversy within the field because of the lack of specific definitions of what are "competencies." The Campus High School, now renamed the A. Philip Randolph Campus High School, represents the collaborative attempt of the City College of the City University of New York City and the Board of Education of New York City to solve some of the problems currently associated with educating the urban student for participation in the world of the future.

The school is fortunate to be named after A. Philip Randolph, who died May 16, 1979, after celebrating his 90th birthday. In a real sense it is bound to the future in that Mr. Randolph was a scholar, civil rights leader, unionist, sage and seer. His entire life was a testimony to one who peered into the future and saw worlds where unity existed and justice prevailed.

The agreement between the City College of New York and the Board of Education of New York City to implement the planning and

operation of the A. Philip Randolph Campus High School is
contained in the Board of Higher Education Resolution, Calendary
#9 of May, 1978; and for the Board of Education in Calendary #LO-
2 of May 24, 1978. The items for operating the school state:

*   that the employer of the staff of the A. Philip Randolph
    Campus High School shall be the Board of Education.
    While all appropriate variances to the contracts should
    be considered and negotiated insofar as they can be
    supportive of innovative efforts in terms of College-
    Board of Education cooperation, City College agrees to
    the observance of contractual arrangements between the
    Board of Education, the U.F.T., and the C.S.A. with
    respect to employees of the A.P.R.C.H.S.

*   that applicants for the principalship will be screened
    by a committee constituted in accordance with the
    established policies and procedures of the Board of
    Education.

*   that the principal will be associated with the City
    College School of Education by holding an appropriate
    adjunct administrative position.

*   that the faculty of the A.P.R.C.H.S. will be appointed
    in the usual manner.

*   that Department Chairmen who function in administrative/
    supervisory positions be eligible to hold adjunct fac-
    ulty status.

*   that an Advisory Policy Board of Curriculum and Instruc-
    tion be established for the A. Philip Randolph Campus
    High School.

The function of the Advisory Policy Board is to make proposals
and recommendations to the principal on the design of instructional programs and curricula. The Advisory Board consists of
these members:

The Dean of the School of Education

The Dean of the College of Liberal Arts

Three members of the City College Faculty--to be designated
by the President

Three teachers, including at least two members of the high
school's professional staff--to be selected by the teachers

Three members of the High School's administrative staff--to be selected by the principal

Four parents[2]

Some of the elements of the Agreement between the Board of Education and the College are cited to illustrate that there is both a legal and formal relationship between the signers of the Agreement. Furthermore, the constraints of the Agreement show that the high school, although experimental in nature, must comply with all of the regulations that every other New York City high school must adhere to. It is, however, apparent that the constitutency of the Advisory Board is unique where faculty members of the college and the high school are to interact with parents as coequals.

There is little doubt that, of all the levels of education, the high school has been the most resistant to educational reform. For the most part, the high school's relationship to college has been characterized by a marked lack of cooperation at best, and by mutual suspicion and recrimination at worst. As a high school of the future, the A. Philip Randolph Campus High School is committed to remedying these conditions through a pioneering venture in cooperation, innovation, enrichment, and institutional assessments.

It is anticipated that among the more unique features characterizing A. Philip Randolph Campus High School will be the following:

1. It is to enroll a cross-section of students from the areas of Manhattan, the South Bronx, Queens, and Brooklyn.

2. The range of student characteristics is to be comparable to that found in other New York City comprehensive high schools.

3. The school is to provide for the student's personal and social growth through a viable program of individual and group counseling.

4. The school will assure that students are graduated with skills important for successful entry into college or those skills that are marketable.

5. Close community relationships will occur through student participation for academic credit in structured internships, apprenticeships, or service activities in community agencies.

6. Career and vocational outlooks may be expanded through involving the students with the diverse programs found in the Center for the Performing Arts, the Urban Legal Center, the Bio-Medical Center, the School of Architecture, the College of Liberal Arts and Sciences, the School of Education, The Black Studies, Puerto Rican Studies and Asian Studies Departments, while making use of the services of ASPIRA, SEEK and the modeling effect of the college's undergraduates.

7. Members of the college faculty will be used in planning curriculum, curriculum materials, and in some instances in teaching in peer relationship with the high school's faculty.

8. The A. Philip Randolph Campus High School will be housed on the campus of the college until it is moved to its permanent site, which is now occupied by the High School of Music and Art.

One may honestly ask at this juncture, how do these elements and programs make the school an institution of the future? The answer is that taken by themselves, the aforementioned elements and programs are exciting, but in no way futuristic. There are other important aspects that have not been discussed that are vital for raising the school from the pedestrian to the lofty heights of the ideal. Two of these factors are the school's philosophy and the school's approach to curriculum.

The school's philosophy might begin with the observation that the true purpose of humankind is to contribute at any level to an ever advancing civilization. Further, we may propose that it is the right of every child to be provided with the opportunity to learn, to develop and to live without fear. This philosophical approach forces the teacher to become aware of certain societal parameters. The child cannot make an adequate contribution to society if he or she is functioning as an illiterate person devoid of basic skills. Nor can an intelligent perspective of the future be developed if he or she is currently unaware of scientific, bio-medical, familial arrangements, ecological system, politico-economical projections and the relationship of humans to their environment--to name a few. For example, humans of the future should have some knowledge of the effects of genetic manipulation on the human organism; genetic implications of population control; the specter of eugenics; control of man's genetic future and the ethics of compulsory sterilization, abortion, and euthanasia.[3]

Some of these subjects may be broken down into modules and included in the biology class, or even in a class developed to discuss problems of the modern human. Yes, future humans must begin their voyage by understanding how present day problems will affect the future world of humankind. The student must also learn about the revolutionary scientific discoveries now being made about aging and dying, and their explicit promise of a vastly extended life span. Also there is the thrill in learning about the almost mystic quality of DNA (deoxyribonucleic acid) and how it seems to live forever.[4]

What I am suggesting here is that some of these subjects once considered sacrosanct, through the expertise of the college faculty may be brought to the students of A. Philip Randolph Campus High School. Students may be programmed to take advanced courses with distinguished professors and be exposed to exciting careers.

In relating components of curriculum to our philosophy, we are forced to identify curriculum domains congruent with our stated philosophy. Four such domains might be:

1. the domain of Self-Realization,

2. the domain of Human Relationship,

3. the domain of Economic Efficiency,

4. the domain of Civic Responsibility.[5]

These domains may be translated into objectives and give flesh to the framework of the philosophy. Such a typography also forces us to ask the question, What should the curriculum do in terms of the behavior of the student? Since we wish to provide the opportunity to enable each child to make his contribution to an ever-advancing civilization, the questions arise: Is the curriculum geared toward making the student a passive accepter of the cultural heritage; does the curriculum motivate the student to become an agent of change; does the curriculum inculcate strong feelings about the oneness of humankind, the equality of men and women and the oneness of the universe? These questions provide the yardstick for measuring whether or not the domain of the curriculum is preparing the youngster to live in and create the future world-society. Since the A. Philip Randolph Campus High School has been in existence only since the fall of 1979, both college and high school faculties still can create models of learning that are flexible enough to be changed, and humanistic enough to inspire humane responses from the student body. In brief, the philosophy of the school influences what is to be taught and sugests how it is to be taught. It serves as the organizational goals and influences the organizational structure as well.

The structured relationship between the Board of Education and the College as currently set up may be diagrammed in this manner.

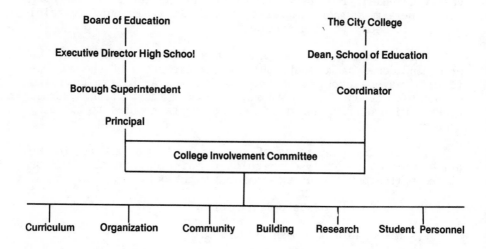

Figure 1

The College Involvement Committee consists of faculty members from the School of Education who have been identified by the Dean of the School of Education to have the expertise, interest and time to serve in six areas: curriculum development, organization, community affairs, building and maintenance, research and evaluation, and student personnel. Some of these professors are chairpersons of departments; others are experts and nationally known for their contribution to diverse fields of education. The important factor is to utilize the talents of the faculty through meaningful involvement in the planning and decision-making process regarding the interrelation of the college and the high school. This simple structure shows how the several areas of the designated involvement centers relate one to another. The College Involvement Committee also serves as the conduit through which decisions flow from the Board of Education or the College. The basic work is done by one of the six sub-committees.

The Curriculum Committee met during the summer of 1979 with members of the faculty of the high school to develop a program

suitable to the needs of the entering ninth year students.   This
was done at what was defined as the Summer Workshop.   Not only
the Curriculum Committee, but also the Organization, Building,
Research, and Student Personnel Committees met with similar
experts from the high school to plan the program for the
September 1979 opening.   The Workshop served to break down
barriers of uncertainty between both faculties as well as to
provide the forum for the exploration of creative approaches to
modeling a school for the future.

The student body and faculty are described to familiarize
the reader with the living elements of this project.   Approximately 300 9th year students were admitted to the A. Philip
Randolph Campus High School in September 1979.   Ninety-five
percent of the students are black.   Four percent of the students
are Hispanic and one percent are white.

The small number of white enrollees disturbs many of the
black parents.   They felt that there would be a diminution of
services directed to the school if the student body was
predominately black.   The thinking was that an excellent
curriculum, creative faculty, and college involvement would
attract students of all racial and ethnic backgrounds to seek
admission to A. Philip Randolph Campus High School.   There is a
great deal of realism in this thinking.   The Fiorello LaGuardia
High School of Music and Art, located adjacent to City College
attracts large numbers of white students because of its excellent
program.   There is no reason that the Campus High School cannot
do the same.

The faculty of the high school consists of 24 people.   They
were screened prior to employment by the principal, coordinator,
and at least one member from the college involved in the area of
study or expertise.   The teachers are energetic, talented,
intelligent, and dedicated toward making A. Philip Randolph
Campus High School one of the best schools in the city.   The
parents, equally enthusiastic and involved, are satisfied with
the faculty at this time.

At present, the high school occupies the second floors of
two buildings.   These buildings are structually sound and safe.
They are being used until the high school moves to its permanent
site in 1983.

The author, observing how some nascent institutions are
destroyed because they are beset on all sides by countless
demands, proposes that the high school adapt a need cycle
breaking model to insure its future.

Such an organizational model is capable of maintaining itself in a shifting environment. Katz and Kahn suggest that there is nothing in the production, supportive, and maintenance subsystems that insures organizational survival in a changing environment. These subsystems are primarily concerned with the internal working of the major systems. Ephemeral changes such as popular taste, cultural norms, group values and the like all reach the organization in the form of demands on the internal system. To refuse to accede to these demands is to risk the possibility that undue strain will be placed on the organization's maintenance system.

To provide for organizational longevity a model should be developed whose substructures can sense and respond to external changes, translating these pressures into organizational objectives without adversely affecting the integrity of the organizational structure. Such a model is called need cycle breaking.[6]

Because A. Philip Randolph Campus High School is new, the college is designing various methods for evaluating its input into the school, as well as discussing criteria for measuring educational output with the high school faculty. Such criteria are to be stated in terms of specific objectives. Further, the use of documentation for analysis of decision making and for describing the life of the organization is one of the techniques that is being utilized to record on a daily basis what occurs in the school. Students, parents, and teachers are involved in the assessing process through their recording of personal observations and impressions and pooling of these findings with other quantitative data. The high school and college staff may make use of the resources of the Computer Center and the statisticians serving at the Center. This Center may also be used by students working on individual projects and needing to determine hard data when needed. This is another element that enhances the modernity of the school and classifies it as a "school of the future."

The question of costs for the operation of the high school is of importance. For if the cost is prohibitive, other educational systems cannot and should not attempt to replicate it. The per pupil cost allotted by the Board of Education is the same given to all other pupils in a comprehensive high school. The in-kind contribution of the college, however, does inflate the per pupil cost when included in the fiscal picture. Not every high school will be able to utilize the resources of a college. What can be replicated, however, are some of the programs and approaches to the teaching-learning process.

One of the most difficult problems to date with regard to the high school-college relationship is the development of a system whereby every interested professor can be involved without long delays. We are aware of the interests of faculty and college students but must guard against system overload.

Not only is there the danger of system overload, but also the possibility of introducing confusion through the entry of additional people who view the school from their individual perspectives. Jay W. Forrester describes this as counter-intuitive behavior of social systems. He contends that social systems, including schools, are complex entities. As such it is difficult for the human mind to comprehend the behavior of the multiple subsystems. Indeed, there are orderly processes at work in the creation of human judgment and intuition that frequently lead people to wrong decisions when faced with complex and highly interacting systems.[7]

The point being addressed here is that the process of introducing more and more new elements into the high school without first insuring that the participants are fully aware of the current state of the art as well as the specific objectives currently under consideration can bring about the opposite of the desired results. To protect against this type of human error, participants in the program must learn how to function in a realistic model of the school. Such a model, although a simplfication of the actual A. Philip Randolph Campus High School, can be far more comprehensive than a conceptual model as perceived by different persons involved in the planning and implementing of programs.

What will make the campus high school a model for the future? How can one predict its continuance as a dynamic future-oriented organism? What are some of the safeguards needed to protect this trend? The author is aware that the answers are not apparent.

By using one of the techniques of the futurist, some of these questions can be answered. For example, by using the Exploratory Forecasting Method, which starts from the present situation and its preceding history, one can attempt to project the future. An observation of the present situation reveals the existence of a school. A review of the antecedents leading up to the school gives this information:

1. A functional cooperative relationship between City College and A. Philip Randolph Campus High School can result in the developing of innovative and stimulating programs, methods, and materials to provide for a broad range of learning activities.

2. Through the practice of exchanging faculty so that the college staff members might teach or join in team-teaching in high school classes, and whereby the high school faculty may receive adjunctive status to become actively involved in the instruction of certain college-based courses.

3. By undertaking a variety of research projects to ascertain the validity of futuristic school goals and objectives, and to examine the degree to which they are being achieved, a system of scientific inquiry is inspired and encouraged.

4. Through the close relationship between the high school and college more of these high school students should aspire to select entering college as a viable option.

5. Student achievement in terms of competencies in reading, writing, mathematical, and oral skills will be enhanced by virtue of the college's success in these areas, as demonstrated by such programs as SEEK, ASPIRA, and Black Studies.

6. Through input by City College, the high school students may explore future careers. The Industrial Arts Program, The Urban Legal Center, Bio-Medical School, Center for the Performing Arts, College of Liberal Arts and Sciences and the School of Education will serve as exploratory experiences and incentive promoters for the high school students.

These are only a few of the ideas that were a part of the pre-planning aspect for the interrelation of the college and high school.

By using another major forecasting method, the Normative Forecasting Method, which starts with some desired or postulated future situation and works backwards to derive feasible routes for transition from the present to this desired future, one can more fully see how the high school is a school of the future.[8]

The network of communication between the college and the high school is so designed that top decision makers in both organizations hold planning meetings where staffing, curricula, teaching strategies for both faculties, introduction of new concepts and personnel into the high school, parental involvement and community input are all discussed. Time lines are developed for the proper phasing in of various elements of the program, and serious critique is given to any area that is not functioning up to the level of the defined objectives. Such an arrangement insures that as many elements as possible have access for meaningful input into the decision-making process. This bears resemblance to a Management by Objectives model. Further, decisions in terms of long range planning and anticipated outcomes are addressed at these sessions.

What will place the A. Philip Randolph Campus High School into the realm of the future will be its futuristic curriculum; teaching-learning processes; staff development program; organizational structure; awareness of current societal problems and their projection into the year 2000; incorporation of the distinguished college faculty into meaningful participatory roles; utilization of such college resources as the Computer Center; utilization of the resources of the total college, and the introduction of futures courses into the high school.

The high school, because of its unique relationship to the college, can develop courses of current and future interest. For example, distinguished professors may work with the high school faculty to develop and present courses dealing with the benefits as well as costs of genetic manipulation; the possible harmful effects of population control; explore the possibility of feeding the world's masses; investigate the concepts of communal living; visit sites utilizing solar energy; and interrelate philosophy, literature and science fiction in attempting to understand 21st century man.

Future courses can be designed where such esoteric terms and concepts as Cryogenics, Cyborg, the Dyson Sphere, Parallel Worlds, Tachyon, Waldo, Ramscoop, PSI, Light-Sail, New Wave, and Grandfather Paradox will become the everyday parlance of the high school students.

By peering into the future and then looking backwards, we become more acutely aware that the 20th century marks the middle period of the second transition in the history of the human race. Kenneth E. Boulding points out, the first transition refers to the phenomenon of the paleolithic and neolithic ages. This transition was from precivilized to civilized society and began some 5 or 10 thousand years ago. The second transition is a 20th century phenomenon, also referred to as the post-industrial era. It is in the 20th century that science has become a substantial, organized part of society, and that the solution to the problem of food gathering, has for the most part, freed man to spend more time in pursuit of aesthetic and scientific matters.[9]

The second transition is mentioned here to highlight some of the attendant problems brought about by the advanced development of technology without the concomitant concern for the spirited development of humankind. In studying family structures like the nuclear extended, single parent, and communal family living, the student will discover that the emotional, psychological, and spiritual attributes of humans have not kept pace with developments in technological fields.

It then becomes important for those who are peering into the future to make certain that courses in English, history, literature, and sociology, specifically deal with the topics of humans' relationships to others and to the universe, as well as the overpowering struggle between ego and subconscious wishes. Indeed, modules teaching the use of mental processes in telekinesis, telepathy, and extra sensory perception must be included as part of the curriculum. Meditation and quiet reflection must also be an integral part of such a futuristic curriculum.

The A. Philip Randolph Campus High School has every potential of demonstrating how the creation of new curriculum, the use of college resources the teaching of systems analysis through computer modeling, meaningful involvement of parents and community, utilization of sound pupil personnel techniques, and the involvement of the students in meaningful decision making, will place and maintain the A. Philip Randolph Campus High School in the position of a futuristically oriented institution.

NOTES

1. H.W. Hertzberg, Competency Based Teacher Education: Does It Have a Past or a Future? (New York: Teacher College Record, Columbia University Press, 1976).

2. See Agreement between the City College and the Board of Education of New York City, May 1978.

3. N.C. Ostheimer and J.M. Ostheimer, eds., Life or Death-- Who Controls (New York: Springer Publishing Company, 1976).

4. Albert Rosenfeld, Prolongevity (New York: Alfred A. Knoff, 1976).

5. Galen J. Saylor and W. Alexander, Planning Curriculum for Schools (New York: Holt, Rinehart and Winston, Inc., 1974).

6. Daniel Katz and Robert L. Kahn, The Social Psychology of Organizations (New York: John Wiley and Sons, Inc., 1966).

7. Jay W. Forrester, "Counterintuitive Behavior of Social Systems." Technology Review, Vol. 73, No. 3 (Boston: MIT Press, 1975).

8. Howard F. Didsbury, Jr. assisted by James J. Crider, _Student Handbook for The Study of the Future_ (Washington, D.C.: World Future Society, 1979).

9. Kenneth E. Boulding, _The Meaning of the 20th Century_ (New York: Harper and Row Publishers, 1965).

A Futures Curriculum for Symmetry

Lenore W. Dickmann

Traditionally, schools have existed for students. Yet, one might raise the question, "To what extent has education made real, as its focus, the person in the educational process?" Too often the emphasis has been placed on content.

A futures curriculum must be holistic in perspective, balanced in its provision for the pupil as well as for the subject matter. The student's future-focused role image must assume an importance equal to his pursuit of knowledge.

Today, with a cry of "return to the basics" receiving currency, educators must concern themselves with the broader issue of balance in the curriculum. The question of balance is receiving little press, however. Emphasis has been placed on the "what" of the curriculum rather than on the "who" in the curricular process. The curriculum, though, doesn't exist as a plan separate from the individual. Its reason for being is to enhance the completeness of an individual in an educational process. Balance in the curriculum must reflect a concern not only with the "3 R's," but with the completeness, wholeness, and symmetry of the person for whom the curriculum is planned.

Symmetry provides a model for considering balance in the curriculum as well as for balance or completeness in the learner.[1] This model presents seven frameworks for expanding the traditional dimensions of curriculum into a pattern to benefit the learner's future-focused role image. It considers the attributes of humankind to offer an organization, or a construct, for them that goes beyond the limits possible when only cognitive development is considered.

The Symmetrical Model suggests seven areas of consideration for those engaged in planning, teaching, or evaluating the curriculum in terms of its completeness or balance. These areas are concerned with seven facets of an individual's being. The

complete person is viewed as alive, purposive, loving, intelligent, truthful, spiritual, and moral. Provision, then, must be
made for fostering each of these seven areas within the
individual and within the curriculum. See Figure 1.

Figure 1

Seven Facets of Symmetry with Attributes
of a Symmetrical Individual

I Alive	II Spiritual	III Purposive	IV Truthful
healthy	resilient	free	precise
sound	alert	rational	candid
progressive	responsive	lawful	authentic
fresh	joyous	creative	sincere
spontaneous	resourceful	individual	perfect
vital	patient	disciplined	factual
invincible	humoristic	perfectible	honest
etc.	etc.	etc.	etc.

V Loving	VI Moral	VII Intelligent
peaceful	loyal	intuitive
merciful	courageous	knowledgeable
unselfish	open	understanding
humble	harmonious	judicious
brotherly	optimistic	apperceptive
faithful	pure	visionary
just	good	scientific
etc.	etc.	etc.

Aliveness as a Framework

To exist, an individual needs life or is alive. Aliveness
is therefore an extremely vital quality of a person's being. Too
often, however, it is accepted consciously or unconsciously as a
given, taken for granted, rather than recognized, cherished, or
considered as a valid area of study.

Aliveness, as an area of direct study, provides an interface between the learner and the "what" that is to be learned. If the subject matter is to have a personal meaning for the "who" then the curriculum must have life. Conversely, for the learner, curriculum without personal application to a person's life is dead to the learner. It is therefore a function of curriculum developers to plan instructional activities that are alive and that help bring personal meaning to the learner in terms of recognizing and understanding aliveness as an important facet in the development of a future focused role image.

In selecting aliveness as a framework, educators must begin with the basic questions. What elements within the present curriculum are growth producing, fostering vitality? What elements need to be stripped away as not conducive to fostering aliveness, leading instead to apathy, lethargy, deadness?

The teacher who fosters aliveness will help students to be vibrantly in tune to the inner and outer world, keenly aware through each of the senses. Such aliveness will be reflected in openness to being. The person experiences each day fully with eager anticipation, thoughtfully involved, and reflective. Apathy, boredom, lethargy are not even a consideration for the alive individual. Gladness to leave the old for the new, to progress, and to make a contribution to the human scene are foremost to the alive person who is also alive to his other facets of completeness.

An educational process consumes many years of a person's lifespan. The aliveness of a human being must, therefore, be an important consideration in curricular decisions. Specific learning activities must be identified and planned to intensify the fullness of life for the individual.

The Framework of Purposiveness

The framework of purposiveness helps the learner to identify the "what" in his or her life. The learner understands self as a goal-seeking individual with a purpose in living and a purpose for being in school.

At issue then, are the individual's goals, plans, and aims in curricular decisioning. The curriculum has as its focus helping the learner in his/her purposiveness as a goal seeker. Curriculum becomes truly personalized, individualized, and goal oriented for the learner.

Love as a Framework

Love is a power in human interaction and may be used for increasing power within the curriculum. It has been identified as a basic human need. It is time, then, to view it as basic in the curriculum, not as a thing apart, to be treated in isolation, but as integral--a way of acting, responding, relating, thinking.

Loving must be viewed as central to an individual's wholeness and therefore central to an individual's curriculum plan. Skills of caring, relating, and responding must be valued, taught, and rewarded.

In valuing love as basic, the school's role is to sensitize students to love as a reality. An awareness of the concept of love is a first consideration. Second, the relation of love to other facets of human behavior is noted, and third, demonstrated behavior is underscored. Learners must be helped to perceive a loving attitude as a basic behavior in their relationships with others.

Intelligence as a Traditional Framework

Intelligence has long had rationality as a prime indicator of a pupil's success with the factual knowledge of the curriculum. It is also the traditional foundation for curriculum planning. Yet, serious omissions have gone almost unnoticed even with the stress that is placed upon intelligence.

These are attributes that cluster comfortably within the framework of intelligent behavior that have scarcely surfaced within a curriculum plan. How much emphasis has been placed upon the visionary, perceptive, or intuitive qualities of learners? How much help have learners been given in understanding these and other such intelligent attributes? It seems that even this area calls for a re-definition.

Studies conducted in Paris at Rene Descartes University point out that "emphasis on academic success and a concept that relates intelligence to factual knowledge and logic have led to the neglect of other important aspects, such as social understanding, and the capacity to deal with both the probable and the uncertain."[2] A curriculum for the future can ill-afford not to help students deal with the probable and the uncertain and manifest social understanding. Such neglect must not continue.

In addition, to plan a curriculum without considering the structure of knowledge with its accelerating change, the nature of the intelligent individual as he copes, the processes by which learning takes place, and the skills for futuristic thinking is to sabotage even this traditional framework for organizing the curriculum. The times call for a new look at this traditional organizer.

Truthfulness Framework

Curriculum planners are often reminded of the truthfulness framework as they plan. The search for truth is held as an objective for an educated person.

A series of questions, however, must be raised for the curriculum planner. What is the relation of truth to a healthy self concept of a future focused role image? Do teachers have the power to make classrooms open arenas for searching into truth and the strength to persevere in the search? Is truth based upon absolutes that should be taught within the schools?

It seems that the framework for truthfulness is a necessary ingredient if the curriculum is to be authentic and relevant. To answer the age old question "What is truth?" however, and to provide for it in the curriculum may be difficult. The exigency of the times mandate truthfulness as a basic framework.

Spirituality as a Framework
for Consideration

The cry to make curriculum relevant is a call to apply the framework of the spiritual to the developmental process. Relevance is gained in the transfer of curriculum content into action in the learner's life. It is the spiritual experience planned within the curriculum that moves the learner from the realm of the mundane into the domain of the preferable.

The curriculum can provide a plan for thinking activities with time to reflect upon what is being learned in order to transfer content into one's life history. For example, curriculum with structured silence provides time for the learner to pass cognitive content through an affective filter.

The spiritual framework sensitizes students to attitudes of joy, patience, humor, and resilience. It provides a criterion for teachers to place thinking and reflecting upon what is taught in a central position within the plan for learning.

It calls for a search for universals that set people apart from the animal instincts and materialism found in life on planet earth.

Moral Criteria as a Framework

The issue of moral education is receiving currency. Parents, teachers, and administrators alike are stressing a need for it. The question is no longer should moral education be included within the school day but rather "how" shall it be included within the curriculum?

Some futurists even warn that, with the many social crises of the present, there is little time to decide moral questions of great import to the future--the future in which students in the schools will spend their lives. Realistically, a futuristic emphasis offers an integrative approach to moral education. Such emphasis deals directly with moral issues, problems, and concerns that are integral parts of broader questions based in the present but with implications for the future. For example, a discussion of the social aspects of food--sharing, pollution, and conserving energy can flow naturally from discussion of current events. Such discussion can lead to inquiry in various areas of the curriculum that are content based.

With this natural approach, fragmentation of thought is lessened for students. Moral issues are not seen as separate from the disciplines. They assume their rightful place as topics for analysis within the established curriculum rather than the hidden or incidental. In using a futuristic focus, the danger of overlooking a direct approach to moral education is minimized. Also, the danger of indoctrination and manipulation through a process approach alone is lessened or negated.

As students identify attitudes held, they can be encouraged to speculate on the consequences of a continuation of these prevailing attitudes. In engaging in trend extrapolation from the news reporting, they can be helped to formulate "What if..." statements for discussion.

When problems are identified either from the news or in personal experiencing, students can be encouraged to generate hypotheses for testing. "If. . .then" statements provide opportunity for reality testing. Manipulation and indoctrination are not easily imposed in an environment of student inquiry and action research that is discipline-based.

Cross-impact analysis, another futuristic technique, offers an excellent framework for an examination of consequences for today's values, choices, and activities. Through checking the effect of one activity on another choice as clarified through

using the cross-impact two-axis grid, students have a tool for
self-appraisal of interests. Questions can be clarified concerning the impact of one activity on another.

The moral criteria framework is concerned with standards of
conduct. Classroom management is an inherent part of the
curriculum and certainly needs a framework for making explicit
the standards of conduct that are conducive to learning within
the school milieu. Character development is a constitutional
charge that would make the framework important in the eyes of the
public. The moral criteria framework offers the learners a
laboratory for making rules of conduct that serve as a corner-
stone in a democratic society. The moral criteria framework
offers a challenge to curriculum developers in a democratic,
multi-cultural society. Further, it calls for students to be
involved in that search as an element in design.

With a discrete focus, students are given tools, and skill
in using them, for dealing with moral questions rather than
having stencils imposed. Transfer of learning may take on added
meaning with the tie to present concerns as well as implications
for the future. With a futuristic emphasis, the affective
emotions students hold concerning moral issues can find
substantive direction within the skills of reasoning provided
through the cognitive areas.

Content of the Curriculum

The seven frameworks of aliveness, purposiveness, loving,
intelligence, truthfulness, spirituality, and morality are
organizing centers for providing for the "who" and a focused role
image.

The eight broad categories of human concerns provide the
"what" or the content:

* War and Peace
* Population and Food
* Resources and Development
* The Environment
* The Economy
* Politics and Government
* Science and Technology
* Terrorism

Curriculum, then, becomes powerful as a check and balance of a
purposive individual in terms of "War and Peace," a loving
individual in terms of "The Environment" and a moral individual
in terms of "Science and Technology."

The seven frameworks of the symmetrical individual and the eight broad categories provide an holistic perspective for viewing curriculum as a plan to help students move toward completeness as human beings in the human scene.

APPENDIX

25 Starter Strategies to Foster an Understanding of Symmetry

* Have students generate questions concerning each facet as leads for study

* Let students brainstorm activities for dealing with each facet

* Help students to make a mural for the seven facets

* Ask students to write poetry for the facets

* Invite students to compile annotated bibliographies for books read, citing relationship to symmetry

* Start students collecting quotations in which attributes of symmetry are used

* Tell students to design posters concerning symmetry

* Give students materials to construct bulletin boards around the symmetrical theme

* Guide students in suggesting additional attributes for each facet

* Involve students in clipping news articles that mention any facet or attribute of symmetry

* Start students in the design of original games for symmetry

* Provide students with the opportunity to make mobiles for the facets

* Suggest students express a facet of symmetry through media they choose
                    * paintings
                    * modeling clay
                    * sculpting
                    * etc.

* Have students write an original story

* Encourage students to invent, design, contrive, compose,
  plan activities with any or all kinds of media for
  symmetry

  * color   * images
  * tone   * world of force
  * movement   * organization
  * space   * social relationships
  * time   * contemplation
  * words

* Start students hypothesizing about each facet

* Have students read biographies to discuss individuals
  in terms of their symmetry

* Let students role play incidents depicting an attribute
  and its opposite

* Suggest students keep a journal of their symmetrical deeds

* Start students collecting pictures for the facets and
  attributes for a personal or class scrapbook

* Ask students to compile a listing of symmetrical
  individuals

* Encourage students to design 1 year, 5 year, 10 year plans
  for their symmetrical development

* Ask students to appraise their own symmetry for each facet
  on a continuum from 1 to 5

* Ask students to suggest songs for each facet or write
  their own

NOTES

1. Edward Weisse, Leonore W. Dickmann, and Kenneth Morrison,
The Symmetrical Teacher: An Introduction to American Education
(Dubuque, Iowa: Kendall/Hunt Publishing Co., 1976).

2. John E. Gibson, "Does Your Mind Affect Your Behavior?"
Family Weekly Magazine in Oshkosh Weekend Northwestern (October
7, 1979), p. 23.

BIBLIOGRAPHY

Dickmann, Leonore W. "Aliveness and The Curriculum," _The Affect Tree_, Vol. II, No. 3, February 1978, pp. 1 & 3.

Dickmann, Leonore W. "Back to the Basic-Love," _Forward_. Wisconsin Association for Supervision and Curriculum Development, Fall 1978.

Dickmann, Leonore W. "Developing Seven Sides of Symmetry Through the Literature," _Wisconsin State Reading Association Journal_, Vol. 16, No. 2, January 1973, pp. 46-55.

Dickmann, Leonore W. "Futuring and the Rule of Reading Teachers," _Wisconsin State Reading Association Journal_, May 1978, pp. 42-46.

Dickmann, Leonore W. "Futurism and Curriculum," _Forward_. Wisconsin Association for Supervision and Curriculum Development, Winter, 1977.

Dickmann, Leonore W. "Moral Education and The Future," _Forward_. Wisconsin Association for Supervision and Curriculum Development, Spring 1978, pp. 40-45.

Dickmann, Leonore W. "Seven Sides of Symmetry A Paradigm for Self-Concept," _Forward_. Wisconsin Association for Supervision and Curriculum Development, Spring 1976.

Gibson, John E. "Does Your Mind Affect Your Behavior?" _Family Weekly Magazine_ in _Oshkosh Weekend Northwestern_, October 7, 1979, p. 23.

Weisse, Edward B., Dickmann, Leonore W., and Morrison, Kenneth. _The Symmetrical Teacher: An Introduction to American Education_. Dubuque, Iowa: Kendall/Hunt Publishing Company, 1976.

Meta-Theoretical Aspects
of Science and Science Education of the Future

Paul A. Wagner

According to the physicist, Thomas Kuhn, science makes its greatest advances during periods of paradigmatic shifts.[1] Or, as Imre Lakatos argues, when one research programme becomes overwhelmed with unaccounted-for anomalies, a new research programme may be instituted by theoretical scientists. These scientists recognize that the present forms of argument are no longer powerful enough to account for the kinds of phenomena the respective disciplines admit as relevant.[2] For Lakatos, a "research programme" is a set of "methodological rules: some tell us what paths of research to avoid (negative heuristic); and others what paths to pursue (positive heuristic)."[3]

The occasions on which new research programmes must be initiated occur only infrequently. Certainly, in the case of physics, Newtonian mechanics seemed adequate enough until about the turn of the 20th century. Following the lead of the young Einstein, a handful of theoretical physicists, including Bohr, Dirac, Heisenberg, Schrodinger, and Born developed the conjectures of Plank, Lorentz and Minkowski into a new research programme. The new research programme was powerful enough to accommodate the theoretical structure upon which all of contemporary macro and micro physics is built. However, once again, physical theory is identifying an unwieldy number of anomalies.[4]

I do not mean to suggest that the scope of the present research programme in physics is exhausted, or even nearly so. Certainly the work of John Archibald Wheeler suggests that much useful insight is yet to be derived from the theories of Einstein.[5] Nor do I mean to suggest that contemporary physics is without its share of theoretically-minded physicists. The work of Richard Feynman would count too heavily against such a claim.[6] However, it is apparent that present physical theory is accumulating anomalies at an uncomfortable rate. And if one is to credit the work of Kuhn and Lakatos with some insight into the nature of scientific progress, then one might anticipate that not too far into the 21st century a new research programme must again be initiated.[7]

The related question for future-minded educators becomes, what sort of education is likely to equip the scientists of tomorrow with the skills and dispositions necessary for developing, adopting and working within a novel research programme? Even the most cursory review of textbooks at all levels of schooling today would give little or no hint that the authors thought it necessary to initiate children to the idea that a paradigm shift in any one of the sciences might occur in their lifetime. There are, of course, a few curricular programs that seem based upon the epistemological anarchism of Feyerabend.[8] Such programs approach science education as if every theory, every hypothesis, every conjecture were of equal worth--regardless of their ability to fit in with relevant current theory or generate a new research programme.[9] If the science students of today will, as adults, have the responsibility of generating new research programmes they must know something about what is entailed in such a venture.

Generating a new research programme in an area such as physics is not merely a matter of accounting for a set of heretofore unaccommodated phenomena, nor is it simply a matter of implementing new mathematical instruments, or new computer software. Generating a new research programme requires that the author of the programme recognize several fundamental features of such a venture. First, it must be reasonably clear that the present research programme is approaching the limits of its powers to account for all phenomena currently considered relevant by scientists practicing in the field. Second, the new research programme must be able to account for nearly all the phenomena accounted for under the programme it is to replace. Third, the new research programme must be able to accommodate much that was regarded as anomolous under the old programme. Fourth, there must be sufficient grounds for believing that the new programme will possess a significantly broader scope of explanatory power than had the previous programme. That is, the new programme must indicate, as relevant, additional _classes_ of phenomena and suggest methods of accounting for such phenomena. And finally, a new research programme must preserve the scientist's respect for simplicity and elegance of explanation.

To ask that education at the elementary and secondary level prepare students for the possibility that they may one day be expected to develop a new research programme is to ask a great deal of the classroom teacher. The classroom teacher is neither a theoretical scientist nor even an experimentalist, but rather a pedagogue who has received a minimal amount of training in a few basic experimental skills along with some relevant background information. In addition one might observe that the young Einstein was able to develop a new research programme in spite of the fact that he had never been exposed to a theoretically-minded physicist in his early education, or even in his undergraduate training. However, the young Einstein did study the works of the leading theoretical physicists and philosophers on his own. For example, Einstein writes that "It was Ernst Mach who, in his History of Mechanics, shook this dogmatic faith; this book exercised a profound influence on me in this regard while I was a student . . . Mach's epistemological position also influenced me very greatly."[10] Einstein subsequently writes that in his later years he found the epistemological position of Mach untenable.[11] The important point to be gleaned from the viewpoints above is that, in Einstein's formative years, he was intensely concerned with the philosophical underpinnings of the entire field of Newtonian physics as it then stood. Einstein's autobiography suggests that he was as much concerned with the epistemological commitments of the Newtonian research programme, as he was with his well-known "thought experiments," through which he considered riding upon a light beam.

Max Born recalls frequent conversations with Einstein in which Einstein attributed much of his intellectual disposition to his familiarity with the epistemological works of philosophers such as David Hume.[12] Several years after Einstein's death, Born himself advised other physicists to take care to familiarize themselves with the philosophic aspect of doing physics.[13] And it should be noted that the Einstein-Heisenberg debate over the principle of uncertainty is again an instance of philosophic discourse. In his book describing the quantum mechanics position in physics, Heinsenberg appropriately used the title, Physics and Philosophy.[14]

The points to be derived from the above are two-fold. First, philosophic discourse has always been fundamental to the doing of science. Second, the essential role of philosophy in science becomes particularly apparent during a period of paradigm shift. When the powers of explanation within a science approach their limits, the theoreticians in the field become increasingly reflective. As theoreticians become more introspective about the nature of their discipline, they find themselves distinctly engaged in philosophic discourse. To the extent that scientists are unfamiliar with philosophic discourse, then to that same extent these efforts to sort out the philosophic dilemmas fundamental to the forming of a new research programme will be impeded.

Kuhn's distinction between normal and revolutionary science is particularly useful to the science educator of the future. For example, Kuhn points out that science is generally characterized by the accumulation of theory and evidence within the confines of a single research paradigm.[15] Consequently much of what we do in science education today in preparing students to work with the research tools and procedures appropriate to present paradigms is adequate. In fact Kuhn seems to go so far as to suggest that science educators should be a bit more rigorous in this regard in their curricular demands.[16]

On the other hand, as the high-energy physicist, Fritjof Capra suggests, we have good reason to suspect that the present language of explanation in physics is approaching its limits.[17] Should the science of physics require a new research programme, it is essential that science educators of the future anticipate this need and take appropriate action in order to prepare students for a productive role in a period of scientific revolution. Hence, the role of future-oriented science education is clear. Science students must be initiated into the philosophic aspects of doing science at each step in their education.

To cause children to ask extraordinary questions does not by itself constitute inclusion of a philosophic dimension in science education. The study of philosophy entails developing skills of logical analysis, both for their own sake and for their usefulness when brought to bear upon problems of related philosophic interest. Science, too, has a basic interest in the use of logic, if only instrumentally. Consequently, if science education is to include the necessary attention to the role of logic in scientific investigation, then the nature of science and logic must be considered together, and from a philosophical perspective. In short, science education ought to be so organized that students learn not only 1) skills of logical analysis, but consider as well 2) the relationship between logically valid statements and the data from the world, 3) the truth-value dependence of logical propositions on the semantic elements they entail, and 4) the programmatic or contextual determinants of meaning for those same propositions.

As I have argued elsewhere, the study of logic remains a distinctive object of philosophic study. Consequently, to the extent that the scientists' activities depend upon his understanding of, and facility with, various logical apparatus, science and science education are dependent upon philosophy and philosophy education.[18]

To suggest that philosophy ought to become a part of science education may sound rather bold. This suggestion is no bolder than the suggestion that a particular science is on the verge of a revolutionary period, or the subsequent claim that future-minded science educators ought to take upon themselves the responsibility of preparing students for this anticipated revolution. Consequently, having argued above that it is reasonable to anticipate a revolution in one of the sciences, physics for example, and, having then argued that as a consequence it is reasonable to demand that science education take into account the needs of the rapidly evolving sciences, it is natural to conclude that the philosophic aspects of a scientific revolution should become both an object and a subject of study within the science curriculum.

The addition of a philosophic component to science education is already being developed in a systematic way by Fred Oscanyan at the Institute for the Advancement of Philosophy for Children, and by myself. Oscanyan's approach is an extention of the philosophy for children model originally spawned by the founder of the IAPC, Matthew Lipman. My own approach varies, in that on occasion it entails more directive elements than do the materials developed by the IAPC.

The idea of including philosophy in an elementary curriculum with the intention of facilitating children's understanding of the sciences has already been put into practice at the Laboratory School at the University of Missouri, Columbia. A rationale for the practice along with a description of some of the activities may be found in an earlier article by Christopher J. Lucas and myself entitled, "Philosophic Inquiry and the Logic of Elementary School Science Education."[19]

Even before any formal attempts had been made to include philosophy as a complement to the present science education curriculum, Lipman and Sharp identified the role of philosophy in developing in children greater adeptness in the making of inferences.[20] Recent studies, which identified improvement of reasoning skills as a consequence of students' initiation into a philosophy program, indicate that any curricular activity dependent upon the child's skill of reasoning can be enhanced if complemented by inclusion of a philosophy component.[21]

The message, then, for the future-oriented science educator is clear. We have good reason to suspect that the nature of the respective sciences may, in the future, be significantly different from what we are accustomed to today. Since we cannot anticipate the specifics that might be involved in a particular paradigm shift, we must content ourselves with a systematic study

of the sorts of things that are involved in such a shift. The
study of the forming and re-forming of research programmes has
long been a practice central to the philosophy of science. As I
have argued elsewhere, "Analysis of the features that distinguish
scientific activity of any sort represents one kind of
philosophic inquiry."[22] Consequently, if the children of today--
who will be the scientists of tomorrow--are to have a mental set
receptive to the demands of forming a new research programme,
then they, too, must be thoroughly familiar with what is involved
in such an activity. Such meta-scientific, or more properly
speaking, philosophic concerns, can only be realized through a
formal systematic practice, in which philosophy becomes an
integral part of the general scientific curriculum, from the
elementary school through graduate school. Through the inclusion
of philosophy, one might expect that the science curriculum will
finally promote science _education_ as opposed to science _training_.
Or, as Gerald Holton concludes after arguing along roughly
similar lines in his discussion of the "Project Physics Program,"
"Training (in the sciences) is achieved by imparting the most
efficient skill for a (single) scientific purpose. Education is
achieved by imparting a point of view that allows generalization
and application in a wide variety of circumstances in one's later
life."[23]

NOTES

1. Thomas Kuhn, The Structure of Scientific Revolutions
(Chicago: University of Chicago Press, 1962). For a similar
characterization of science see also, Gerald Holton, Thematic
Origins of Scientific Thought (Cambridge, Massachusetts: Harvard
University Press, 1973).

2. Imre Lakatos, "Falsification and the Methodology of
Scientific Research Programmes," in Criticism and the Growth of
Knowledge, eds. Imre Lakatos and Alan Musgrave (Cambridge:
Cambridge University Press, 1970), pp. 91-197. For a similar
line of argument see also: Larry Laudan, Progress and Its
Problems: Towards a Theory of Scientific Growth (Berkeley:
University of California Press, 1977).

3. Ibid., p. 132.

4. For an extended discussion of the nature and role of
anomalies in scientific theory see: Willard C. Humphreys,
Anomalies and Scientific Theories (San Francisco: Freeman,
Cooper and Company, 1968).

5. See, for example, John Archibald Wheeler, "Superspace and the Nature of Quantum Geometrodynamics," in <u>Batelle Rencontres</u>, eds. C.M. de Witt and John Archibald Wheeler (New York: Benjamin Company, 1968), pp. 242-307. For further discussion of the scope of Einsteinian relativity see: S.W. Hawking, <u>The</u> <u>Large</u> <u>Scale</u> <u>Structure</u> <u>of</u> <u>Space-Time</u> (Cambridge: Cambridge University Press, 1973).

6. Richard Feynman, <u>The</u> <u>Character</u> <u>of</u> <u>Physical</u> <u>Law</u> (Cambridge, Massachusetts: Massachusetts Institute of Technology Press, 1965).

7. Stephen Toulmin reaches a similar conclusion in his "From Form to Function: Philosophy and History of Science in the 1950's and Now," <u>Daedulus</u>, Summer, 1977, pp. 143-162.

8. See, for example, Paul Feyerabend, <u>Against</u> <u>Method</u> (New York: Verso Publishing Company, 1975).

9. For further discussion of this issue see: Michael Martin, <u>Concepts</u> <u>of</u> <u>Science</u> <u>Education</u> (Glenview, Illinois: Scott Foresman and Company, 1972), chapter one.

10. Albert Einstein, "Autobiography," in <u>Albert</u> <u>Einstein:</u> <u>Philosopher-Scientist</u>, ed. P.A. Schilpp (La Salle, Illinois: Open Court Press, 1949), p. 21.

11. Ibid., p. 21.

12. Max Born, <u>Physics</u> <u>in</u> <u>My</u> <u>Generation</u> (New York: Springer Verlag, 1969), p. 156.

13. Ibid., p. 77.

14. Werner Heisenberg, <u>Physics</u> <u>and</u> <u>Philosophy</u> (New York: Harper and Row, 1958).

15. Thomas Kuhn, <u>The</u> <u>Essential</u> <u>Tension</u> (Chicago: University of Chicago Press, 1978), pp. 225-239.

16. Ibid., pp. 240-265.

17. Fritjof Capra, <u>The</u> <u>Tao</u> <u>of</u> <u>Physics</u> (Berkeley, California: Shambala Publishing Company, 1975).

18. Paul A. Wagner, "Philosophy, Children and 'Doing Science,'" <u>Thinking</u>, Vol. I, No. 1 (1979), pp. 55-57.

19. Paul A. Wagner and Christopher J. Lucas, "Philosophic Inquiry and the Logic of Elementary School Science Education," Science Education, Vol. 61, No. 4 (1977), pp. 549-558.

20. Matthew Lipman and A. Sharp, et al., Instructor's Manual to Harry Stottlemeir's Discovery (Upper Montclair, New Jersey: Institute for the Advancement of Philosophy for Children, 1975), p. 14.

21. M. Lipman, A. Sharp, and F. Oscanyan, Philosophy in the Classroom (Upper Montclair, New Jersey: Institute for the Advancement of Philosophy for Chidren, 1977).

22. Wagner and Lucas, pp. 550-551.

23. Gerald Holton, The Scientific Imagination (Cambridge: Cambridge University Press, 1978), p. 298.

Futuristics and the Professional Education of Social Workers

Dennis R. Falk

Application of the Futuristic Perspective to Social Work

The School of Social Development (SSD), as it currently exists at the University of Minnesota-Duluth, is the result of applying several components of futuristic orientation to the traditional model of social work. By describing the emergence of SSD during the past eight years, we can gain an understanding of how a futuristic orientation has been incorporated within the School. A more complete description of the concept of social development and of the educational program will be provided in the next sections.

The School of Social Development at the University of Minnesota-Duluth began as the new School of Social Work in 1971. It was initially expected that SSD would develop along the lines of other traditional social work schools of that time. A brief description of social work during this time follows.

One common definition of social work used in the early 1970s was as follows:

Social work is concerned with the interactions between people and their social environment which affect the ability of people to accomplish their life tasks, alleviate distress, and realize their aspirations and values. The purpose of social work therefore is to (1) enhance the problem-solving and coping capacities of people, (2) link people with systems that provide them with resources, services, and opportunities, (3) promote the effective and humane operation of these systems, and (4) contribute to the development and improvement of social policy.[1]

Social work traditionally focused on the first two purposes described above, with a lesser emphasis on the third, and a limited emphasis on the fourth.

The three basic approaches to social work at that time were casework, group work, and community organization. In casework, social workers used interviews to identify problems of individuals and families. They then helped these people to understand and to solve their problems and to receive needed services, education, or training. In group work, social workers helped people to understand both themselves and others better, to overcome racial and cultural prejudices, and to work together with others in achieving a common goal. They planned and conducted activities for children, adolescents, older persons, and other adults in a variety of settings. In community organization, the social workers coordinated the efforts of various groups to combat serious problems through community programs. During the early 1970s casework was the dominant approach of social workers, followed by group work and community organization.

As you will discover, SSD did not become a traditional school of social work. Several factors contributed to the emergence of SSD (the name was changed in 1974), among them the futuristic orientation of some of its faculty. A primary influence was the literature concerning international social development. This literature emerged from the United Nations and emphasized the futuristic concepts of a holistic (systems) approach to development and a long-term time-perspective.[2] In the holistic approach, it is contended that political, economic, and social systems must develop simultaneously if societies are to develop in positive ways. In focusing on the development of entire societies, it was necessary to adopt an extended time perspective, as experience demonstrated that societal development is a lengthy process. The U.N. literature on social development thus expanded and extended the relatively limited view the social work profession had taken on as its purpose.

The futurist concept of imaging the future emerged within SSD in an attempt to find direction for social development. Development implies change, but questions surrounding the consequences of change arose: "In what areas should this change occur?" and "Toward what end is change directed?" In attempting to answer these questions, the faculty and students in SSD began to image a future characterized by relatively abstract concepts such as fulfillment of basic human needs, social justice, and social equality. This image of the future was at first quite nebulous, but it is continually being refined and clarified.

As images of the future developed, it became apparent that appropriate models for creating the future in the area of social services were needed. While social work skills aimed at system change were recognized in the social work literature and some of these skills were taught at schools scattered throughout the country, no existing school of social work emphasized these skills. SSD became the first school of social work in the U.S. to emphasize social policy analysis and development, social planning, human service administration, community organizing, and social research as social work skills which can be incorporated to create the future within the domain of the social services.

Social work in general and SSD in particular have had a continuing interest in the values which serve as guidelines for the professionals in these fields. It became apparent within SSD that the expanded role envisioned for the social worker/developer required a value base which extended the values of traditional social work. In 1977 a futures methodology, the Delphi technique, was used to identify and clarify the values which serve as criteria for the process and outcome of social development. The results of this study will be described next.

The Delphi-Based Social Development Approach

The application of futuristic concepts to traditional social work practice drastically altered the focus of the SSD orientation to social services, as may be partially understood from the preceding section. The systems orientation, the long-term time-perspective, the concepts of imaging and creating the future, and the emphasis on values were all critical in the emergence of the social development approach.

Social development is defined within SSD as the process of planned institutional change to bring about a better fit between human needs and social policies and programs. The emphasis on planned or purposive change grows out of the futurist ideas of imaging and creating the future. It is recognized that change occurs constantly and that much of the change that currently exists is without purpose or direction. Social development emphasized the need to make conscious decisions about the direction of change and to undertake activities to produce the desired change.

The systems approach adopted by SSD has led to a focus on institutional, structural, or macro level change. In the past there has been a tendency to blame the victim for the negative situation in which he or she was found. For example, the resident of a black ghetto was held by many to be totally responsible for his or her place in society. Increasingly, the institutions or systems in a society have been identified as primary determinants of many social problems. Institutional racism may therefore be viewed as the primary cause of the black ghetto. Social development is aimed primarily at changing institutions and systems--i.e., policies, agencies, programs, and social roles and expectations--and not at changing individuals.

The term social development implies that it is necessary to focus on the distinctively human aspects of development. Previously in the United States we have emphasized economic development, that is planning and change efforts directed primarily at maximizing the efficient use of physical resources. Social development emphasizes a need for more comprehensive and coordinated policy and planning on a regional and national basis to address the social needs and enhance the human potential of everyone in the society.

Social development also promotes primary prevention of social problems. Primary prevention refers to action taken to prevent individual problems from occurring before they start. In contrast, secondary prevention refers to early intervention once a problem has been identified, and tertiary prevention is an extension of secondary prevention wherein action is taken after a problem becomes more serious. Using chemical dependency as an example, drug education may be viewed as primary prevention, crisis intervention and responsible use groups are examples of secondary prevention, and treatment for chronic alcoholism may be viewed as tertiary prevention. Social development advocates primary prevention as the appropriate response in attempting to address the root causes of a variety of social problems.

In many ways, values are central to the social development approach. Obviously, in developing an image of a desirable future and in deciding on methods to create that future, several value judgments must be made. A Delphi study of social development values polled the views of 38 people associated with SSD who were selected for their expert knowledge of social development values. In questionnaire #1 each participant was asked to list four values which could be used as guidelines for 1) the process of social development and 2) the goals of social development. In questionnaire #2 each respondent ranked the seven most important process values and the seven most important goal values which were obtained from the first questionnaire. They were also requested to comment on each list of values. The preliminary ranking results and a listing of previous comments were included

in questionnaire #3. Respondents were again asked to rank the
seven most important process and goal values. The seven highest
ranked process values and their definitions were as follows:

1. PARTICIPATION

People possessing equally the
opportunity to participate in the
decisions that affect their
lives.

2. RESPECT FOR HUMAN DIGNITY

Recognizing and accepting as
valid the basic worth of each
human being.

3. GLOBAL AWARENESS

Recognizing that the consequences
of change can go far beyond the
persons and situations most
directly affected (i.e., secondary and tertiary consequences).

4. NONDISCRIMINATION

Treating others equally, regardless of sex, race or other
ascribed characteristics.

5. HUMANISM

Focusing on the needs of individual human beings as opposed to
the needs of institutions.

6. COLLECTIVITY

Having consideration of the
common good take precedence over
the pursuit of individual rights.

7. SELF-DETERMINATION

Guaranteeing the right of
individuals to pursue personal
and group goals.

The seven highest ranked end-state (or goal) values and
their definitions were as follows:

1. FULFILLMENT OF BASIC
   HUMAN NEEDS

An end-state where each person
has adequate housing, food,
health care, shelter and safety.

2. HUMAN DIGNITY

Inherent value in each
individual is recognized and
respected.

3. EQUALITY OF MEANS
   (Freedom from Oppression)

Each person has equal access to
social political and economic
opportunities.

4. PARTICIPATORY DEMOCRACY

A structure in which everyone can join in the decision-making process in all matters affecting their lives and interests.

5. PEACE

The absence of war, non-violent coexistence.

6. SOCIALLY RESPONSIBLE HUMAN INSTITUTIONS

The purpose of institutions is to meet human needs, not to preserve themselves.

7. HEALTHY HUMAN ECOLOGY

A balanced interrelationship between society and the natural environment.

The values described above are related to social work values, but demonstrate the influence of a futuristic orientation as well.[3]

As can be seen from the description above, the futuristic concepts incorporated by SSD resulted in a social development orientation quite different from the traditional social work approach. Social work has traditionally focused on providing direct service to individuals and small groups in an attempt to solve current problems. Social development has emphasized macro level change which will develop policies and programs to better meet the needs of people for the future. The social development approach has supplemented and complemented the orientation of traditional social work.

Education for Social Development

Because of the unique focus within SSD, an educational program very different from that of traditional social work has developed. Traditional social work curricula primarily provided students with the skills and knowledge such as interviewing, individual program diagnosis, contracting, and treatment modalities, necessary to work directly with individuals and small groups. In introductory SSD classes, by contrast, students are exposed to systems theory, to opportunities to image the future that is most desirable to them, and to general models of creating the future (planned social change). Students are encouraged to develop a knowledge of the political and economic processes related to social development. The SSD curriculum encourages students to develop skills in social policy development, social planning, administration, community organization, and social research. Throughout their classes, students are encouraged to explore the values they hold with regard to the processes and goals of planned change. In addition, students are exposed to some futuristic methodologies as they pursue to their learning objectives. A more thorough description of the SSD curriculum is provided elsewhere.[4]

The SSD educational program differs significantly from the other schools granting an M.S.W. degree. While the social work profession and the SSD curriculum has by no means been completely "futurized," the profession of social work has been partially reconceptualized from a futuristic viewpoint, and the educational program has been redefined to educate the type of professional who can contribute within this new conception.

Implications for Professional Education

The preceding description provides an example of how a futuristic perspective can transform the conception of a profession and consequently redefine the nature of professional education. While the profession of social work is used in the example, a futuristic orientation can be (and probably has been) applied to other professions as well. Persons involved in medicine, nursing, law, education, engineering, business, and other professions can similarly incorporate a futuristic perspective, reconceptualize the role of their profession, and alter their professional education programs accordingly.

In incorporating a futuristic perspective, other professions may find similar components of futuristics to be useful. A systems approach, long-term time-perspective, concepts like imaging the future and creating the future, futures methodologies, and a focus on values will be appropriate to examine a variety of professions. A new conceptualization of the role of a profession can thereby be developed.

It is my speculation that the reconceptualized role of other professions may be similar to several aspects of the social development focus. Most often the image of the future that is developed will differ significantly from the world that currently exists. For this reason, the change function of the profession will most likely be emphasized. Given the futuristic orientation it is probable that systems (as opposed to individual) change will be emphasized and primary prevention will be given more consideration by the profession. The values promoted by the profession may similarly reflect a futuristic orientation.

A new educational program will most likely be designed to provide professionals to fill newly conceptualized professional roles in society. Chances are good that these programs will focus on the skills and knowledge necessary to create the future within the domain of the profession. In addition, futuristic concepts and methodologies will be incorporated into the educational programs.

The professions in general and professional school in particular have the potential to become self-serving and to become stagnant within a changing society. Some writers have gone so far as to view the professions as groups which restrict progressive change within society.[5] It is hoped that in incorporating a futuristic orientation into the professions, professional education can contribute to creating a future world which approximates the idealized images which so many of us hold for the future.

NOTES

1. Allen Pincus and Anne Minahan, Social Work Practice: Model and Method (Itasca, Illinois: Peacock Publishers, Inc., 1973).

2. Commission on Social Development, "Popular Participation and Its Practical Implications for Development" (New York: United Nations Economic and Social Council, 1975); and, Commission on Social Development, "Report on a Unified Approach to Development Analysis and Planning" (New York: United Nations Economic and Social Council, 1974).

3. Values in Social Work: A Re-examination (New York: National Association of Social Workers, 1967).

4. C.D. Hollister, "Social Work Skills for Social Development," Social Development Issues, Vol. 1, No. 1 (Spring 1977), pp. 9-20; and School of Social Development Bulletin 1977-79 (Duluth: University of Minnesota--Duluth, 1977).

5. Jeffrey Galper, The Politics of Social Services (Englewood Cliffs, N.J.: Prentice-Hall, 1975); and Ronald Gross and Paul Osterman, The New Professionals (New York: Simon and Schuster, 1972).

Forecasting the Speech Communication Curriculum of the Future

Phoebe P. Hollis

The field of speech communication encompasses the study of communication as both an art and a science. Throughout its history, the discipline has provided activities in the arts and humanities, the social sciences, and the natural sciences. These diverse concerns range from scientific investigation of communicative disorders through the humanistic studies in rhetoric, public address, oral interpretation and theater, to the social sciences in the study of communication behavior. With this diversification, the very <u>breadth</u> of the speech communication arts and sciences poses a dilemma for the constituents of the discipline. As a result, members not only encounter problems <u>within</u> the discipline, but also face obstacles outside the discipline, particularly in meeting the demands and the needs for adaptation resulting from the changes experienced by society.

This descriptive study was an investigation of issues existing within the discipline of speech communication and their implications for the speech communication curriculum. When left unconfronted, these issues may leave the discipline unprepared for the future. A growing fragmentation has been noticed within the discipline. There seems to be dissatisfaction and discontent among the members as there have emerged five or six discrete sub-disciplines (such as theater, oral interpretation, rhetoric, debate, communication behavior) within the one. In addition there is a lack of defined objectives for the discipline in relationship to the total academic arena and even to sub-areas of study within the discipline. Also noticeable is the lack of consensus regarding a specific purpose relating to what the speech curriculum is supposed to accomplish. And probably the most important because of its impact is the difference in research approaches to human communication, mainly exemplified by the contrast in the scientific and the humanistic method.

From this division, the discipline suffers from a "two-world" view represented by these two distinct groups who have different names and who conduct different investigations. This dichotomous view implies that the discipline actually contains two distinct theories of communication. The discontent resulting from this division between scientific and humanistic orientations has led members of the discipline to question the status of the profession and of the curriculum in institutions of higher learning. This division has led to a lack of agreement in curricular and, also, discipline goals.[1]

The principal purpose of this study was to reach a consensus of attitudes from the highest administrative officers of the speech communication areas on future curriculum goals of the discipline. Also, the study identified the major research orientation of these officers and explored the relationship between the identified orientation and the focus of the future speech communication curriculum. Administrators of the speech communication academic areas in the 996 public and private four-year institutions listed in the Speech Commmunication Directory, who were identified as offering course sequences or degree programs in speech communication, were asked to respond to this curriculum study using the Delphi Technique. The total population, as defined, made each member of the population a potential respondent; consequently, no sampling procedure was necessary.

Delphi Technique

The Delphi Technique, which is a method of attaining consensus from a large number of anonymous participants, was employed in this investigation. This technique is suited to futures forecasting since it allowed the respondents to indicate the opinion, probability, and desirability of the elements of speech communication curriculum of the future. Its classic definition is "a carefully designed program of sequential individual interrogations (best conducted by questionnaire) interspersed with information and opinion feedback."[2] The technique elicits and refines the opinions of a group of individuals to arrive at "convergent" or "polarized" views of one or more possible future events. It is highly valuable, particularly in the decision making process where major difficulties have always been present when a large number of influential individuals pool their opinions in face-to-face interaction.[3]

Each Delphi study requires the development of a specific instrument or series of instruments to elicit responses to questions for which consensus is sought. The Delphi instrument used in this study underwent a sequence of three developmental steps which synthesized items from a selected panel of judges and from the professional literature. The final questionnaire consisted of 24 items that stated areas of curriculum concern within the speech communication discipline. Two rounds were conducted for the study with 303 usable responses for Round I and 220 usable responses for Round II.

Results

The respondents indicated consensus on 22 of the 24 Delphi statements with two statements remaining in a polarized manner (see Appendix for details). Of those on which consensus was reached, agreement with 10 statements and disagreement with 12 statements gives clear indications of the direction they feel the speech communication of the future should take. They judged, as desirable and necessary, specific skill development, such as decision making, problem solving, adjusting to societal change, and communication skills for prospective teachers. They viewed many of the methodological and technological directions, including self-paced content, use of educational technology, and modular scheduling, as being adverse. The respondents indicated as undesirable any direction to merge with other professional groups and preferred to remain within the organizational structure of Arts and Sciences. They would not choose to limit the discipline by eliminating it as an academic major or to effect any extensive changes in hour requirements or reassignment course levels. They agreed to expanding the undergraduate opportunities in research and providing a curriculum based upon empirical research conclusions. They indicated as desirable the blending of behavioral and rhetorical research techniques. Those participating in the project emphasized a need for inter disciplinary study and clearly defined curriculum objectives; however, they did not see the curriculum organized around skills for specific vocational preparation.

Speech Communication Curriculum of
the Future

The data obtained in this research provide a basis for forecasting the future curriculum of the speech communication discipline and the possible directions of the discipline. Responses to the Delphi instrument serve to project the type of curriculum which might be expected, and the results indicate the possible directions of the discipline. Certainly the responses of the administrative officers to the questionnaire give some indication of what is likely to occur. Since the future speech communication curriculum is influenced by their decisions, a curriculum projection can be formulated.

The speech communication discipline of the future is projected to be a strong, independent field of study which will include a vast array of interests. However, these specific areas will probably contribute to increased specialization, which may only serve to dramatize the differences that will exist among speech scholars within the next ten years. The division of the scholars will be in the different approaches to research resulting in two distinct camps: those loyal to the scientific approach and those loyal to the humanistic approach. The orientation division, accompanied by the increased specialization, may be a harbinger for the separation of pure speech subjects and the social science oriented subjects by 1990. Certainly there is nothing that foreshadows a major reconciliation of the two orientations before 1990 to the extent that the discipline of the future is likely to be identified significantly with one of the two approaches.

Another expectation of this condition will be the different focus of curricula offered depending upon institutional characteristics. A difference will be expected in the larger institutions, particularly those with graduate programs. These schools will have a sound scientific orientation and will offer more courses in quantitative methods designed to enhance their research programs. The smaller institutions, however, will be traditionally oriented, but will be sensitive to the demands of society by revising many of their traditional courses. They will offer a curriculum reflecting vocational concerns. There will be no major difference in the speech communication curriculum of the future between public and private institutions given comparable size and program level. By 1990 the speech curriculum within individual institutions will definitely reflect the dominant philosophical position of either the scientific or the humanistic orientation to the study of human communication. This position will very likely coincide with the orientation of the administrative officer.

This curriculum of the future, derived from this Delphi Study, indicates that by 1988 the curriculum will respond to changes in society by increasing situation-oriented courses. As societal changes produce new demands, the speech communication curriculum will be made adaptable to societal needs. Basically, classroom procedures will insure that students will receive instruction that will enable them to cope with the rapid rate of change. The resulting curriculum will be student-oriented which will facilitate the acquisition of these needed skills.

Generally, this Delphi study foretells little change in the future for the speech communication discipline as reflected in its curriculum. It portends that the two dominant orientations within the discipline will hamper agreement on future curriculum goals. Probably the most perplexing problems faced by the discipline is recognition of the demand for change. How the discipline will actually respond to the demands of society remains to be seen, but if its supporters align according to past occurrences, then the discipline will respond and will change where the need is evident. Change must occur in order to avoid stagnation, and the refusal to recognize the needed change by clinging to tradition often results in a future created by fate.

The constituents of speech communication must face the areas of concern, must recognize the need for change, and must be willing to change where necessary for the survival of the discipline. They must adapt and grow in fruitful directions. The decisions made today produce the consequences of tomorrow-- undoubtedly the wisdom of the profession is at stake and the future depends upon the wisdom in the choices.

APPENDIX

Speech Communication Curriculum Delphi Questionnaire Results

1. The speech communication curriculum should be oriented around the skills necessary for decision-making and problem-solving.

    A. Agree 78.6%; Disagree 21.4%
    B. Will occur by: Mean Year 1984; Median Year 1984
    C. Desirable 81.3%; Undesirable 18.8%

2. The undergraduate curriculum should provide opportunities for participation in speech communication research.

    A. Agree 87.3%; Disagree 12.7%
    B. Will occur by: Mean Year 1984; Median Year 1984
    C. Desirable 86.8%; Undesirable 13.2%

3. Individualized instruction and self-paced programs should diminish the amount of classroom activity in speech communication.

    A. Agree 12.3%; Disagree 87.7%
    B. Will occur by: Mean Year 1993; Median Year 1990
    C. Desirable 12.9%; Undesirable 87.1%

4. Instruction in speech communication should adopt the use of
    clearly defined objectives and measurable outcomes.

    A. Agree 87.1%; Disagree 12.9%
    B. Will occur by: Mean Year 1986;Median Year 1984
    C. Desirable 86.2%; Undesirable 13.8%

5. Speech communication research efforts should be directed
    primarily to the resolution of current social problems.

    A. Agree 17.7%; Disagree 82.3%
    B. Will occur by: Mean Year 1990; Median Year 1986
    C. Desirable 26.2%; Undesirable 78.8%

6. The curriculum in speech communication should be organized
    around courses which are designed to enhance job
    opportunities for speech communication graduates.

    A. Agree 54.1%; Disagree 45.9%
    B. Will occur by: Mean Year 1895; Median Year 1984
    C. Desirable 55.9%; Undesirable 44.1%

7. Efforts should be devoted to severing organizational ties
    with Arts and Sciences and Humanities by moving to establish
    Schools of Communication.

    A. Agree 17.4%; Disagree 82.6%
    B. Will occur by: Mean Year 1993; Median Year 1991
    C. Desirable 21.5%; Undesirable 78.5%

8. Efforts in speech communication curriculum revision should
    be devoted to making speech courses an essential part of all
    educational programs rather than promoting the speech
    communication major as a field of study.

    A. Agree 36.0%; Disagree 64.0%
    B. Will occur by: Mean Year 1991; Median Year 1990
    C. Desirable 39.6%; Undesirable 60.4%

9.   The speech communication curriculum should be revised to
     emphasize the interdisciplinary nature of the course
     content.

     A.   Agree 80.3%; Disagree 19.7%
     B.   Will occur by: Mean Year 1986; Median Year 1985
     C.   Desirable 83.5%; Undesirable 16.4%

10. The scientific method of investigating spoken symbolic
     interaction should be the major theoretical base for the
     speech communication discipline.

     A.   Agree 10.0%; Disagree 90.0%
     B.   Will occur by: Mean Year 1993; Median Year 1990
     C.   Desirable 12.1%; Undesirable 87.9%

11. Enrollment in speech communication courses should be limited
     to those for whom the content has direct vocational
     application.

     A.   Agree 1.7%; Disagree 98.3%
     B.   Will occur by: Mean Year 1999; Median Year 2002
     C.   Desirable 2.7%; Undesirable 97.3%

12. A significant core of the speech communication curriculum
     should be based on research conclusions regarding strategies
     and constraints in message choice, communication
     environments, and speech functions.

     A.   Agree 89.4%; Disagree 10.6%
     B.   Will occur by: Mean Year 1985; Median Year 1985
     C.   Desirable 91.1%; Undesirable 8.9%

13. Speech communication should be based on a "source-message"
     centered curriculum as opposed to a "message-audience"
     curriculum.

     A.   Agree 13.3%; Disagree 86.7%
     B.   Will occur by: Mean Year 1993; Median Year 1990
     C.   Desirable 15.0%; Undesirable 85.0%

14.   Major elements in the course content of speech communication
      should insure that students are prepared to adapt to the
      constant rate of change reflected in the society.

      A.   Agree 89.5%; Disagree 10.5%
      B.   Will occur by: Mean Year 1986; Median Year 1984
      C.   Desirable 90.4%; Undesirable 9.6%

15.   The speech communication curriculum of the future should
      eliminate those traditional performance areas such as oral
      interpretation, voice and articulation, debate, and
      parliamentary procedure.

      A.   Agree 11.4%; Disagree 88.6%
      B.   Will occur by: Mean Year 1995; Median Year 1992
      C.   Desirable 1.9%; Undesirable 98.1%

16.   The application of educational technology should replace the
      classroom teacher as the medium of instruction in speech
      communication.

      A.   Agree 2.4%; Disagree 97.6%
      B.   Will occur by: Mean Year 2001; Median Year 2005
      C.   Desirable 1.9%; Undesirable 98.1%

17.   Within the practical framework of institutional scheduling,
      the speech communication curriculum should be structured on
      a modular approach.

      A.   Agree 11.1%; Disagree 88.9%
      B.   Will occur by: Mean Year 1994; Median Year 1992
      C.   Desirable 12.8%; Undesirable 87.2%

18.   Credit hour requirements in speech communication should be
      reduced in order that students have greater opportunities
      for interdisciplinary study.

      A.   Agree 19.7%; Disagree 80.3%
      B.   Will occur by: Mean Year 1992; Median Year 1989
      C.   Desirable 23.9%; Undesirable 76.1%

19.   Speech communication should be fused with the subject matter
       content of the social sciences (psychology, sociology,
       political science) rather than continue as a separate
       discipline.

       A.   Agree 12.1%; Disagree 87.9%
       B.   Will occur by: Mean Year 1996; Median Year 1996
       C.   Desirable 14.2%; Undesirable 85.8%

20.   The instructional program in speech communication should be
       revised to reflect more empirical research.

       A.   Agree 68.1%; Disagree 31.9%
       B.   Will occur by: Mean Year 1987; Median Year 1986
       C.   Desirable 71.3%; Undesirable 28.7%

21.   The speech communication curriculum should be revised to
       include specific context courses such as political communi-
       cation, organizational communication, and legal communica-
       tion.

       A.   Agree 82.8%; Disagree 17.2%
       B.   Will occur by: Mean Year 1986; Median Year 1984
       C.   Desirable 83.0%; Undesirable 17.0%

22.   Much of the content of speech communication graduate courses
       should be incorporated into the undergraduate program.

       A.   Agree 20.2%; Disagree 79.8%
       B.   Will occur by: Mean Year 1992; Median Year 1990
       C.   Desirable 22.7%; Undesirable 77.3%

23.   Speech communication research efforts should be directed
       toward merging behavioral and rhetorical approaches in a
       common approach to research design.

       A.   Agree 92.1%; Disagree 7.9%
       B.   Will occur by: Mean Year 1987; Median Year 1987
       C.   Desirable 92.7%; Undesirable 7.3%

24. The speech communication curriculum should provide a course
     concerning the relationship of classroom communication to
     learning and instruction for all prospective teachers.

     A. Agree 94.9%; Disagree 5.1%
     B. Will occur by: Mean Year 1986; Median Year 1984
     C. Desirable 95.6%; Undesirable 4.4%

             Individual and Institutional Information:

Sex: Male 83.5%; Female 16.5%

Highest Degree: Bachelor's 0.8%; Master's 20.9%; Doctorate
78.3%

Years Since Highest Degree: 1-5 36.3%; 6-10 27.4%; 11-15
16.1%; 16-20 7.7%; Above 20 12.5%

SCA Individual Member: Yes 82.2%; No 17.8%

SCA Regional Member: ECA 11.9%; SSCA 32.7%; CSSA 36.5%;
WSCA 18.9%

SCA Regional Association Meetings Attended in Last Five
Years: 0 33.1%; 1 14.5%; 2 17.3%; 3 11.7%; 4 9.3%; 5 14.1%

SCA National Conventions Attended in Last Five Years:
0 28.9%; 1 16.1%; 2 21.3%; 3 13.3%; 4 9.2%; 5 11.2%

Institutional Size: Up to 5,000 54.4%; 5,000-10,000 22.0%;
10,000-15,000 8.4%; 15,000-20,000 6.4%; Over 20,000 8.8%

Institutional Support: Public 58.0%; Private 42.0%

Institutional Type: Four Year 55.2%; Graduate 44.8%

Speech Communication Organization: Major Area Only 29.6%;
Department 59.9%; Division 10.5%

Speech Communication Degree Offered: None 20.5%; Bachelors
49.4%; Masters 23.7%; Doctorate 6.4%

Speech Communication Full Time Equivalent Faculty Members:
1-5 58.6%; 6-10 20.9%; 11-15 11.6%; 16-20 3.6%; Over 20 5.2%

NOTES

1. For a guide to understanding the status of the Speech Communication discipline, see Waldo W. Braden, "An Uncommon Profession," The Southern Speech Journal, 36 (Fall 1970), pp. 1-10; Robert C. Jeffrey, "Speech and the Humanities," The Southern Speech Communication Journal, 4 (Winter 1976), pp. 158-164; Carroll C. Arnold, "Rhetorical and Communication Studies: Two Worlds Or One?" Western Speech, 35 (Spring 1972), pp. 75-81; Eugene E. White, "Prospects for the Future: Changing Continuity," The Speech Teacher, 23 (March 1974), pp. 139-143; Robert J. Kibler and Larry L. Barker (eds.), Conceptual Frontiers in Speech-Communication (New York: Speech Association of America, 1969); James E. Roever, "New Orleans, Wingspread, and Pheasant Run Briefly Revisited," Western Speech, 37 (Winter 1974), pp. 7-12; Donald K. Smith, "Speech for Tomorrow: Concepts and Context," The Speech Teacher, 15 (January 1966), 30-33; Kenneth R. Williams, "Speech Communication Research: One World or Two?" Central States Speech Journal, 21 (Fall 1970), pp. 175-180; Phoebe P. Hollis, "Speech Communication Curriculum of the Future: A Delphi Profile" (Ph.D. dissertation, Texas Tech University, 1977).

2. Olaf Helmer and Nicholas Rescher, "On the Epistemology of the Inexact Sciences," Management Science, 6(October 1959), p. 37.

3. For use of the Delphi Technique see N.C. Dalkey, The Delphi Method: An Experimental Study of Group Opinion (The Rand Corporation, RM-5888-Pr, June 1969); Olaf Helmer, The Use of the Delphi Techniques in Problems of Educational Innovations (The Rand Corporation, P-3499, December 1966); Harold A. Linstone and Murray Turoff, The Delphi Method: Techniques and Application (Reading, Massachusetts: Addison-Wesley Publishing Company, 1975).

Cybernetics of Communication in Academic Life

Carlos Torre

Social Cybernetics: A Brief History

In 1970, at the University of Sao Paulo's School of Sociology and Politics, Dr. Waldemar De Gregori designed and developed a method for training people to consciously cultivate their ways of thinking, and to train their mental functions. He calls this process "Social Cybernetics"--social, because it utilizes Antonio Rubbo Muller's "Theory of Human Organization" as its particular systems theory; cybernetic in that it has borrowed and adapted the electronic engineering concepts of holistic system, communication, and feedback loop for purposive self-direction and regulation of individuals, groups and institutions.

Initially, the method was used with interdisciplinary groups for community development. Later, sessions were organized for developing trainers. Simultaneously, the School of Sociology and Politics opened extensions in several Latin American countries. In 1973, laboratory groups from several Latin American countries were compared and contrasted. The experimental group (using Social Cybernetics) proved superior in its members' ability to think, to reason, and to carry out investigations, while the members of the control group were more disorganized, confused, and disoriented. Since 1976, the Social Cybernetics method has been applied to a variety of specific disciplines (including scientific writing for university students called the "Cybernetics of Communication" at Northeastern Illinois University in 1979). And in 1978, the Sao Paulo School of Sociology and Politics opened an extension--The Sao Paulo-Chicago School of Sociology and Politics--Chicago campus.

Theoretical Structure and Principles of Social Cybernetics

The theoretical base for the Social Cybernetics approach to the training of the mental functions is a synthesis of various established scientific theories and concepts together with new scientific contributions.   It has combined Darwin's evolutionary process with Wiener's concepts of cybernetics and feedback, Christianity's idea of collective work and an innovation on Marx's Dialectics called "triadic thinking."   Using the scientific method, De Gregori then added new steps for the mental process applicable to a wide variety of learning, research and problem-solving situations.   The uniqueness here comes in putting the steps together and in sequencing them.

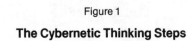

Figure 1

The Cybernetic Thinking Steps

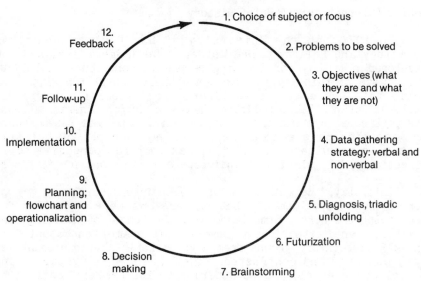

An epigenesis of Gestalt psychology, called the "Global Theory" is then incorporated in order to suggest a holistic conceptual intrument.

A "Theory of Programming" is introduced to help the individual understand the societal and institutional socialization he/she receives from birth through the life cycles.   Finally, De Gregori bases his Social Cybernetics approach on the following principles:

* that the thinking process has steps which can be mastered and used for intellectual, mental and self development;

* that no one can write effectively if there is no internal organization of the message that he/she wishes to communicate;

* thus, rather than giving students facts and data, they should be trained to develop their mental process by providing them with instruments so they themselves can collect the facts and data available around them (from books, people, institutions, and archives);

* that education should be an interdisciplinary process with students learning through involvement and mutual feedback among the participants;

* that learning how to approach a situation should be a gradual, progressive process where student achievement is explicitly self-directed rather than left to chance.

The Cybernetics of Communication

De Gregori and this writer have adapted the theoretical structure and principles of Social Cybernetics to the process of writing the kind of scientific works universities demand of their students. The program is called "The Cybernetics of Communication." The format follows:

A Social Cybernetics weekend training workshop is held (Saturday and Sunday--seven and a half hours each day, or any other equivalent module). At this workshop the participants are exposed to systems theory and are trained in the use of the model.

After the weekend workshop the participants begin meeting in regularly scheduled sessions. Using the model and Social Cybernetics concepts, the facilitator demonstrates how to organize mentally the message that one wishes to communicate (internal organization of message) and how to define a theme. In most cases, students select topics they are working on for other courses.

At this point the participants begin to work on developing and communicating their themes. An interdisciplinary teaching team is formed by bringing in a specialist on basic communication skills (who provides information on sentence structure, grammar vocabulary, etc.) and a Social Cybernetics facilitator (who supervises students on their projects, acts as an animator during each session, provides clarification and examples of how to use the Social Cybernetics instruments, and progressively provides more advanced techniques and information about the process). Most sessions consist of students reporting on their themes and receiving feedback from fellow classmates and from the inter-disciplinary team. The specific issues dealt with during this stage of the program are:

* how to think out the theme;

* how to edit;

* how to communicate one's topic verbally;

* how to differentiate the quality of information obtained through texts, popular magazines, articles, news, and commentary.

In summary, the Cybernetics of Communication course is an innovative approach to basic communication skills acquisition for academic life. Its procedures are based on a synthesis of previously tested and newly developed scientific theory. It is developmental in nature rather than remedial, and holistic rather than fragmented. Social Cybernetics involves the student directly in his/her own process of simultaneous self-development and skills acquisition. The method is highly structured and organized, yet as one participant stated during a session, "it's really quite digestible."

POSTSCRIPT
Systems Thinking for the Educational Futurist

Arthur M. Harkins

Educators everywhere are realizing that increased choices for tomorrow constitute a kind of cultural evolution; that merely by having more choices at hand we have increased the complexity, and perhaps the survivability, of ourselves, our society, and humankind.

Alternative educational futures tend to increase choices, not only for our futures, but also for how we view alternative presents and pasts. Alternative educational futures are the source of our hopes for better futures, for the resources and skills to "push back" negative futures.

Interestingly, many educators do not seem to be aware that alternative educational futures have poor chances of success if "environmental" conditions do not support them. An educational innovation's environment is everything "significant" that has, or could, come into contact with it. Many educational futurists are learning that the innovation environment interaction is the "system" that can easily be overlooked in the excitement of designing and implementing change. Such a perspective is often referred to as the "systems" approach.

There is a need to bring "systems thinking" into the complex of issues, ideas, problems, and opportunities wrestled with by educational futurists. Why? Because the complex of factors making up past and present realities and future possibilities/ probabilities is so vast and so intractable as to make piecemeal "solutions" questionable, sometimes even dangerous. What are some of the main ideas in systems thinking and why would/should they be of use to educational futurists?

First, systems thinking allows us to view pieces of problems and whole problems together. Why is this important? Because

very often a "solution" at one level of an educational problem
produces reactions that lead to a worsening of the total
situation. Despite whether the solution is attempted at a
"holistic" or "lower" level of the problem, we do not know enough
about the interactive nature of human educational and other
systems to know for certain what effects the "solution" will
have. Systems thinking encourages skepticism about "quick
fixes," using either reductionistic approaches, or facile
holistic approaches.

Second, systems thinking encourages us to think of the role
of human invention in creating conceptions of systems. Systems
may be thought of as "hard" or "soft," meaning that some are
weighable, as in the case of a school building, and some are not,
as in the case of an idea for developing approaches to controlling delinquency. Human beings are the only source of "truth"
about the configurations and behaviors of all systems--past,
present or future. Humans are the source of systemic educational
philosophies, organized sports, world religions, and student
handbooks emphasizing ethical conduct. If humans can invent
schools that produce dropouts and semi-literate graduates, it is
theoretically reasonable to assert that humans can redesign or
recreate such systems to produce different results.

Third, all conceptions of hard and soft systems developed by
humans can be viewed as the fundamental content of our cultures.
It is pragmatically useful for persons to know the difference
between apples and oranges, schools and governmental institutions, and families and hockey teams. These inventions allow
humans to distinguish one type of system from another system.
They also allow people to ask, How does sytem A interact with
system B? And how do both interact with system C? How does a
school in the Soviet Union interact with the Communist Party
headquarters nearby? How does a group of adolescent girls in a
small New Guinea tribal village interact with the mission school
teacher, and both with short wave radio stations, many of them
busily transmitting rock music and secular messages? How does a
major rocket scientist boast that he has no college credits to
his name, when many people assume that all rocket scientists
should (or must?) have at least one college degree? How can
teachers without knowledge of computers work effectively with
children from homes where computer learning experiences are
commonplace? And how do either these children or their teachers
interact with children from homes where computers are called
"machines of the devil?" These conceptions of systems in
interaction make up both the content and processes of cultural
and personal views of reality.

Fourth, enhancement of numbers and varieties of systems
conceptions creates more complexity, and thereby more choice, in
humans. Enhancements in complexity underlie all forms of human

attempts to educate, because education adds to our knowledge of culture and self. This increase in complexity theoretically and practically enhances the ways in which people are able to view past, present, and future events in their lives and in the lives of others. Imagine how different the future images of children who have been encouraged to think that "all things are possible" might be, from those who have been warned not to "think the unthinkable," whatever that may be. The future is driven by the existence of amounts and types of complexity in the present, and in the past, but, of course, it is not completely determined by either.

What we have outlined is more common sense than theoretical or mysterious. But virtually everything we have suggested above is, to some degree, perceivable as closely associated with the stuff of ideology and power. Nothing could be more useful or dangerous to cultures than alternative conceptions of reality, which is what systems thinking is all about. If some conceptions of future directions for a culture do not fit within the boundaries of the status quo, the results could be culturally destabilizing, or perhaps disastrous. In fact, it might be necessary for the perceived common good of the culture to limit the development and expression of past, present and future realities in order to maintain control of the situation. Is this what underlies the slow development of alternative futures curricula in some public schools as compared to others? Is the fact that only three or four graduate programs in alternative educational or social futures exist in America a possible source of concern about excessive limitation of futurist thinking and education? Or is it because change is slow and does not occur at the same rate--that culture lag, "futures shock," uneven psychological adaptations to change, and the like, are involved?

What is _your_ construction of reality? Your notion of the natures of interaction systems will allow you to answer such questions one way or another, or perhaps not to take them seriously at all. You could even be unaware of such questions by virtue of your place in the "system of systems" that constitutes the ecology of _world_ cultures.

I would like to suggest some more specific ways to employ systems thinking in educational futures work. A systems approach to educational futures is worth serious consideration because systems thinking allows both cultural analysis and cultural creation. Cultural analysis and creation are central to all phases of educational futures, whether in one society or another, and whether at one level of education or another.

Systems _teleology_. By systems teleology we mean a system's capacity to create. Human systems are the best example we (as humans) can now identify as sources of creativity. You are a human system. Are you able to create the educational future that you want for yourself? For your students? Your children? Much of the creation effort starts with a sense of self that is power_ful_ as opposed to power_less_. Often this sense of power is hard to develop in individuals who are pressured by fellow teachers, administrators and union personnel to conform to collective standards. Yet collective standards can be changed by the individual who has a sense of purpose and a clear image of alternative educational futures. Some of the most important educational futures of the 1980s may well occur outside the public or even the private schools. Direct broadcast satellites, small, wearable teaching devices, and such socioeconomic innovations as corporate schools and vouchers may make the educational landscape far more pluralistic in the near future. Teleology will have as much to do with educational success in the 1980s as ever before, whether the success is inside or outside schools as we know them today.

Systems _evolution_. By systems evolution we mean an increase in the complexity of the system. Such new complexity may or may not "fit" the nature of the environment in such a way as to enhance the survivability of the system or even the environment. The notion of systems evolution is very complex. Evolution does not succeed simply because an innovation has occurred; the innovation must fit the environment and/or change the environment so that both may survive. The implications for educational futures are many. If we want a curriculum on alternative futures to be introduced successfully in our schools, we may have to pay as much or more attention to preparing the environment for the innovation as in preparing the innovation itself. The idea is to regard the innovation process broadly enough to include the reactions of the environment that will be affected by the change. Both innovation and environment may have to be altered to allow this to occur, and both innovation and environment will continue to change in the future.

Requisite _adaptability_. By requisite adaptability we mean the capacity of the system to survive changes in itself or the environment because it has, or can develop, sufficient complexity to do so. For an educational innovation to succeed, we may have to make it more complex so that it can adapt successfully to the environment. A curriculum on alternative futures may have to be "tailored" to fit not only the school, but the beliefs and values of some of the members of the community in which the school operates. Requisite adaptability means that the innovation must have a certain amount of complexity in order to succeed in a particular environment. The requisite adaptability for one classroom environment may be quite different from another, perhaps one right down the corridor in the same school building.

"Zero sum" systems orientation. By this we mean a view of the situation that focuses on scarcity of resources, such as textbooks, money, or teaching positions. This view is sometimes called the "limited good theory"; it assumes that when System A gains part of a resource, System B automatically loses that part. This orientation is deadly to those who wish to open their minds to alternative educational futures. Why? Because the zero sum systems orientation tends to close the imagination to new definitions of resources and strategic and tactical change potentials. Educators with a zero sum approach to their professional situations are often cynical and defeated. They tend to see change potential in very narrow, institutionally limited terms. Worst of all, they tend to judge themselves very harshly and negatively, so that they see little in themselves that can change or be developed as a new kind of personal resource. They believe that there are only so many facets of self, school, and other resources, and that if these are already in use and efforts to change already have failed, nothing further can be done.

"Non-zero sum" systems orientation. A non-zero sum systems orientation allows for everyone to get a piece of the pie without consuming that resource entirely ("all win"). But it also allows for the possibility that no one could get a piece of the pie, or that the pie could disappear ("all lose"). The non-zero sum systems orientation allows for movement off dead center. It is a risky orientation because it not only allows for fantastic success, but catastrophic failure and everything imaginable in between. Zero-sum systems thinkers often admire and envy non-zero sum systems thinkers because they seem to be more "alive"; that is, they seem to be much more able to imagine change, for better or worse, than the static, leveled-out thinking characteristic of "fixed pie" people. Non-zero sum thinking and non-zero sum people are behind the changes that occur in all human institutions. Trying to implant a futures curriculum in a school may seen "impossible" to zero-sum systems thinkers, but it is always something that seems possible to non-zero sum thinkers.

Systems information underload. Have you heard of the notion of "information overload" concerning future educational alternatives? This notion is based on the assumption that the system cannot handle certain kinds of complexity, in this case those concerning alternative educational futures. Information overload is not really the problem when a future alternative cannot be managed by people. Information underload is really the problem.

We cannot undertake to think constructively about alternative educational futures unless we have sufficient information to do so. Every instance of our incapacity to deal with an alternative future for education or anything else is an instance wherein our information underload does not permit us to consider, and possibly to take advantage of, an alternative future. Information underload about alternative educational futures is exactly what this book and many other publications, films, television programs, and other information inputs can help to dispel.

WHAT WE HAVE TRIED TO DO by discussing a few general systems concepts is to suggest a possible language of professional change analysis and management. It is the futurist's task to produce alternative ideas and plans for educational and other future choices. Formulating a language of change and change management is important, because such language can serve as a "glue" to hold together the efforts of human change agents. Systems language is being tied to an emerging profession concerned with alternative futures. The language of general systems thinking is a prime candidate for facilitating the carefully orchestrated emergence of a true profession of change and change management in society, culture, and education.

*   *   *   *

IN THE TRUE SENSE OF SHARED VISION AND NETWORKING, the editors and contributors to Sourcebook II invite comments, criticism, and other types of feedback on this second effort. General responses should be addressed to: Dr. K.M. Redd, Stewart Hall, St. Cloud State University, St. Cloud, MN 56301 and/or Dr. A.M. Harkins, Burton Hall, University of Minnesota, Minneapolis, MN 55455. Reactions or comments about specific papers should be sent directly to the author(s) [see About the Authors]. Succeeding volumes and conferences of the Education Section will benefit by such interactions. Copies of this book and future conference volumes will be available through the WFS Book Service. The Education Section is planning yearly conferences to share ideas and efforts of educators throughout the world. The 1980 meeting will be at the University of Massachusetts at Amherst. All individuals are invited to attend these and other conferences of the World Future Society. For information about conference registration and WFS membership, write to: World Future Society, 4916 St. Elmo Avenue, Washington, D.C. 20014 (ask for Education Section membership information).

About the Authors

EDWARD F. CARPENTER is a professor of Educational Administration, and Teacher Education in the Graduate School of Education of the City College of New York. He earned his doctorate in Education from the University of Massachusetts. He also holds advanced certificates in Counseling, Mathematics and English. Dr. Carpenter is best known for having been the pioneer founder of Harlem Prep. This school gained international fame for working with "dropouts" or "potential dropouts" who demonstrated an interest in obtaining the high school diploma and then attending a college or university. He was awarded an LL.D. by Iona College, the Distinguished Alumnus Award by Long Island University, and served as a member of the Governor's Commission to Study Campus Unrest from 1969-1974. He has written numerous articles on education and the future and has served as consultant for the NEA, National Urban League, and colleges throughout the U.S. and Africa. He has also been a member of the World Future Society since its inception. Address responses to: Dr. Edward F. Carpenter, 96 Van Aradale Place, Teaneck, N.J. 07666.

CHRISTOPHER J. DEDE is Associate Professor of Science Education and Futures Research at the University of Houston at Clear Lake City, and is President of the Education Section, World Future Society. He was previously an Assistant Professor at the University of Massachusetts, Amherst, where he co-founded and directed the first graduate futures research program in the United States. This past year, he has been on leave, working in the Planning Office, National Institute of Education under a policy fellowship from the Institute for Educational Leadership, George Washington University. His publications include The Far Side of the Future and Educational Futures: Sourcebook I (both published by the World Future Society), as well as numerous articles. Address responses to: Dr. Christopher Dede, University of Houston at Clear Lake City, 2700 Bay Area Boulevard, Houston, TX 77058.

JOHN F. DEETHARDT is Associate Professor of Speech Communication at Texas Tech University Complex. He is currently inventing the details of new platforms for political communication: a bi-weekly university forum in an audience participation debate format; a university cross-disciplinary interaction center; the Lubbock community forum--a prime-time, televised public affairs program; a communication network of Texas academicians in speech communication for political influence; and an annual town-hall meeting for a national professional association. He has chaired two international conferences, in Stuttgart and Vienna, the speech education section of the 4th International Congress of Applied Linguistics, and the 6th Biennial International Colloquium on Verbal Communication. Address responses to: Dr. John F. Deethardt, Division of Speech Communication, Texas Tech University Complex, Lubbock, TX 79409.

LEONORE W. DICKMANN, Ph.D. is Professor of Education and Coordinator of the Curriculum and Instruction Program, and of the MS Curriculum and Supervision degree program at the University of Wisconsin-Oshkosh. She has been an elementary teacher, vice-principal, and supervisor of curriculum and instruction with the Milwaukee Public Schools. In a joint appointment, she served as a Visiting Lecturer and Coordinator of the Intern Program with both the University of Wisconsin-Milwaukee and Marquette University. She has received the Johnson Foundation Award for Distinguished Teaching (1971), the Danforth Foundation Award for Humanistic Concerns (1974), and the Outstanding Educator's Award (1972). Presently, she teaches three courses in futurism on her campus, and is a member of the World Future Society. She is active in in-service and consultant work in the areas of futures, creativity, and affective education. Address responses to: Dr. Leonore W. Dickmann, Curriculum and Instruction, College of Education, University of Wisconsin--Oshkosh, Oshkosh, WI 54901.

DENNIS R. FALK is an Assistant Professor in the School of Social Development at the University of Minnesota-Duluth. The School of Social Development offers social work programs that have developed around a futuristic orientation. His current activities involve teaching interdisciplinary courses, including a course on alternative futures. He is the author of articles on the dissemination and adoption of innovative curriculum models and on small group functioning. He is interested in the integration of futuristic principles, concepts, and methodologies into professional education programs and believes that futuristics can make significant contributions in promoting planned social change within the professions. Address responses to: Dennis R. Falk, School of Social Development, Marshall W. Alworth Hall Room 295, University of Minnesota--Duluth, Duluth, MN 55812.

ARTHUR M. HARKINS is an Associate Professor of Education and Sociology at the University of Minnesota where he also directs the program in Alternative Social and Educational Futures. He is a Director and past President of Minnesota Futurists and serves on the Board of Editors of Futurics. His Ph.D. is in Sociology from the University of Kansas. His special interests are in anthropological and sociological aspects of culture transmission and the creation and design of alternative futures. With Magorah Maruyama, he has edited Cultures of the Future and Cultures Beyond the Earth. Dr. Harkins has directed several Delphic research projects as well as being actively involved in a U.S. Office of Education project on the future of K-12 education. Address responses to: Dr. Arthur M. Harkins, College of Education, University of Minnesota, 203-B Burton Hall, Minneapolis, MN 55455.

PHOEBE P. HOLLIS is an Assistant Professor of Communication in the Department of Communication at the University of Nebraska at Omaha, Omaha, Nebraska, where she teaches courses in communication and education. She is the author of several papers about societal change and subsequent implications for education, and has appeared on several panels regarding futures research in communication. Her research interest is in assessing the impact of change upon society and the educational system, particularly higher education. She has been active in the Speech Communication Association where she is currently serving as chairperson of the Futures Studies in Human Communication Committee. Address responses to: Dr. Phoebe P. Hollis, Department of Communication, University of Nebraska at Omaha, Omaha, Nebraska 68182.

FLORENCE F. HOOD is an Associate Professor in the Department of Home Economics at Norfolk State University in Virginia. Her teaching experience is quite diverse; she has taught at the elementary, junior high, secondary, undergraduate and graduate levels. She received her Ph.D. from Texas A & M University where she was the first woman president of a college chapter of Iota Lambda Sigma, an Industrial Education honorary fraternity. She is currently Secretary-Treasurer of the Adult Vocational Education Association, American Vocational Association. In addition to having published and made presentations on education, change, and the future, Dr. Hood has developed and taught various courses in the Master's Urban Studies program, including one on the "Dynamics of the Change Process." Address responses to: Dr. Florence F. Hood, School of Social Sciences, Norfolk State University, Norfolk, Virginia 23504.

JEAN HOUSTON has served on the faculties of psychology, religion, and philosophy at Columbia, Hunter, and Marymount College and is presently teaching at The New School for Social Research. Dr. Houston is the developer of, and chief consultant for, the curriculum in Human Capacities at The New School for Social Research—at present the only advanced training offered by an accredited university in the study and application of human potential. For some time now, she has been training teachers and introducing her methods into primary and secondary schools for more effective education, as well as working in programs for rehabilitating the elderly and ex-prisoners. Dr. Houston is currently interested in extending arts curricula in the schools as a means to improve learning and psychophysical development in children. With Robert Masters, she has written, among other works, Mind Games and Listening to the Body. Dr. Houston is past President of the Association for Humanistic Psychology and Director of the Foundation for Mind Research. Address responses to: Dr. Jean Houston, The Foundation for Mind Research, PO Box 600, Pomona, New York 10970.

GAYLE HUDGENS, Ph.D., is Director General of Transdisciplinary Services, an independent futures research and consulting firm, and is the former Associate Director of the Project on Literacy Development at The University of Texas at Austin, a project funded by the National Institute of Education. She has a transdisciplinary and global background in research and writing, has published in The Nation and Americas, has been an active member of the Governance Task Force of the Education Section of the World Future Society, and pursues with vigor her special interests in ethics and professional responsibility, grant writing, public affairs, international relations, and alternative futures. Listed in Contemporary Authors, Dr. Hudgens receives mail at P.O. Box 25561, Dallas Texas 75225.

EARL C. JOSEPH is Staff Scientist-Futurist with Sperry Univac. His fields of specialization and interest include technology forecasting, future value systems, educational futures, basic futures research, and computer futures. He is a Director and past President of Minnesota Futurists, a chapter of the World Future Society, and a member of the Board of Editors of Futurics. He is a Visiting Lecturer in future studies at the University of Minnesota and a Futurist-in-Residence at the Science Museum of Minnesota. For more than seventeen years he has been active in basic futures research and long-range planning at Sperry Univac. His publications are numerous, including more than 100 papers and chapters in 20 books. Address responses to: Dr. Earl C. Joseph, Staff Scientist-Futurist, Sperry Univac U 2L28, PO Box 3525, St. Paul, MN 55165.

ELEONORA BARBIERI MASINI is Secretary-General of the World Future Studies Federation. She earned a degree in law from the Universita di Roma and has engaged in additional studies in comparative law, philosophy and psychology. In addition to her responsibilities with WFSF, Dr. Masini directed the course in social forecasting at Universita Gregoriana and has worked with IRADES where she was responsible for social forecasting studies. Dr. Masini has directed research on "children's images of the future" for UNESCO and on "women's changing role in Italy" for Centro Italiano Femminile. In addition, she has been actively involved in a study of "Visions of Desirable Societies" as part of the U.N. University's project on "Goals, Processes, and Indicators of Development." Address correspondence to: Dr. Eleonora Masini, Secretary General, World Future Studies Federation, Casella Postale 6203, Roma-Prati, Italy.

GERRI PERREAULT is Co-Chair of Minnesota Women in Higher Education; a consultant in the areas of adult development, adult learning, women's studies, and curriculum development; and a Community Faculty member at Metropolitan State University where she teaches courses on "The Development of the Adult: A Neglected Species." She is presently completing her doctorate at the University of Minnesota. Her research is on development of a typology which outlines different feminist perspectives on higher education. Past experiences have included positions at the University of Minnesota as an Administrative Fellow in the graduate Higher Education Program, an Administrative Assistant on Project BORN FREE, and an educational consultant in the School of Public Health master's programs. Address responses to: Gerri Perreault, 3224 Harriet Avenue South, Minneapolis, MN 55408.

HAROLD G. SHANE holds a distinguished professorship at Indiana University with the title of University Professor of Education. Dr. Shane's professional experiences are many and varied, including work in nursery school, in grades three and four, at the junior-senior high school level, as an elementary principal, as a city superintendant of schools, as a state curriculum director and as Dean of the School of Education at Indiana University from 1951 to 1965. Dr. Shane's Indiana University teaching assignments at present are in the fields of elementary education, curriculum development, English education, and futures research. He is a past President of the Association for Supervision and Curriculum Development and has served on the governing boards of the National Association for Nursery Education and the John Dewey Society, as well as many other organizations. Dr. Shane has been an editor and consultant for many publications, including the Phi Delta Kappan and Futurics. Address responses to: Dr. Harold Shane, School of Education, Room 328, Indiana University, Bloomington, IN 47401.

MICHELE GESLIN SMALL is an Assistant Professor of English at Northland College, Ashland, Wisconsin. Prior to coming to Northland in 1972 she taught French for three years at the State University of New York at Albay. She holds a licence d'Anglais from the University of Nice, France, and a Master's Degree in English from the State University of New York at Albany. She is presently pursuing a Doctoral Degree in Future Studies at the University of Minnesota-Minneapolis. She came to the United States in 1967 on a Fulbright Scholarship and has lived and taught in this country since that time. A world traveler, she was born in the New Hebrides and spent most of her youth in Madagascar. She has also lived in Europe, Africa and the South Pacific and has traveled extensively in other parts of the world. In addition to her teaching she is experienced in both simultaneous and written translation in French and English. She started a Futures Studies Program at Northland College and has taught courses in Alternative Futures and Science Fiction since 1974. She is extremely interested in interdisciplinary studies and feels that the field of Future Studies must play a major role in transcending and unifying the many separate cultures in higher education and in helping society ease its way into the 21st century. Address responses to: Michele Small, Route #1, PO Box 255, Washburn, WI 54891.

WILLIAM L. SMITH was sworn in as the 24th United States Commissioner of Education on January 9, 1980. As Commissioner of Education, he heads the 113-year-old Office of Education, which has more than 4,000 employees who administer 110 education programs with a budget of $12.4 billion. Prior to this, Dr. Smith served as Director of the Teacher Corps. Since coming to the Office of Education in August 1969, he has served in a variety of posts including Acting Deputy Commissioner for Development, Associate Commissioner for Career Education, Associate Commissioner for Educational Personnel Development, and Director for Improvement of Educational Systems. Previously, Dr. Smith was executive director of Programs of Action by Citizens in Education (PACE), an independent organization which promotes educational innovation in 32 greater Cleveland public school districts. From 1963 to 1968 he was principal of Patrick Henry Junior High, Ohio's largest junior high school located in the Hough Section of Cleveland. From 1960-63 Dr. Smith taught social studies and served as a vocational placement and guidance counselor in a technical high school. Smith's Ph.D. is from Case Western Reserve University. Address responses to: Dr. William L. Smith, U.S. Commissioner of Education, Department of Education, Washington, D.C. 20202.

THOMAS J. SORK is an Assistant Professor in the Department of Adult and Continuing Education at the University of Nebraska-Lincoln. He received his doctorate in adult education from Florida State University where he first became interested in futuristics. His teaching and research interests focus on educational planning for adults in both school and non-school settings. Each summer he directs a workshop on educational futuristics. As a futurist, he considers himself a "skeptical optimist" because, although he feels the quality of life will improve in the future, it will not do so in ways forecast by most prominent futurists. He is committed to the futures invention process as a means of empowerment and believes our greatest challenge in the 1980s will be to foster a sense of hope. Address responses to: Dr. Thomas J. Sork, Department of Adult and Continuing Education, Room 61 Henzlik Hall, University of Nebraska, Lincoln, NE 68588.

CARLOS ANTONIO TORRE is an Associate Professor of Human Services at Northeastern Illinois University in Chicago. He received his doctorate from the Graduate School of Education at Harvard University. He has also taught sociology at Roxbury Community College in Massachusetts and worked as a National Science Foundation Grant Project Director. In addition to teaching at Northeastern Illinois University, he is presently offering courses and workshops in social cybernetics through the Sao Paulo School of Sociology and Politics, of which he is President of the Board of Directors. He is also making a 16mm documentary film on Puerto Rican migration. Address responses to: Dr. Carlos A. Torre, Human Services Department, Northeastern Illinois University, 5500 N. St. Louis Avenue, Chicago, IL 60625.

PAUL A. WAGNER, Ph.D., Assistant Professor, Professional Studies in Education and Philosophy, University of Houston at Clear Lake City. Formerly Professor Wagner was the Director of the Philosophy for Children Project at the University of Missouri at Columbia. He is presently a consultant with the Clear Creek Independent School District and is developing for them a philosophy for children program for the gifted. He has published two dozen articles in the last three years on a variety of topics including creativity, science education, philosophy for children and criminal rehabilitation. He is presently completing a book to be used by third graders in learning logic and other associated reading skills. Address responses to: Dr. Paul A. Wagner, University of Houston at Clear Lake City, 2700 Bay Area Boulevard, Houston, Texas 77058.

WINIFRED I. WARNAT is Professor of Education, The American University, Washington, D.C. During much of her career she has specialized in research on staff development and inservice education. She is also founder and Director of American University's Adult Learning Potential Institute, a research and development operation that concentrates on adult learning processes, family as educator, and human resources development. Before coming to The American University, Dr. Warnat was a Professor at Howard University. While there, she served as Chairman, Department of Curriculum and Instruction, School of Education; Assistant Dean for Advanced Studies and Research, Graduate School of Arts and Sciences; and Clinical Professor, Department of Pediatrics and Child Health, College of Medicine. She has conducted numerous research projects focusing on various adult learner populations, as well as on adult development, education of the handicapped, child care services, and early childhood education. In addition, she has addressed many professional organizations and has published numerous journal articles. Address responses to: Dr. Winifred I. Warnat, Director, Adult Learning Potential Institute, American University, Washington, D.C. 20016.

EDITH WEINER is Executive Vice President of Weiner, Edrich, Brown, Inc., consultants in the management of change and strategic planning. Prior to the formation of WEB in 1977, she was director of the Trend Analysis Program (TAP) at the American Council of Life Insurance. Under her leadership, TAP became known as the foremost environmental scanning program in American business, and she acquired an international reputation as an outstanding futurist. Articles by Edith Weiner have appeared in a number of publications, including the Harvard Business Review. In 1978, Ms. Weiner was elected to the Board of Directors of the Union Mutual Life Insurance Company. She is a member of the U.S. Association for the Club of Rome. In addition, she serves on the editorial board of Business Tomorrow. Ms. Weiner has been a guest lecturer at the Harvard Business School, the Wharton School, the University of Massachusetts, Georgia State University, the New School for Social Research, and other educational institutions. Address responses to: Edith Weiner, Weiner, Edrich, Brown, Inc., 303 Lexington Avenue, New York, NY 10016.

About the Editors

Kathleen Redd is Associate Professor of Interdisciplinary Studies at St. Cloud State Univeresity where she teaches courses in futures studies and general social science. She has been actively involved in preparing a proposed undergraduate futures studies minor at St. Cloud State. In addition she is an associate editor for the journal Futurics and has recently completed her term as Vice President for Academics of the Minnesota Futurists, a chapter of the World Future Society.

Arthur Harkins is Associate Professor of Education and Sociology in the Department of Social, Psychological, and Philosophical Foundations of Education at the University of Minnesota. He was one of the founders of the Minnesota Futurists as well as of the journals Futurics and the Journal of Cultural and Educational Futures. He is Director of the Graduate Concentration in Future Cultural and Educational Systems at the University of Minnesota, and co-President of the Minnesota Chapter of the Society for General Systems Research.

Contributors to the Conference

I. <u>General Sessions</u>

Education and Its Transformations
Jean Houston, Foundation for Mind Research, Pomona, New York

WFS Perspectives: Education and the Future
Edward Cornish, President, World Future Society

Presidential Address: The 1980s--Crisis for Education
Christopher J. Dede, President, Education Section--
World Future Society

Importance of Future Studies' Perspectives in Education and in Society
Edith Weiner, Vice President, Weiner, Edrich and Brown, New York

Decoding the Future
Earl Joseph, Sperry-Univac and University of Minnesota, Minneapolis, Minnesota

Learning to be Better Choosers
Willis Harman, Stanford Research Institute, Palo Alto, California

Bridging the Future
William L. Smith, Director, Teacher Corps, Washington, D.C.

Social Change and Educational Outcomes 1980-2000
Harold G. Shane, Indiana University, Bloomington

II. Clinics--Full Day or Half Day

Student Designed Simulations: An In-Class Opportunity to
Experience the Future Today
Edward M. Greb, Billie Betler, Judith DeFilippis,
Washington and Jefferson College, Washington, Pennsylvania

Designing a Future Living Curriculum for Schools and
Classrooms (K-12)
Elliott Seif, Temple University, Philadelphia, Pennsylvania

Teacher Training in Educational Futuristics: A Practicum
in the Way It's Spozed To Be
Diane N. Battung, University of Southern California,
Los Angeles, California

Preparing Today's Youth to Deal Effectively With
Tomorrow's World: A Proposed Methodology
Louis A. Iozzi, Rutgers-The State University, New Brunswick,
New Jersey

Introductory Practicum on Ethnographic Futures Research
Robert B. Textor, Stanford University, Stanford, California

"Fast Forum" Technique and Zeitgeist ("Spirit of the
Time") Communication
Richard J. Spady, Forum Foundation, Bellevue, Washington
Pat Sablatura, Sisters of St. Francis, Rochester, Minnesota

The Universal Action Pattern of the Mind and Self: A
Unifier and Simplifier for All Forms of Learning
R. Duncan Wallace, Rick Davis, Certainty, Inc., Salt Lake
City, Utah

Social Cybernetics Interdisciplinary Seminars
Waldemar DeGregori, The Sao Paulo School of Sociology and
Politics, Chicago, Illinois

Inventing Alternative Approaches for Inventing Desirable
Futures
Gerald L. Kincaid, Minnesota State Department of Education,
St. Paul, Minnesota;
Roger Wangen, Minnesota State Department of Education,
St. Paul, Minnesota

Future Bowl for Gifted Problem Solvers
Michael L. Gates, Newton Community School District, Newton,
Iowa;
Lois Fingerman, Iowa State Future Bowl Director and Judge

Unity Alternative School...Educating for the 21st Century
Carol I. Marshall, ISD #709, Duluth, Minnesota;
Myra DeByle, Unity Alternative School, ISD #709, Duluth,
Minnesota

Health Care Futures: Implications for Professional
Education
Stanley L. Freeman, Jr., University of Maine, Orono, Maine;
Robert C. Briertson, Michigan State University;
Robert L. Patrick, Alvin Community College, Alvin, Texas;
Jack D. Arters, Middle Tennessee State University;
Anne Niemiec, Medical Care Development, Inc., August, Maine

Creating and Evaluating Alternative Images of Childhood
Glen Palm, University of Minnesota, Minneapolis, Minnesota

Options for Implementing Futures Programs in Schools,
School Districts, and Teacher Education
Don E. Glines, Educational Futures Projects and California
State Department of Education, Sacramento, California

Community Education: A New Direction
Don Kramlinger, Minnesota Community Education Association,
Buffalo, Minnesota

The Process of Creating and Implementing a Future Fair
Dean A. Haledjian, Northern Virginia Community College,
Annandale, Virginia

Futurizing Your Curriculum: Creating Multidisciplinary,
Problem-Centered, Multi-Cultural and Future Oriented
Activities for Primary Ages Through Adult in School and
Non-School Activities
Peter Barnet, Northfield, Minnesota;
Judith M. Barnet, Director, Judith Barnet Associates,
Barnstable, Massachusetts

The Image-Making Picture Art Process--An Art Event
Bruce Breland, Carnegie-Mellon University, Pittsburgh,
Pennsylvania

III. Sectionals--One or Two Hour

Futuristics and Professional Education
Dennis R. Falk, University of Minnesota, Duluth, Minnesota

The Emerging Futurists--Perspectives From Graduate
Programs
Linda Armstrong, Glen Palm, University of Minnesota,
Minneapolis, Minnesota

A Futuristics Program for Middle School Gifted and
Talented Students
Elizabeth Stafford, Anne Arundel County Board of Education,
Annapolis, Maryland

Conflict Anticipation: A Tool for Environmental Problem
Solving
Susan Carpenter, W.J.D. Kennedy, ROMCOE-Center for Environ-
mental Problem Solving, Denver, Colorado

Speculative Fiction in Non-Literature Curriculums
Lawrence S. Luton, Rust College, Holly Springs, Mississippi;
Philippe Cohen, University of Minnesota, Minneapolis,
Minnesota;
Sharon Nickel Snowiss, Pitzer College and Claremont Graduate
School;
Joseph D. Olander, Florida International University;
Albert Somit, State University of New York, Buffalo,
New York;
Patricia Warrick, University of Wisconsin

A Metro Network for Educational Futures: State of the
Process
Berenice Bleedorn, Minneapolis, Minnesota

Visual Documentation of Conference: Designed Space
Modifiers
J.A. Kula, V.M. Brouch, Florida State University,
Tallahassee, Florida

Twenty-Year Countdown: Attitudes of Teachers About the
Future
Charles E. Sherman, Jeanne B. Morris, Illinois State
University, Normal, Illinois

Futures and the Fundamentals
Mary Kay Howard, Betty B. Franks, John Carroll University,
University Heights, Ohio

Futurism Components for Local Inservice Education Programs
K. Fred Daniel, Florida Department of Education,
Tallahassee, Florida;
Arthur J. Lewis, University of Florida, Gainesville,
Florida;
E. Ward Thomas, Pinellas County School District, Clearwater,
Florida

Some Futures for Occupational Education
Charles F. Adams, Onondaga-Madison Boces, Syracuse,
New York;
Thomas Mecca, Tompkins-Cortland Community College, Syracuse,
New York

Education to Meet Needs for Living in the Future
Eldon M. Meyer, U.S. International University, Lemon Grove,
California

Zest Groups: A Rebirth of Liberal Learning for Adults
Janet Hagberg, Human Renewal, Inc., Minneapolis, Minnesota;
Carol Heen;
Charlie Boone, WCCO Radio, Minneapolis, Minnesota;
Mike Finck, Lakewood Pub., Inc.

Implications of the Future--Teacher Attitudes and
Implementation
Jean Nicholsen, Indiana University-Purdue, Indianapolis,
Indiana

Project Outer Limits
Doris Lyons, Ron Stadsklev, The University of Alabama

Is Literacy Passe in a Pushbutton World?
A. Gayle Hudgens, University of Texas, Austin, Texas

Futuristic World Views: Modern Physics, Feminist
Education, and Native Americans
Gerri Perreault, Metropolitan State University, St. Paul,
Minnesota;
Flo Wiger, University of Minnesota, Minneapolis, Minnesota

Toward a Systematic Integration of Global Perspectives
Into all Major Fields of Learning
Erika Vora, St. Cloud State University, St. Cloud,
Minnesota;
Molefi K. Asante, State University of New York, Buffalo,
New York

A Fast Round Trip to the Future: Creative Problem Solving
Win Wenger, Gaithersburg, Maryland

Alternative Futures in Education
Robert E. Hendricks, University of Miami, Coral Gables,
Florida

Adaptation of Federally Funded Secondary Futuristics
Course
Louis Gass, Faribault Senior High School, Northfield,
Minnesota

Workshop on Teaching How to Develop Scenarios
Robert J. Doyle, University of Windsor, Windsor, Ontario,
Canada

The Campus High School: School for the Future
Edward F. Carpenter, The City College of New York, New York,
New York

Educational Applications of Computerized Conferencing
Murray Turoff, Starr R. Hiltz, Newark, New Jersey

Everybody Loves a Winner: Long-Range Planning and Effective
Intervention Help Private Schools Grow in Students and
Funding
Genevieve A. Schillo, Archdiocese of Omaha, Omaha, Nebraska

Elementary Education: The Present as Future
Harlan S. Hansen, University of Minnesota, Minneapolis,
Minnesota;
David C. Davis, University of Wisconsin

Ethnoelectronics and Learning Futures
Earl Joseph, University of Minnesota and Sperry-Univac,
Minneapolis, Minnesota;
Arthur Harkins, University of Minnesota, Minneapolis,
Minnesota;
William Norris, Control Data Corporation;
Robert Miller, University of Wisconsin;
Robert Textor, Stanford University

Teaching Cooperation to Enhance Creativity
James E. Herrick, University of Washington, Seattle,
Washington;
Penelope Herrick, Union Graduate School

Future Educational Process
Toni Farrenkopf, California State University System, Pomona,
California

Student Demand for the Study of the Future
Dwight W. Allen, Old Dominion University, Norfolk, Virginia;
W. Brett Parent, Teaching Corps Project, Paterson,
New Jersey

Crimes Against the Future: The Educator as Change-Agent
Jim Bowman, University of Houston at Clear Lake City,
Houston, Texas

"The Little House on the Prairie" Paradigm for the Future
Nicholas D. Bevilacqua, University of California-Berkeley,
Walnut Creek, California

Interaction Center for the University of the Future
John F. Deethardt, Texas Tech University, Lubbock, Texas

Futures Designs and Their Implications to Education
Fred D. Kierstead, University of Houston at Clear Lake City,
Houston, Texas

Educational Policies for a Sustainable Society
Rodger W. Bybee, Carleton College, Northfield, Minnesota

Technological Languages: Reading What We Make
Molefi Kete Asante, Howard University, Silver Spring,
Maryland

General Education for "The Too Late Generation"
Jack Quistwater, Sheridan College, Oakville, Ontario, Canada

Arts Network Meeting
V.M. Brouch, Florida State University, Tallahassee, Florida

Aspects of Theoretical Science and Science Education of
the Future
Paul A. Wagner, Jr., University of Houston at Clear Lake
City, Houston, Texas

From Closed Disciplines to Open Systems
Ruth Allen, Brooklyn College, Brooklyn, New York

Community Development Simulation
Wilbur R. Maki, Minneapolis, Minnesota;
Randolph Cantrill, University of Minnesota, Minneapolis,
Minnesota;
James Krele, University of Minnesota, Minneapolis,
Minnesota;
Thomas Stinson, University of Minnesota, Minneapolis,
Minnesota;
Robert Eyestone, University of Minnesota, Minneapolis,
Minnesota

Transdisciplinary Thrusts of Educational Futures:
Rhetorical or Realizable Goals?
A. Gayle Hudgens, The University of Texas, Austin, Texas

Suggestive-Accelerative Learning and Teaching (SALT):
Enhancing Classroom Learning
L. Palmer, Winona, Minnesota;
Doris Lyons, Ron Stadsklev, The University of Alabama

Concepts of Time and the Future in Early Childhood
Education
Richard D. Wood, Central Washington University, Ellensburg,
Washington;
Orval E. Putoff and Jacqueline T. Bates, Central Washington
University, Ellensburg, Washington

Introducing Futures to K-12 Education: The Michigan Plan
Sherry Schiller, Waterford Public Schools, Pontiac,
Michigan;
Lawrence B. Schlack, Barry Intermediate School District,
Hastings, Michigan

Education for Achieving a New Societal Paradigm
Ronald W. Hull, Atlanta University, Austell, Georgia;
Clayvon Croom, Atlanta University, Austell, Georgia

How the Future Was Won: A Scenario
Leland Hott, St. Cloud State University, St. Cloud,
Minnesota

The International Dimensions of Future Studies
Abdul Al-Rubaiy, University of Akron;
Magda McHale, Houston, Texas;
Molefi Asante, Silver Spring , Maryland

Smuggling in the Future Via the Basics: Elementary
John R. Eggers, University of Northern Iowa, Mason City,
Iowa

**Futurism as Therapy: Interface of Social Networking,
Bodywork and Futurism**
Joe W. Hart, University of Arkansas, Little Rock, Arkansas

Ethics in Future Studies
Suleiman I. Cohen, University of Rotterdam, Rotterdam,
Holland

**New Linkages: Building a Futurists Network Among
Professional/Industrial Organizations**
Dennis VanAvery, Westminster College, Salt Lake City, Utah

**Futures: With Or Without Shock--Organizing at the Grass
Roots Level in the Public Schools**
Richard R. Green and Gerry Sell, Minneapolis Public Schools,
Minneapolis, Minnesota.
Co-presenters: Moira Rummel, Becky Yarlott, Don Imsland,
Lauri Isaacson, Geraldine Burns, Paula Taylor, Jan Hively,
Caroline Marks, and Timi Stevens

Developing and Evaluating a Futures Study Curriculum
Geoffrey H. Fletcher and Gary D. Wooddell, Milford
Futurology Program/Milford Public Schools;
Ted Dixon, Milford Futurology Program, Milford, Ohio

A Model of Education for the 80's and 90's
G. Barry Morris, University of Saskatchewan, Saskatoon,
Saskatchewan, Canada

**Designing and Implementing the Regional Education Service
Agency of the Future**
Lawrence B. Schlack, Barry Intermediate School District,
Hastings, Michigan

Designing Learning Environments for the Future
Stephen L. Albert, St. Louis University, University City,
Missouri

Networking: A Synergistic Support and Information System
Carol Marshall, ISD #709, Duluth, Minnesota;
Mary Ann Lucas, ISD #709, Duluth, Minnesota

**Futurizing the Elementary Classroom: An Interdisciplinary
Learning Approach**
Jill Reicher, Castle Rock, Colorado, and Karen Peterson,
Aurora, Colorado

Gifted/Talented in Futuristics Education
Phyllis Maul, Kalamazoo Valley Intermediate School District,
Kalamazoo, Michigan

Futures Theory in Education and Mass Media Values
John D. Pulliam, University of Oklahoma, Norman, Oklahoma

Appropriate Technology (A slide-tape presentation on)
Carol A. Christensen, Christensen Associates, Newark,
Delaware

Students: A Resource for Solution of Campus Problems
Robert J. Falk, University of Minnesota, Duluth, Minnesota

Crucial Issues for Education in the 21st Century
Christopher Dede, University of Houston at Clear Lake City,
Houston, Texas;
Dwight Allen, Old Dominion University, Norfolk, Virginia

The Future of the Residential Liberal Arts College
Samuel L. Dunn, Seattle Pacific University, Seattle,
Washington;
Ray Reglin, Mid-America Nazarene College, Kansas;
Joseph Nielson, Olivet Nazarene College, Illinois

Preview of a Forthcoming Book, The Whole Future Catalog
for Kids
Paula Taylor, Minneapolis, Minnesota;
Cy DeCosse, Cy DeCosse Creative Department, Minnetonka,
Minnesota

Forecasting Demand for International Languages:
Brainstorming
John A. Brownell, East-West Center, Inc., Honolulu, Hawaii

The Community Forum and Networking the State
John F. Deethardt, Texas Tech University, Lubbock, Texas

Futuristic Information Resources Networks
Gary Walz, University of Michigan, Ann Arbor, Michigan;
Jane Leu, University of Michigan, Ann Arbor, Michigan

Argument and Action for Gifted and Talented Leadership
in Tomorrow's world
Berenice B. Bleedorn, Metro State University and College of
St. Thomas, Minneapolis, Minnesota;
Linda Jeska, Regional Inservice Training Project for
Educators of High Potential;
Representatives of Educational Funding Agencies

Ongoing Education: Identifying Needs--Anticipatory or
Reactionary?
Linda Armstrong, University of Minnesota, Minneapolis,
Minnesota;
Bill Nelson, University of Minnesota Technical College,
Waseca, Minnesota;
Terrence MacTaggart, St. Cloud State University, St. Cloud,
Minnesota;
Dimitri Gat, University of Massachusetts, Amherst,
Massachusetts

Graduate Futures Study in a College of Education, 1971-1979
Arthur M. Harkins, University of Minnesota, Minneapolis,
Minnesota;
Earl Joseph, University of Minnesota and Sperry-Univac,
Minneapolis, Minnesota;
William Gardner, University of Minnesota, Minneapolis,
Minnesota;
Harold Shane, Indiana University, Bloomington, Indiana;
Christopher Dede, University of Houston at Clear Lake City,
Houston, Texas;
Jerry Jinks, Eastern Montana College

Learning Resource Management: Creating Alternative
Educational Outcomes for Post-Secondary Education
Mary E. Sudholt, E.F. Hutton, Boulder, Colorado

Planning a Futures Course: A Simulation
Jim Reynolds, East Texas State University, Commerce, Texas

Intuitive Decision Guiding: New Powers of the Mind
Doris Lyons, The University of Alabama, Tuscaloosa, Alabama;
Ron Stadsklev, The University of Alabama, Tuscaloosa,
Alabama

Long-Range Planning in Higher Education
Mary G. Weisensee, University of Minnesota, Minneapolis,
Minnesota

Forecasting the Speech Communication of the Future
Phoebe P. Hollis, University of Nebraska, Omaha, Nebraska

A Futures Curriculum for Symmetry
Leonore W. Dickmann, University of Wisconsin, Oshkosh,
Wisconsin

Avoiding Futures Burn-Out
John R. Eggers, University of Northern Iowa, Mason City,
Iowa

A Network of Learning Systems--Theory and Practice
Arthur J. Lewis, University of Florida, Gainesville, Florida

Comprehensive Planning in Two-Year Colleges for the 1980s
Steven L. Van Ausdle, Ohio State University, Columbus, Ohio

Laying the Foundation: Basic Theories for a High School
Futuristics Course
David E. Smith, Lamphere High School, Madison Heights,
Michigan

1999: A Futures Exploration
Eileen Brown, Catholic Schools, Fairbanks, Alaska, and
Marilyn Guldan, Marylhurst Education Center, Marylhurst,
Oregon

Higher Education for Higher Consciousness: Rediscovering
the Missing Dimension in Education
Robert Winquist, Maharishi International University,
Fairfield, Iowa

Values' Clarification: Future Shock and the Growth Debate
Lawrence Litecky, Metropolitan Community College,
Minneapolis, Minnesota

Training for the Pure, Electronically Mediated Democracy
John F. Deethardt, Texas Tech University, Lubbock, Texas

Boredom and Its Implications for the Future of Education
William C. Leikam, Fremont Union High School District,
Palo Alto, California

The Element of Change: Impact, Implications, and
Recommendations
Phoebe P. Hollis, University of Nebraska, Omaha, Nebraska

Getting Future Teachers to Think About Teaching in the
Future
Eileen Rice, Siena Heights College, Adrian, Michigan

Future Families as Household School Institutions
Winifred I. Warnat, American University, Washington, D.C.

The Future of Faculty Development: A Proposed Cost-
Effective Approach
Jon M. Anastasio, Rutgers State University of New Jersey,
Piscataway, New Jersey

Colloquium: Curriculum Alternative for the Future
Jean Meyer, St. Edward's University, Austin, Texas

Illusions: Visions of New Realities
David G. Gueulette, Northern Illinois University, Dekalb,
Illinois

Long Term Impact of the Silicon Revolution on Education
Earl C. Joseph, Sperry-Univac, St. Paul, Minnesota

Planning Change in Education: Futuristic Trends and
Images
Florence F. Hood, Norfolk State University, Portsmouth,
Virginia

Developing a Futures Perspective: Variables of Interest to
Educators
Thomas J. Sork, University of Nebraska, Lincoln, Nebraska

New Ways of Being: Holistic Education
Doris Lyons and Ron Stadsklev, The University of Alabama;
Diane Battung, University of Southern California

Forecasting in the Futures Studies Classroom: A Second
Generation Approach
Penny Damlo, Burnsville High School, Burnsville, Minnesota

Student Sensitization to Career Trends of the Future
Jon F. Sobecki, Montclair State College, Denville,
New Jersey

IV. Special Events

The Club of Rome Learning Project: The Human Gap
Eleonora Masini, Secretary-General, World Future Studies
Federation

Symposium: Women as Futurists and Educators
Moderator: Penny Damlo, Senior Vice President, Minnesota
Futurists, Burnsville, Minnesota.
Invited Participants: Carol Christensen, President,
Christensen Associates, Newark, Delaware; O.W. Markley,
University of Houston at Clear Lake City, Houston, Texas;
Eleonora Masini, Secretary-General, World Future Studies
Federation, Rome, Italy; and Magda McHale, Vice President,
World Future Studies Federation, and Director, Center for
Integrative Studies, University of Houston, Houston, Texas

Women, Children, and the Future: The Future of Us All
Speakers: Eleonora Masini, Secretary-General, World Future
Studies Federation, Rome, Italy; and Magda McHale, Vice
President, World Future Studies Federation, and Director,
Center for Integrative Studies, University of Houston.

Trends in Futurist Journals' Publication
Edward Cornish, Editor, The Futurist; Scott Erickson,
Editor, Futurics; Arthur Harkins, Editor, Journal of
Cultural and Educational Futures; and Lane Jennings,
Editor, World Future Society Bulletin.

Futures in the Classroom: Halfway There?
Joel Barker, President, Functional Futures and Integrative
Thinking, Inc., St. Paul, Minnesota

Venezuelan Government Project on Human Intelligence
Jose Dominguez, Advisor-General to the Minister of State for
the Development of Human Intelligence, Caracas, Venezuela

Symposium: Futures Studies Beyond the United States
Moderator: Jim Dator, University of Hawaii, Honolulu,
Hawaii.
Participants: Luis Alberto Machado, Minister of State for
the Development of Human Intelligence, Caracas, Venezuela;
and Eleonora Masini, Secretary-General, World Future Studies
Federation, Rome, Italy, and others.

**Advanced Methodology in Futures Studies and Futures
Education**
O.W. Markley, University of Houston at Clear Lake City,
Houston, Texas

BUSINESS MEETING
EDUCATION SECTION—World Future Society
Presiding: Chris Dede, President

RESEARCH ROUNDTABLE
Chaired by Scott Erickson, President of Minnesota Futurists
    Papers included in this session: Varying Responses to
Global Scarcity and Limits, Linda J. Groff, California State
University, Dominguez Hills, California; Politics in the
Futures Literature, William C. Johnson, Bethel College, St.
Paul, Minnesota; Higher Education Curricula in Futures
Studies: A Proposal,Donald F. Mulvihill, Kent State
University, Kent, Ohio; What's Wrong with Systems?, Michelle
Small, Northland College, Ashland, Wisconsin; Piagetian
Theory--A New Force in Education, William Sweeters,

Morningside College, Sioux City, Iowa; _Prejudice Reduction in the Changing Society of Tomorrow_, Joshua Weinstein, University of Houston, Houston, Texas.

V. Working Groups

WORKING GROUP I: MISSING COMPONENTS IN FUTURISTS' EDUCATION
Coordinator: Marian Dobbert, University of Minnesota, Minneapolis, Minnesota.
Invited Participants: Linda Armstrong, Jim Dator, Leandra Eckelkamp, Geof Fletcher, Marlene Goldsmith, Barbara Howard, Michelle Small, Elizabeth Wroblinski, Bill Nelson, and Scott Erickson

WORKING GROUP II: THEORIES OF SOCIAL CHANGE
Coordinator: Jim Dator, University of Hawaii, Honolulu, Hawaii.
Invited Participants: Dwight Allen, Chris Dede, O.W. Markley, Kathleen Redd

WORKING GROUP III: FUTURES IN THE CLASSROOM--WHERE DO WE GO
   FROM HERE?
Coordinator: Joel Barker, President, Functional Futures and Integrative Thinking, St. Paul, Minnesota.
Invited Participants: Jim Bowman, Carol Christensen, Penny Damlo, Betty Franks, Fred Kierstead, Al Peakes, Sherry Schiller

WORKING GROUP IV: MINORITY YOUTH--VIABLE OPTIONS FOR THE
   FUTURE
Coordinator: Edward Carpenter, City University of New York, New York City.
Invited Participants: Dwight Allen, Wayne Jennings, Al Peakes, Jerri Sellers, Charles Sherman, Moira Rummel, Bill Owens, Judith Barnet, Brett Jansen and others.

IV. Commissions and Tasks Forces

Adhoc Group on Young People's Organization: Interim Report

Commission on Alternative Learning Environments: Initial Meeting

Convocations Task Force: Interim Report

Commission on Emerging Issues and Concerns in Education:
Initial Meeting

Governance Task force: Interim Report

Commission on Futures Research Implications for Educational
Practice: Initial Meeting

Communications Task Force: Interim Report

Commission on Teaching for the Future: Initial Meeting

International Liason Task Force: Interim Report

Commission on Organizational Planning and Networking:
Initial Meeting

Commission on Developments in Educational Technology:
Initial Meeting